# COMPUTER APPLICATIONS IN OPERATIONS ANALYSIS

# COMPUTER APPLICATIONS IN OPERATIONS ANALYSIS

BENNET P. LIENTZ
*University of California, Los Angeles*

PRENTICE-HALL INC., Englewood Cliffs, New Jersey

*Library of Congress Cataloging in Publication Data*

LIENTZ, BENNET P
  Computer applications in operations analysis.

  Includes bibliographical references.
  1. Electronic data processing—Operations research.
I. Title.
T57. 6. L53 1974     658.4'034'02854     74-8959
ISBN 0-13-164103-4

©1975 by Prentice-Hall, Inc.
Englewood Cliffs, New Jersey

All rights reserved. No part of this book
may be reproduced in any form or by any means
without permission in writing from the publisher.

10 9 8 7 6 5 4 3 2 1

Printed in the United States of America

PRENTICE-HALL INTERNATIONAL, INC., *London*
PRENTICE-HALL OF AUSTRALIA, PTY. LTD., *Sydney*
PRENTICE-HALL OF CANADA, LTD., *Toronto*
PRENTICE-HALL OF INDIA PRIVATE LIMITED, *New Delhi*
PRENTICE-HALL OF JAPAN, INC., *Tokyo*

To my wife, Martha, and our children—
Bennet Jr., Andrew, Charles, and Herman

# CONTENTS

Preface　　xi

**1  Introduction to Computer Systems and Operations Systems**　　1
　1.1  Computer Hardware　　1
　1.2  Computer Processing　　6
　1.3  Program Construction　　8
　1.4  Operations Systems　　9
　1.5  Applications of Computer Based Models　　11
　1.6  Remarks　　14
　　　References　　15

**2  Data Management and Information Systems**　　18
　2.1  Introduction and Data Handling　　18
　2.2  Searching and Sorting Procedures　　24
　　　*2.2.1  Overview and examples*　　24
　　　*2.2.2  Search procedures*　　25
　　　*2.2.3  Sorting and merging procedures*　　31
　2.3  File Structures and Selection　　34
　2.4  Management Information Systems　　39
　2.5  Programs　　43
　　　References　　45
　　　Problems　　46

## 3 Mathematical Programming — 49
- 3.1 Introduction   49
  - 3.1.1 *Overview*   49
  - 3.1.2 *Establishing the mathematical form of the problem*   52
- 3.2 Definitions and Basic Methods of Linear Programming   56
  - 3.2.1 *Basic problem and geometry*   56
  - 3.2.2 *Simplex method*   60
  - 3.2.3 *Computational methods*   65
- 3.3 Methods in Integer Programming   67
- 3.4 Applications   79
- 3.5 Programs   92
- References   96
- Problems   98

## 4 Network Analysis — 102
- 4.1 Formulation of Networks Definition   102
- 4.2 Maximal Flow in a Network   105
- 4.3 Shortest Path   113
- 4.4 Program Planning and Applications   118
- 4.5 Programs   123
- References   125
- Problems   126

## 5 Statistics — 131
- 5.1 Overview of Probability and Statistics   131
  - 5.1.1 *Probability*   131
  - 5.1.2 *Estimation*   138
  - 5.1.3 *Testing hypotheses*   139
- 5.2 Statistical Methods   143
  - 5.2.1 *Regression analysis*   143
  - 5.2.2 *Fitting procedures*   145
  - 5.2.3 *Analysis of variance*   149
  - 5.2.4 *Nonparametric statistics*   152
- 5.3 Applications   157
  - 5.3.1 *Traffic flow*   158
  - 5.3.2 *Insecticide testing*   159
  - 5.3.3 *Credit card and investment analysis*   159
- 5.4 Programs   160
- References   161
- Problems   162

## 6 Simulation and Queuing Theory — 167
- 6.1 Introduction   167

    6.2  Simulation and Queuing Analysis    170
         6.2.1  *Nonstochastic simulation*    170
         6.2.2  *Pseudo-Random and random number generation*    180
         6.2.3  *Queuing theory*    185
         6.2.4  *Simulation modeling*    194
    6.3  Applications    198
    6.4  Languages    203
         References    207
         Problems    209

## 7  Numerical Analysis    214

    7.1  Introduction    214
    7.2  Methods in Numerical Analysis    217
         7.2.1  *Interpolation*    217
         7.2.2  *Differentiation and quadrative*    223
         7.2.3  *Linear systems of equations*    227
         7.2.4  *Solution of ordinary differential equations*    232
         7.2.5  *Numerical analysis and operations research*    235
    7.3  Programs    236
         References    238
         Problems    238

## Appendices

## A  Linear Algebra and Matrices    243

    A.1  Definitions and Relationships    243
    A.2  Programs    255
         References    255
         Problems    256

## B  Networks and Graph Theory    258

    B.1  Network Concepts    258
    B.2  Tree Structures    266
         References    267
         Problems    268

## C  Tables of Statistics and Pseudo-Random Numbers    272

    C-1  Binomial Coefficients    272
    C-2  Exponential Distribution    273
    C-3  Normal Distribution    274
    C-4  Chi-Square Distribution    275
    C-5  $F$ Distribution    276
    C-6  Pseudo-Random Numbers    279

## Index    285

# PREFACE

Computer applications are aimed at the partial and total automation of tasks related to decision making at all levels ranging from production processes and daily decision problems to generalized planning. Viewed in perspective, mathematical methods aided by computer machinery have made progress in the first area. In the area of general decision-making, automated planning is still in the formative stage. The reason for this and for the lack of computer-aided technology in some scheduling and production problems lies in part in the difficulty of the situation and in the value of human judgment and experience. In the future, advances in these areas will often be based on heuristic or experience related systems. Examined in these chapters are a number of mathematically based methods and techniques. These methods are valuable not only in production and daily scheduling, statistics, and other applications but also as realized in programs in high level planning.

The approach here is to develop procedures that are not overly sensitive to existing computer technology; instead, some of the major thrusts are devoted at methodologies that are now in part computerized. New results can be imbedded in this framework. References include not only journals and textbooks but also encompass review journals of new programs and sources and libraries of available programs. To many future and present practitioners of operations research and numerical methods, these latter sources are most important. A reason is that frequently in physical sciences neither the time nor resources are available for a complete program to be developed, programmed, debugged, and tested. This is also true of researchers in social, behavioral, and other sciences who need to apply an existing method for rapid evaluation of data.

The scope of this book is based on a one-year course at the undergraduate level or as a supplement to graduate level courses outside mathematics. The logical relationship of the chapters is shown in Fig. F-1. The dotted line connecting Chapter 5 and 6 indicates that some familiarity with basic definition and results of probability theory is assumed in Chapter 6.

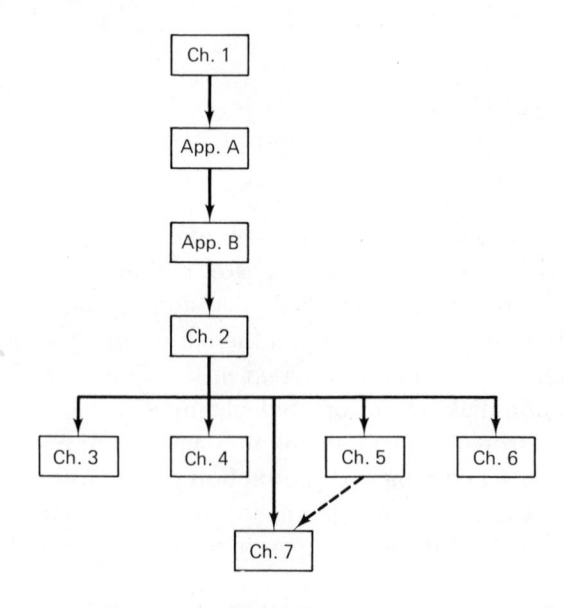

Figure F-1

The first semester could include Chapters 1 and 2, Appendices A and B, and one or two additional chapters. The remainder would constitute part of the course for the second semester. In a one-year time span, it is possible to introduce additional applications in a particular area from technical journals. It should be noted here that the content and use of the chapters also depend on the particular field of study of the students.

In a single semester, the material depends on the programming background of the students. For students with an adequate knowledge of a programming language, Chapter 1 to 5 and the appendices may be generally covered.

The purpose of this book is to expose the student to some of the major fields of operation research and statistics which utilize the computer and which are applied in a variety of disciplines. Emphasis is on the methods and the how rather than the proofs of results or the why. It is emphasized that no chapter pretends to be exhaustive in terms of results in an area; rather, several major methods and problems are addressed. References and Problems appear at the conclusion of each chapter and appendix.

A subsidiary purpose is to point out the need for considering the whole problem before plunging in and programming parts of methods. Of primary concern in applications is the usability and the general efficiency of the entire procedure, not just the algorithm. This includes the interface of data management and operations research tools. A section in Chapter 2 is devoted to this.

Another aim is to point out the existence of running program codes and sources of information. Often for a single use or application of a method, it is too expensive and time consuming to construct error-free codes from scratch. For many areas, tested and experienced programs exist. Many of these are free except for a nominal cost for a manual or copy of a tape.

The reader is assumed to be familiar with set theory, functions, and algebra and calculus in some chapters. This is usually the first course in college or advanced high school mathematics. Of importance is a working knowledge of a computer language. Most of the programs described in this text are of the scientific programming variety and exist in FORTRAN. An exception is the collection of simulation programs. For a reader who needs to review FORTRAN, several references are given here.

1. Blatt, J. M., *Introduction to FORTRAN IV Programming Using the WATFOR Compiler*. Pacific Palisades, Calif.: Goodyear Publishing Co., 1968.
2. Ledley, R. S., *FORTRAN IV Programming*. New York: McGraw-Hill Book Co., 1968.
3. Lee, R. M., *A Short Course in FORTRAN IV Programming*. New York: McGraw-Hill Book Co., 1967.
4. McCracken, D. D., *Guide to FORTRAN IV Programming*. New York: John Wiley & Sons, Inc., 1965.
5. Dorn, W. S., *Numerical Methods and FORTRAN Programming*. New York: John Wiley & Sons, Inc., 1964.

To summarize, computer applications will be a growing area of interest and development for some time to come. This will be as a result of advances in the methods and algorithms themselves, in computer hardware, and in the programming systems and concepts that govern computer operations. Computer applications is an exciting and rewarding area that impacts social and physical sciences, law, medicine, biological sciences, and other disciplines.

Finally I wish to take this opportunity to say this book could not have been written without the encouragement and assistance of my wife and family. I am also indebted to Ms. Mary Margaret Benson for her editorial assistance and to Ms. Alice Kamiyama, Linda Mauldin, and Rebecca Bimmerman for their typing assistance. Finally, I am most grateful to Professor Joe Mize for his help in organization and his encouragement.

BENNET P. LEINTZ

# 1

# INTRODUCTION TO COMPUTER SYSTEMS AND OPERATIONS SYSTEMS

## 1.1 Computer Hardware

This chapter introduces and reviews computer systems in general and computer programs (software) in particular. Computer systems and programs are aimed at solving problems in operations systems. This is a system of some type that exists or will exist in a real-world operational environment.

A computer system is the computing machinery, the operating system that controls the machines, and the software to be run on the computer. A knowledge of these factors and their interrelation is necessary to be able to apply computer based resources to specific application areas.

A computer is an electronic device for performing mathematical operations. Computers are of three general categories: digital, with discrete numbers; analog, with continuous values of quantities; and hybrid, which combines digital and analog portions. Our attention will focus on digital computers. Electronic Data Processing (EDP) is the general title for all operations with the computer.

The input might consist of data as well as a program for manipulating the data. Within the computer, the data is stored in the memory. The memory is called *core*, since it is made of ferrite cores. The general memory is divided into ferrite cores and registers. Core is where variables and instructions are kept. *Registers* are locations for numbers. The control unit is the master of computer operations to be performed by the processing.

Some applications of EDP occur in inventory control, scheduling of personnel and equipment, accounting, and simulation of physical processes. The range of applications is from simple file maintenance tasks to complex simulation and analysis for such projects as that of the Apollo moon landing.

As in any electronic device, there is a basic unit that is called here a *bit*. A bit is an abbreviation for a binary digit, which is either 0 or 1. From number theory we know any number can be represented in binary form as an array of bits, called a *word*. The data or numbers are input into the computer and then converted into binary form. The number of bits to compose a word varies with the computer manufacturer. IBM 360 and 370 uses a 32-bit word where a byte or character is 8 bits. CDC uses 60- and 36-bit words. Univac uses 36 bits per word. Other word sizes are 12, 16, and 18 bits. Storage in the machine is expressed in the total number of words. A constant $K$ has been introduced in labeling ($K = 2^{10}$ bits). Storage is then expressed in multiples of $K$ (e.g., 124$K$, 500$K$). An address is a location key to find a word. Letters are stored as characters. From this basic unit of storage, we can express data aggregations. Items are groupings of contiguous data. A *field* is part of a word in an item. Packing is combining of items smaller than words into words. In a language, we combine characters and symbols to form words. The set of rules for determining character combinations is called *syntax*.

Input and output operations (often denoted by I/O) are procedures by which data are put into and extracted from the computer. This can take several forms. With a simple program, the data and instructions for handling the data are put on standardized cards. The symbols are typed on a keypunch machine that then perforates the punch card with a code for each symbol. Cards are read into the computer by a reading device.

Alternative forms of input are from magnetic tape, disk, and drums. Usually information is first punched on cards and transformed onto a tape or disk. These alternative forms are preferred for large problems since the physical area needed for storage of information is much reduced.

A magnetic tape resembles a large recording tape. It is coated with an oxide to maintain data. The tape itself appears as in Fig. 1-1.

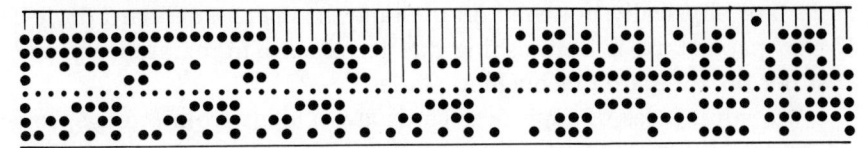

Figure 1-1. Section of magnetic tape.

Data characters are stored in the columns. The number of cells (rows) in a tape column is the number of tracks on the tape. A tape is mounted on a tape drive and reeled through to an empty tape spool. The data are read through the head (Fig. 1-2). The tape can be moved *forward* or *reverse*.

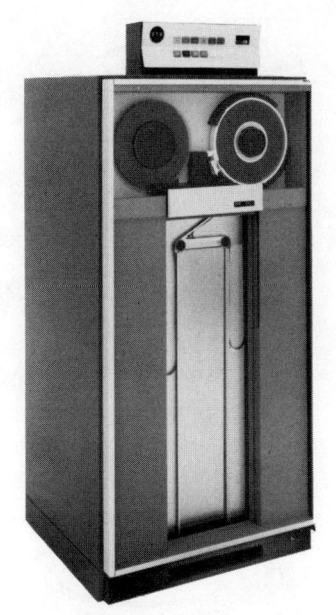

Figure 1-2. Tape drive.

A tape stores data sequentially as a recording tape or cassette. The program instructs the computer system on which part of the tape to read or write on.

Data are stored on a tape in *files*. A file is broken into a collection of records. For a dictionary, a file could be all words beginning

4 / Introduction to Computer Systems and Operation Systems

with a $D$ and a record could be every word beginning with $D$. Like a dictionary, the files are stored sequentially on tape. A label appears at the beginning and end of the file to mark the file boundaries.

Another kind of tape is paper tape. This appears as a ticker tape. Holes are physically punched on the tape through a keyboard device. Use of paper tape is diminishing due to expense in maintenance and cost per bit compared to magnetic tape.

The advantages of tape over cards are evident from storage, loss of cards, and misordering; however, running repeatedly through a tape consumes time. In the middle 1960's the spread of more rapid peripheral storage media began. Two such rapid access media will be considered here.

A disk unit is commonly called a *pack* (see Fig. 1-3). The pack consists of layers as in Fig. 1-4. Each layer is a *disk*. Both sides of

Figure 1-3. Disk pack.

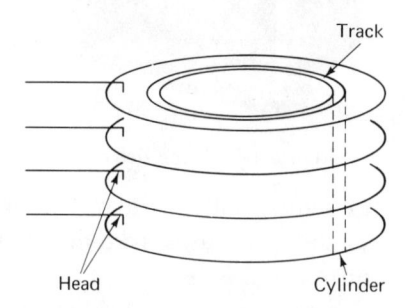

Figure 1-4. Disk unit.

disk are coated to store data. Data are stored on concentric circles on the top and bottom of each disk. The top side of the top disk and bottom side of the bottom disk are left blank. These circles are called *tracks*. Each track is then composed of records as a tape.

The disk pack is read and accessed by heads that are attached to access arms somewhat like a stack of record players. The access arms on each level move as a unit. We remark that some disk units have one head per track so that there is no arm movement time for setup. Because of this arrangement, it would appear that time could be saved by storing information vertically to reduce the number of arm movements. This is the case. A vertical unit of storage is called a *cylinder*. A cylinder consists of the positions on the disk pack referenced at a single position of access arm. Tracks are then grouped into cylinders.

A magnetic drum appears as in Fig. 1-5. The drum or cylinder stores information in the exterior coated surface. Tracks are then columns (or slices) on the cylinder. The heads are positioned in a single place while the drum rotates. There is one head per track. The average access time is then one-half of the time necessary for a revolution of the drum (neglecting the time for moving the head).

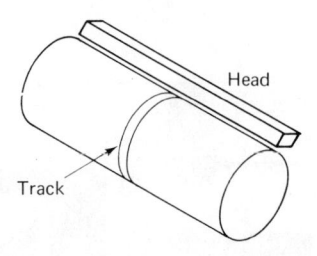

**Figure 1-5.** Magnetic drum.

Disk and drum devices are called *rapid access* because through the program they are set up and begin to rotate prior to and during the entire execution of the program. Access time is much faster than tapes, which access the required data and then stop rotation.

The difference between rapid access storage and core storage is that in main storage we may execute instructions and access words in main memory directly. For disk and drum, we must call information by its address on the device. A computer charge formula is usually very sensitive to the number of I/O calls to either a tape or a rapid access device. Thus, at times it is most economical to use core.

6 / Introduction to Computer Systems and Operation Systems

These memory devices will be changing and evolving over time. In the not too distant future, much larger core areas are anticipated in the application of advanced technology. Virtual memory has been added to some machines. This feature permits a program to think it has almost unlimited core storage available.

In addition to the input forms above, the output can be in printout format. Here the results of the program run are printed by a high-speed printing device using specially formated paper.

We have referred to some of the hardware devices present at a computer center. These include the computer itself; printing and reading devices; and tape, disk, and drum devices. A sample system configuration appears in Fig. 1-6. The configuration includes a main computer, operator console, printer, card reader and punch, and disk and tape drives. Additional equipment includes a sorting machine for classifying punched cards and terminal devices. For example, it is possible to have results displayed on a cathode-ray tube (referred to as a CRT). There may also be special purpose output and display terminals. Here a *terminal* is a console that may resemble a large typewriter.

Figure 1-6. Computer center configuration.

## 1.2 Computer Processing

Computer processing can be classified as batch or on-line. Batch processing is when a number of jobs are input and processed to be returned several minutes or hours later. On-line processing gives the user or programmer more immediate results, usually through a terminal device. Time-sharing computer processing is when many users simultaneously share the time of a computer to process jobs.

In time sharing, the users each "talk" to the computer individually. A control unit sequences the programs to efficiently utilize processing power and memory.

The execution time for a program is measured in microseconds ($10^{-6}$ seconds) and nanoseconds ($10^{-9}$ seconds). This is measured by an internal clock that monitors time by the number of internal cycles. Thus, the execution of an individual instruction consumes some number of cycles. The time per cycle depends on the machinery.

The time from submitting a program until its return is called *turnaround time*. Short turnaround time is advantageous for the rapid correction of errors in a program. This is a feature of a time-sharing system that permits many users to interact simultaneously with the computer through individual terminals. Time sharing is frequently expensive, however, especially with large programs, due to core and CPU (central processing unit) requirements.

Computer processing is not yet at the stage where a user can communicate to a computer in natural English or voice. At present, we must resort to a standardized language and format for programs and data. A program that is written in a given language is converted to a machine language for manipulation directly by the computer. The converter or translator is called a *compiler*. Because a program's efficiency depends in part on the computer and its ability to set up and store arrays, tables, and instructions, compilers are revised periodically. Compilers can detect many errors in format and some errors in logic. Correcting errors is given the label *debugging*. If a program is compiled without error, it can enter the *execution phase* where the actual operations as specified by the program are performed.

There are a number of programming languages now in use. FORTRAN IV is commonly used for scientific problems. COBOL is used for accounting and routine business operations. Some languages are designed for simulation. Other languages are PL/1, BASIC, APL, and ALGOL. Some of these are dynamic, in that changes and modifications are frequently introduced.

Because we wish to concentrate on operations research and statistical areas, we shall be mainly concerned with FORTRAN IV programming except for simulation languages.

The compiler is considered to be part of the general software for the computer. The controlling software is called the *operating system*. This software includes I/O control, editing, and program coordination.

When setting up a program, the user must insert job control cards at the beginning of his deck of punched cards to be identified by the software so that proper compilers, storage, and I/O devices can be set up to handle the program. These job control cards are followed by the program. If there are data that are not in the program itself, they must be placed after the program and preceded by a job control card in order to identify them as data. At the end of the data, additional cards are needed to notify the operating system that the data has ended.

## 1.3 Program Construction

We have talked about errors in formating. Once the program is run, the errors may be very subtle to detect due to the gradual accumulation of roundoff and truncation errors. Termed *numerical contamination*, it is a major problem with complex programs. A method may theoretically converge to a solution but contamination may lead to an erroneous solution or no solution at all.

Another class of errors is related to optimal construction of programs. To solve a given problem, many different programs can be written. Each may require a different amount of storage and may have a different sequence of operations. For example, matrices can be stored in a matrix form or as a one-dimensional array with pointers to indicate the beginning of each row. If a problem is simple, many programs can reach a correct solution in reasonable time. The problems arise in large, complex, or operating system-dependent programs. An example of the last is a program that has been constructed around the properties of an operating system.

Much work has been expended on automated programming and design. Unfortunately, the results have not kept pace with the developments in hardware. As a result, many computer projects run afoul with software errors so that costs mount and deadlines are not met. In one navigation program, for example, a comma was omitted. The result was a satellite that went off track, leading to an unsuccessful mission.

Available to the programmer are, however, several program checkout aids. One is a program that automatically flowcharts a program written in a high level language. Another is the check-out compiler that not only detects simple errors but also blocks of code that cannot be reached because of the program structure as well as locations for internal locking in a do loop.

The specific steps in program construction are

> General layout of methods.
> Flowcharting.
> Programming.
> Debugging and modifications.

The last two steps have already been examined. Method layout consists of a general specification of the algorithms and techniques to be used. Parameter ranges may be specified. Flowcharting consists of designing the various modules of the program and producing a flow of information through the program.

## 1.4 Operations Systems

Previously we have examined computer systems that provide a framework within which we attempt to solve problems. Computing systems are but one example of a general system.

A *system* can be viewed as a collection of units or modules that interact and interface with each other according to a partially or totally specified plan. Almost all operations problems deal with some system that is dynamic in some sense (hence, the name *operations system*). Dynamic is meant to convey a sense of time dependence. Decisions based on data will be implemented at a later time. Observations of a satellite can be used to estimate the position of the satellite at some future time. For data collected on several drugs and their effectiveness, statistical tests can reveal which are ineffective and should not be marketed in the future. Based on traffic statistics, a network analysis method can measure the shortest path and best route for bus riders. Stored for rapid access, the bus rider can call and be given the best route to suit his needs. School or election boundaries can be modified to satisfy certain population conditions. Mathematical programming can find the least disruptive alteration that can then be implemented for the next school year or election. Using simulation, inventory policies and storage for a future factory can be specified. Seen in this light the operations analysis tools of this book provide a means that, when supported by computer systems, can address these decision-making problems. The objectives of decision making include obtaining the best configuration of parts of operations and establishing policies for economical and efficient operation.

Implicit in the analysis of an operations system is the connection between the system and the surrounding environment. This environment can be represented by noise, random arrivals or events, demands, and conditions that constrain the scope of the decision maker.

At this point we could inquire as to the need for these operation analysis methods. After all, if an operations system is real, it can be studied and modified. This is true for some systems but, for moderate-sized systems, working with the system directly in an active role may have a detrimental economic effect. This is not to say, however, that operations analysis is not involved in the present system. Passive observation and small-scale experimentation are an integral part of operations analysis. To test alternative strategies, a model is constructed that represents the operations systems to be studied. The model is then combined with the appropriate mathematical tools and embodied in a computer program. The program is processed and run repeatedly to evaluate alternatives.

For a model to be useful, it must be representative of the operations system. Validation and sample runs must be done with the model to test the fit between the model output and the actual system performance. Errors uncovered in this stage often lead to modifying assumptions on which the model is based. In statistics this could lead to modifying the assumption on the behavior of some variable. In network analysis, simulation, and mathematical programming this could result in a modified framework of conditions or constraints.

Because of the complexity and size of many problems in operations systems, even a correct model may flounder because of faulty or incomplete implementation. Implementation of a model for an operations system involves much more than correct programming. It involves the handling of information within the model and the communication with the user of the model. Too little emphasis has been placed on data management and handling. Selection of proper arrangements of data within the computer can provide flexibility and adaptability for many uses of the model. It can also be so constructed that if hardware or data input format is changed even slightly, most of the model must be reimplemented. This leads to data management being of paramount importance in the design and construction of a model.

Just as subsystems can be combined to form larger systems, models can be constructed from component models that analyze the corresponding subsystems. This modular method of construction and analysis is another key to obtaining usable models. In programming this is represented by management wherein a master programmer directs the construction of subprograms that can then be tested individually and validated. After validation, subprograms can then be composed. This approach in model design and construction together with data handling are two primary ingredients in analyzing large and complex systems. Several examples in later chapters are based on models that embody several operations analysis tools.

## 1.5 Applications of Computer Based Models

Computer programming and computer-dependent decision making are spreading to almost all areas of research, business, and government. Part of this increase is due to the growth of information and data. Hardware development has also made computer time, in general, cheaper and more available. Finally, various segments of science, medicine, and economics employ technical methods with computing devices. The medical sciences employ a variety of statistical methods, simulation, and data management. Satellite and aircraft tracking employ numerical analysis and data retrieval. Transportation uses statistics for estimation, network analysis, and reliability. Fuel-producing industries utilize linear programming and integer programming. In Chapters 2 to 7, we shall study topics in data management, mathematical programming, networks, statistics, simulation, and numerical analysis and detail some of these applications along with available programs for analysis.

When considering any available programs, attention should be paid to the size of problem it can solve, the running time as a function of size, and the ease with which the program can be used. Manuals should indicate formats of data cards, control cards, and error messages. Sample printouts of problems should be displayed.

The size of the software-producing industry for these various disciplines has led to journals exclusively devoted to disseminating information on available programs and advancements in technology.

The periodical *Software World* is an international report on the software market, production, and business applications as well as state-of-the-art in software. International Computer Programs, Inc. publishes the *ICP Quarterly*, which is a catalog of computer programs which are commercially available.

A description of many programs available through computer user groups appears in the *Computer Programs Directory 1971*.[1] Published by the Joint User Group of the Association of Computing Machinery, this provides for each program the acronym, documentation, author, price, and a short description. The sources of these programs are groups of users of a given manufacturer. These include

SHARE (IBM Users of 360, 370)

RCA-CUA (Computer User Association)

XDS Users

FOCUS (Control Data Corporation)

UUA (Univac Users Society)

CUBE (Cooperative Users of Burroughs Equipment)

H-400/1400, H-800 (Honeywell User Groups)

Addresses of these and other user groups appear in Section 1.6.

Several universities have created a library called Educational Information Network (EIN).

Programs include business applications, operations research, matrix operations, statistics, numerical analysis and data management. Addresses and contacts appear in the *Computer Programs Directory*.

In addition to periodicals and user groups, there are sources where many existing programs can be obtained. For example, many programs written under contract to NASA can be obtained from the Computer Software Management and Information Center (COSMIC) at the University of Georgia. COSMIC also handles some of the SHARE programs. When evaluating available software from user groups, manufacturers, or software firms, several criteria apply. First is the question of compatibility. Can the program function on the available machine and peripheral equipment? Is the core storage sufficient? This can be determined by examining the user's guide or manual that is usually available with the program. A rewrite of a major program may consume more resources than are available for a one-time application. A second criterion in evaluation is the language. If a program is acquired, is it in source or object code? An object code written in assembly language is difficult to work with unless the specific problem fits easily into the program framework. A third aid in evaluation is to contact existing users who have applied it in similar circumstances. Some programs are written especially for applications in business, civil engineering, and astronautics. In evaluation it is also important to examine the available error messages and corrections. A fifth question relates to the level of usage. A popular program employed by many users will be more experienced and checked out. Program support after evaluation and selection is another criterion. A number of articles have been written on the subject of evaluation. One appeared in the April, 1970 issue of the *ICP Quarterly*. This article lists some of the detailed characteristics of vendors and software.

There are a number of technical journals devoted to computation, computer sciences, and their applications. A partial listing appears below:

Computer Sciences

> *Computing Reviews*
> 
> *Journal of the Association for Computing Machinery*
> 
> *Computer Journal*
> 
> *Computer Bulletin*
> 
> *Computing Report*

Applications

> *Computer Physics Communications*
> 
> *Computers and Biomedical Research*
> 
> *Management Science*
> 
> *Operations Research*

This list will be expanded in later chapters.

In this chapter, computers and operations systems have been discussed. It should be pointed out that there are limitations and shortcomings to computers and their use. Computers have been overused in some cases in that data and reports have been produced that have been little utilized. It is possible to characterize situations in which computer systems can be employed. First, the problem should be either repetitive or of such importance that the cost of building and running the programs can be justified from the standpoint of costs. Second, the problem should remain in the same mathematical form over time so that the system can be employed over a sufficient time horizon. This also means that the size of the problem does not radically change so as to affect the reliability of the operations system in obtaining a solution. The problem should be of such a size and/or complexity that it can be most effectively solved by an operations system. The value of the program should be measurable in cost savings, performance gains, or understanding relationships and satisfying research goals.

## 1.6 Remarks

Having discussed the computer, software, sources, and applications, it might be appropriate to examine several other computer-related topics. For a number of uses of the computer, it is unnecessary to have large processing capabilities. Also, there may be physical space limitations. This has led to the development of *minicomputers*, which are small computers that sometimes have special capabilities for handling a limited class of problems. The hardware development has been rapid and software for mini's is now progressing.

Other advances are being made in memory design and computer sharing of hardware and software across a communication network. These portend even more utilization of computers in both scope and depth, as resources are made available on a wider basis. This will lead to greater dependence on computers for handling routine tasks and investigating the behavior of physical systems using as tools the methods of mathematical sciences.

References in this chapter are to texts that deal with general computer techniques and computer science at an elementary or intermediate level. Rice and Rice[6] is a basic level course for introduction to computers. Flores[2] examines the internal structure of computers. References 3, 4, and 7 examine general aspects of computer sciences. Knuth[5] is a collection of several volumes that examines in detail computer applications and structure.

# REFERENCES

*Textbooks*

1. FADEN, B. R. (ED.), *Computer Programs Directory—1971*. New York: CCM Information Corp., 1971.
2. FLORES, I., *Computer Logic: The Functional Design of Digital Computers*. Englewood Cliffs, N. J.: Prentice-Hall, Inc., 1960.
3. —,*Computer Software: Programming Systems for Digital Computers*. Englewood Cliffs, N. J.: Prentice-Hall, Inc., 1965.
4. HULL, T. E., AND D. D. F. DAY, *Computers and Problem Solving*. Reading, Mass.: Addison-Wesley, Pub. Co., Inc., 1970.
5. KNUTH, B. E., *The Art of Computer Programming*, Vol. 1–3. Reading, Mass.: Addison-Wesley Pub. Co., Inc., 1964.
6. RICE, J. K. AND J. R. RICE, *Introduction to Computer Science*. New York: Holt, Reinhart and Winston, Inc., 1969.
7. WEGNER, P., *Programming Languages, Information Structures, and Machine Organization*. New York: McGraw-Hill Book Co., 1968.

Table 1-1. COMPUTER USER ORGANIZATIONS HARDWARE SPECIFIC ORGANIZATIONS

| | | |
|---|---|---|
| CAP | Council to Advance Programming<br>Honeywell CAP User's Group<br>Honeywell Computer Control Division<br>Framingham, Mass. 01701 | |
| COMMON | Users Group for Small IBM Computers<br>Computer Center<br>University of South Dakota<br>Vermillion, S. D. 57069 | |
| DECUS | Digital Equipment Computer Users Society<br>DECUS<br>Main Street<br>Maynard, Mass. 01754 | |
| DEUA | Digitronics Equipment Users Assn.<br>Systems Research and Development<br>Continental Insurance Co.<br>80 Maiden Lane<br>New York, N. Y. 10038 | |
| FOCUS | Forum of Control Data Users<br>Control Data Corporation<br>13145 Porter Drive<br>Palo Alto, Calif. 94304 | |
| GET | GE Computer Users Association<br>Penn Park Building<br>General Electric Company<br>P.O. Box 8555<br>Philadelphia, Pa. 19104 | |

16 / Introduction to Computer Systems and Operation Systems

GUIDE — IBM Large Scale Computer Users Group
University of Wisconsin
1220 Linden Drive
Madison, Wis. 53706

H-400/1400 — Honeywell 400/1400 Users Association
National Industry Conference Board
345 Third Avenue
New York, N. Y. 10022

HUG — Honeywell 800/1200 Users Association
Philadelphia Electric Company
2301 Market Street
Philadelphia, Pa. 19103

SERCUS — Raytheon Computer Users Group
Raytheon Computer
2700 South Fairview Street
Santa Ana, Calif. 92704

SHARE — IBM 360, 370 Users Group
Share, Inc.
Suite 750
25 Broadway
New York, N. Y. 10004

SNUG — Scientific Users of NCR Computer
40 National Cash Reporter Company
Main and K Streets
Dayton, Ohio 45409

USE — Univac Scientific Exchange
Univac Division, Sperry Rand Corp.
P.O. Box 8100
Philadelphia, Pa. 19101

UUA — Univac Users Society
Harris Trust and Savings Bank
P.O. Box 755, 111 Monroe Street
Chicago, Ill. 60690

VIM — Users of Control Data Series Computers
Westinghouse Electric Corp.
Bettes Atomic Power Laboratory
P.O. Box 79
West Mifflin, Pa. 15122

XDS Users — Users of Xerox Data Systems Computers
701 South Aviation
El Segundo, Calif.

*Other User Organizations*

ACUTE — Accountants Computer Users for Technical Exchange
P. O. Box 4076, Grand Central Station
New York, N. Y. 10017

| | |
|---|---|
| AIChE | Machine Computation Committee<br>American Institute of Chemical Engineers<br>Engineering Department<br>E. I. DuPont de Nemours<br>Lonvier Building<br>Wilmington, Del. 19898 |
| BIO | Biological Information-Processing Organization<br>Department of Biophysics<br>University of North Carolina<br>Chapel Hill, N. C. 27514 |
| CEPA | Civil Engineering Program Applications<br>Tibbette, Abbett, McCarthy, and Stratton<br>375 Park Avenue<br>New York, N. Y. 10022 |
| ECHO | Electronic Computing—Hospital Oriented<br>McHorel Reese Hospital and Medical Center<br>29th Street and Ellis Avenue<br>Chicago, Ill. 60616 |
| EDUCOM | Educational Information Network (EIN)<br>100 Charles River Plaza<br>Boston, Mass. 02114 |
| JUG | Joint Users Group<br>DECUS<br>Maynard, Mass. 01754 |

# 2

# DATA MANAGEMENT AND INFORMATION SYSTEMS

## 2.1 Introduction and Data Handling

Data management systems appear to be simple to understand and implement. This appearance is not only deceptive but also has cost corporations and governments millions of dollars with hardly any return. This is due to faulty design, overly ambitious goals, and incomplete construction. In this chapter we examine several aspects of data management including sorting, searching, file structure, and relationship to operations analysis. Data management is concerned with the storage, manipulation, and retrieval of information. Whereas numerical methods have to solve a specific problem quickly, data management must be flexible and capable of handling a variety of commands and queries from different users over a longer period of time. Because of this generality, data management systems are so complex and represent one of the most difficult parts of software development.

Involved in data management are the control of the data, the structure, a comprehensive language for users, performance, and security. Sections of this chapter will address some of these topics. The struggle for a general, useful data management language resulted in the formation of the Conference on Data Systems Languages (CODASYL). A result of research and analysis was the COBOL (*C*ommon *B*usiness *O*riented *L*anguage) language. It, too, possessed shortcomings, however, and so the search continues.

Of growing importance to data systems is the security of the information from unauthorized users. Security means here that each user is not allowed to access information to which he should not have knowledge. The security or integrity problem is intense because many firms and government agencies are now storing personnel records, business accounts, and classified information on magnetic tape or other secondary storage devices. A common security requirement is that each potential user identify himself as to a code. There may be several codes required. This password system permits access to sensitive files. Growth of security research was spurred by the development of time sharing. If many persons are using the same computer via terminals, the danger exists for one user to access another user's file.

The actual coding and encrypting methods are descendents of codes developed long before the computer. Coding can be for individual parts of the data. This requires a user who wishes access to information to enter a sequence of code words.

Data structure centers around the data base. A *data base* is a centralized ordered grouping of information. It includes the totality of information that the user will need to access. It is stored for at least one user or application. Some examples are given below.

**Example 2.1.** At a company each employee's record is computerized to contain social security number, address, telephone number, monthly earnings, classification, and accumulated earnings and deductions. The file is the collection of employee records. A user of the system might wish to know the percent of employees making over or under a certain amount. Another use would be to correlate salary and personnel classification.

**Example 2.2.** A library maintains a record on every book including the identity of its borrower and the key words identifying the book as well as title, author, publisher, and date of publication. This

20 / Data Management and Information Systems

data base can be queried so as to determine the most popular category of books, to locate all sources with certain key words, and to list all available books by a certain author.

**Example 2.3.** An airline operates a computer-based reservation system, a route maintenance file, and a flight crew-scheduling method. The route structure is first determined and becomes part of the data base. This is then accessed by the crew-scheduling method that allocates flight crews against the schedule. The reservation system accesses the schedule to provide customers with knowledge of future flights.

Each of these examples contains a data base which consists of a file(s) which is (are) a collection(s) of records. The *record* named or labeled and the remainder of the record contains properties or attributes of the subject. Similar records become a *file*. In Example 2.3, application programs function using a central schedule of flights. These applications are called *management information systems*.

The arrangement of a data base resembles a tree diagram. (We shall use the definitions and notation of Appendix B.) The nodes in the tree are viewed as points. A single parent point is the name of the record. The properties of the name are aggregated in categories. To see this, consider a record in Table 2-1.

The levels in the tree correspond to the hierarchy and aggregation of the data. Note that because of the aggregation only the leaf points have exact information. This is the reason for allowing the leaf points to be nodes and by restricting the other vertices to be points. It would appear that if the height of the tree were great, the number of levels would be large, and the time to search and retrieve information would be great. The radix is the number of records. The process of extracting partial files and records is really then that of obtaining subtree structures. From this comparison, it is evident that there is a correspondence between procedures for accessing a data base and searching and subdividing tree structures. This correspondence will aid in the development in the next sections. Chapin,[11] for example, applies tree theory in comparing file organizations.

In Fig. 2-1. we notice that several of the leaf points have the same label (e.g., a, b, and c). In a storage context, this is inconsistent. At a minimum, we would like to move leftward in the tree from a leaf point to a parent point. Using a decimal labeling procedure, we would obtain Fig. 2-2.

**Table 2-1**

    John Doe

A. Personal Information
    1. Domicile                      (a) Address
                                     (b) Telephone
    2. Marital status           (a) Married
       Family                            i. Name of wife
                                     ii. Number of children
                                   (b) Single
                                   (c) Divorced
    3. Physical appearance    (a) Height
                                   (b) Weight
                                   (c) Defects

B. Employment Information
    1. Classification           (a) Position
                                   (b) Date classified
    2. Salary                     (a) Date of increase
                                   (b) Previous salary
    3. Record                   (a) Days of vacation
                                   (b) Days of illness

In a tree this would be arranged as shown in Fig. 2-1.

This labeling is based on adding a dimension to a vector with each level attained. Thus, level-four points are represented by four-dimensional vectors. This labeling reduces the storage of the entire tree. Only the leaf points or nodes need to be kept since by the labeling process we can trace our way to the beginning. An example is

$$(1, 1, 2, 1, 2) \rightarrow (1, 1, 2, 1) \rightarrow (1, 1, 2) \rightarrow (1, 1) \rightarrow (1)$$

In passing, we note that other labeling schemes are possible.

    A large part of a data management system is that of dealing with information retrieval. We seek to extract information efficiently out of a file. Response time here is the time to locate and retrieve the desired information and present it to the user. Location of information is discussed in Section 2.3. Retrieval depends on the structure of the file and the application program accessing the file. File structures are discussed in Section 2.2. The efficiency and form of a system depends on the percentage of the file accessed and the frequency of changes, additions, and deletions of records in the file. Some file organizations are very inefficient with many changes.

22 / Data Management and Information Systems

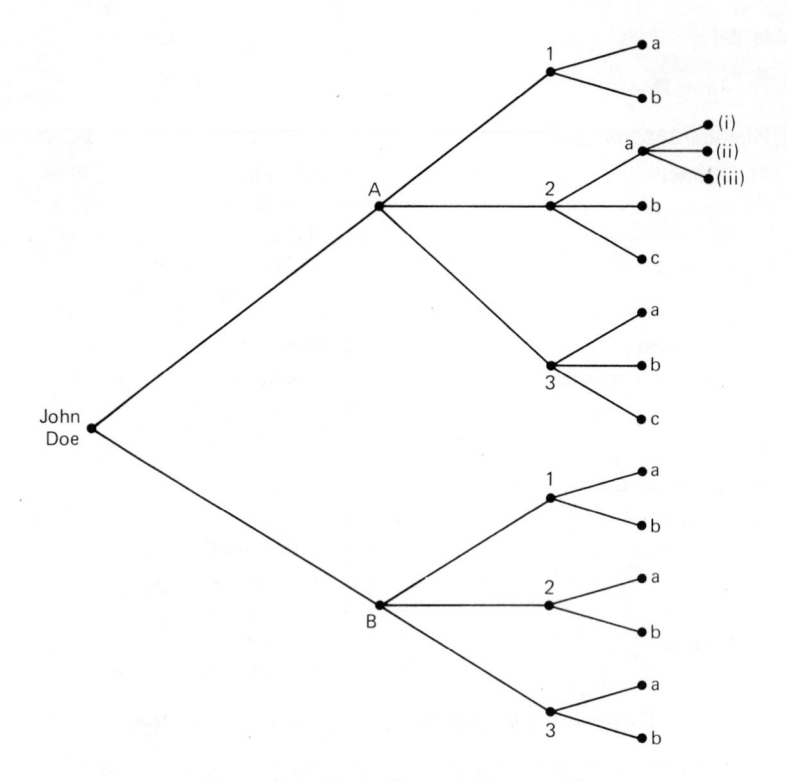

Figure 2-1. Tree diagram of a record.

Another operation with records is their sorting and arranging based on a collection of attributes. The aggregation of several files into one file is called *merging*. This is examined in Section 2.3.

There are several ways of storing a set of numbers that are logically connected in core memory. One way is by an array. An *array* is a fixed sequence of numbers, say, $a_1, ..., a_k$, such that to find $a_{i+1}$ we add one to an index associated with the previous entry ($a_i$). Arrays are restrictive in that the sequence of entries in the array must be contiguous. A more useful method of storage is a list structure. In a *list structure*, each record contains a pointer to the next item in the sequence. List records, because of these pointers, do not require consecutive addresses in core. That flexibility in a list is beneficial is borne out in considering the addition or deletion of elements in the list. A record can be added by inserting the record and changing the pointer of the predecessor record. Deletion is accomplished in a similar manner. In an array the element would have to be removed and a new array constructed.

A *sorted list* is a list arranged in order (descending or ascending). This order is a precedence relationship between elements of the list. A *sublist* is a list within a list. A list structure is a collection of lists within lists. If several lists share a common sublist, then it is wasteful in storage to replicate the sublist for each list in which it is contained. Because of the list properties, we can keep it once and point to it from each list. A list can have its records point forward and backward in the sequence. This means that inserted in the record are two pointers: one to the preceding entry and one to the following entry. This costs storage for pointers, but allows us to search both ways for an item instead of going through the records to the end of the file and restarting.

In some restaurants, plates are stacked on top of previously cleaned plates. When plates are needed, they are removed from the

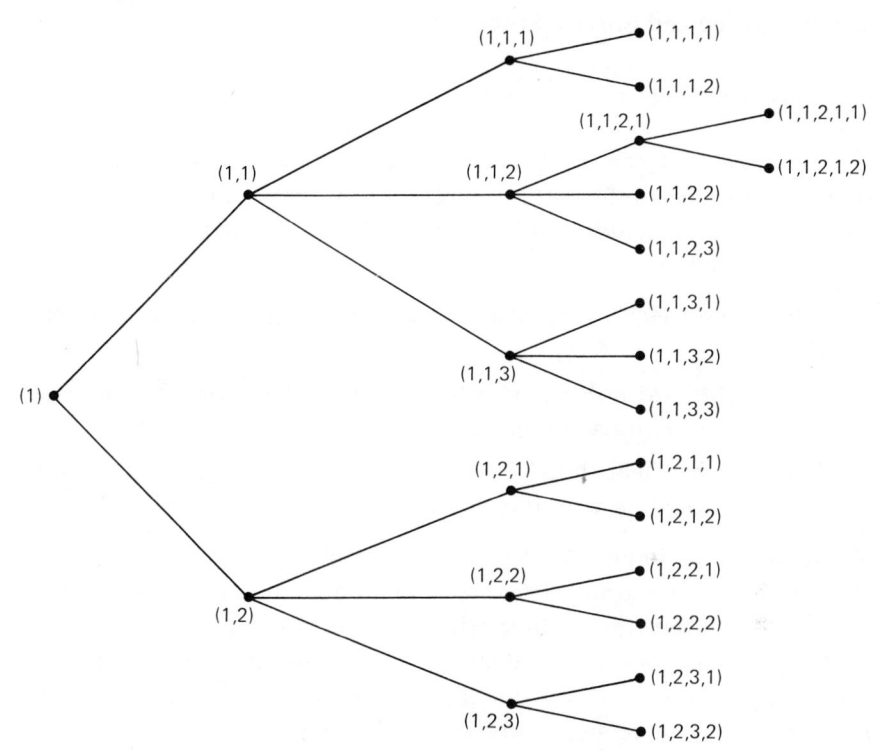

Figure 2-2. Labeled tree of a record.

top of the stack. This is an example of a push-down table or stack. A *push-down list* is one that can only be modified by modifying the item at the top of the list. It follows that additions and removals to the list occur when the affected items are at the head of the list.

To see how a push-down list functions, let us consider searching through a data base. As the search progresses in the structure, the removed or searched items are stored in another push-down list. Thus, when we wish to back up to the previous level, we go to the new push-down list.

List structures are common enough to warrant a language, LISP. One text on LISP is Weissman.[14] A language like LISP is oriented toward processing lists as units. Communication between the compiler and the user is list oriented in structure.

## 2.2 Searching and Sorting Procedures

### 2.2.1 *Overview and examples*

An important part of a data management system is its ability to transfer and access information in response to user commands. These requests might include asking some of the following queries of appropriate data bases:

Who owns a 1970 Chevrolet with Nevada license plates containing a"9"?

Are credit card holders who have been in debt for 10 years and who are married bad credit risks?

How much wheat did Canada ship to England in 1965 and how did that compare with the annual shipments from 1950 to 1964?

These questions require the system to systematically search through the files until the proper records and items are found. After the search, the system then either prints out the information or else provides it to a subroutine for analysis. The query on wheat shipments not only requires retrieval but also comparison by some statistical method such as regression analysis (see Chapter 5).

Questions can be efficiently answered by requiring the arrangement of records in the data base to be in a specified order. For example, the wheat shipments could be stored increasingly by volume (ascending) or decreasing by year (descending). A tracking system for aircraft may store aircraft records in order of ascending distance from a central point. A corporation may want to arrange customers by metropolitan area first and then within the area by volume level and subsequently by alphabetical order. These are examples of sorting problems. A sorting procedure is a method by which information is arranged according to a set of criteria specified by the user.

Suppose now that several government agencies are pooling their data bases for economy of scale. This appears like a merger of information. A sorting procedure for two or more separate files is called a *merging procedure.* On a less global scale, a person may be connected to an information network on nonfatal accidents. Information is stored at seven computer sites across the United States. The user queries each center to obtain a subfile of the information desired. After performing this seven times, he wishes to put these records in order on the basis of the year and make of automobile. This would entail merging procedures for seven files.

The examples above indicate the importance of searching, sorting, and merging routines for the user of a data management system. These operations are among the prime ingredients in the failure or success of the system. For example, inefficient sorting procedures may take excessive computer time and resources that could occur if sorting had been done on an infrequently accessed attribute.

In selecting and using these procedures, several points should be kept in mind. First, there are the constraints of the existing system. Many sorting routines require additional core areas for storing intermediate or partial lists or arrays. Second, it makes a difference whether a search is through a sorted array or list and whether it is a list structure. Third, if the process is a one-time use or use with a small amount of data, then the sorting routine in the supporting software can be used. This is accessed by the user as a utility program using job control cards. Another point to consider is that many operations research and statistical methods require the arrangement of data for efficiency of a solutions procedure or estimation method. We shall consider several examples of this in the next chapters.

### 2.2.2 Search procedures

A search procedure is a method for examining a file structure for an item(s) satisfying a given set of conditions. Usually the method will stop when it encounters the first entry that satisfies the condition. Here we shall examine several of the basic search methods. More elaborate methods have been constructed by combining features of two or more methods.

A simple search procedure for an array or list is a linear search. In a *linear search* we test the value of a given attribute in each record. If this value equals the value that the user has specified, then the search ends. If it is not equal to the value, it goes to the next record. This is possible in a list since each record contains a pointer to the next record in the list. If the array or list is not ordered on this attribute, then the search must continue until a match occurs or until the end of the list is reached. If a search fails and there is no match, the preset test entry can be inserted. The drawback to this insertion is that if the memory space is limited, there is some chance of an overflow. That is, the information being input overflows the preset allocated capacity.

As an example of a linear search, consider the following array:

|     |     |
| --- | --- |
| YYT | SLQ |
| XJC | APP |
| FXH | SLJ |
| CTW | SLQ |
| DUQ | EYT |

The sixth item is the SLQ on the top of the second column. Suppose we wish to see if SLQ is in the array. We begin in a linear search at the top and test each item. We would terminate the search after six items have been tested.

If the test had been for BJR, then the search would have tested every item in the array. Failure would have occurred and the item BJR could have been added to the bottom of the list.

Now consider the case where the array is ordered alphabetically so that the array appears as

|     |     |
| --- | --- |
| APP | SLJ |
| CTW | SLQ |
| DUQ | SLQ |
| EYT | XJC |
| FXH | YYT |

In the first search SLQ would be found after seven tests or probes while the absence of BJR would have been detected after two tests. On the average, a sorted array or list can be searched with fewer tests than an unsorted one. Indeed, if this had been a two-way list (a list where each record has two pointers), then knowing that S is near the end of the alphabet, we could have started the search with YYT and ended after three tests.

Termination in a sorted file would occur in general when the item tested exceeds the test value. If the test value was higher than that being probed, the search would continue.

Another property of a linear search is that a file can be run across or traversed. This means that items in the file can be skipped. The logic of the linear search permits this.

For a sorted array, the linear search appears slow in the sense that we should not be forced to start at the beginning of the array. For SLQ, it would be better to start in the middle and then move out in the proper direction. This is called a *skip search* where the items are not scanned successively. We shall consider a specific skip searching procedure here, namely, a *binary search*. This search will not work with lists or unsorted arrays because it depends on the adjacency of items and on the ordered structure of the array.

Suppose we have the sorted array of the previous example. The binary search takes the number of items (10), divides it in half to obtain 5, and examines either the fifth or sixth entry. The fifth entry is the largest entry in the first half of the array (when the array is sorted in an ascending order), while the sixth element is the smallest entry of the second half of the array. If the fifth element is tested and found to be larger than the test element, we know that the search must continue in this half. If it is equal to the fifth element, then we stop searching. If it is greater than the fifth element, the search continues in the second half of the array. A similar argument holds for testing the sixth element. The first test has thus reduced the array where we must search by one-half.

If we had tested the fifth element (FXH) with SLQ, we would move to the second half of the array. At the next stage, we divide the half of the array remaining into two parts. Since 5 (the array length) is odd, we can divide it after 2 or 3 elements. We then repeat the same procedure as above with the second or third element. For our example, we see that either way we complete our search since both the second and third elements are equal to SLQ.

28 / Data Management and Information Systems

The search for SLQ took two tests in the example above. In general, with each test, we reduce the size of the part of the array to be searched by one-half. Suppose the search terminated after $k$ steps; then because of this successive one-half reduction, the length of the array $N$ is approximately $2^k$ or $k = lnN$ is an upper bound to the number of tests required. This is the reason for using a binary search for a sorted array.

The binary search can also be modified to test an inequality as well as equality. In the example above, we can ask to find the first entry $\leqslant$ or $\geqslant$ SLQ. Each test consumes slightly more time but termination may occur earlier. Surprisingly, a linear search is more efficient than a binary search if an array is very short since then the mechanics of dividing a small array and testing exceed the time to methodically test successive items.

With the efficiency of the binary search for large arrays, it would be desirable to adapt the method for list structures that have been presorted by some order relationship. In a list structure, the arrangement has to permit a binary choice and then at each point the remainder of the number of records remaining in the list must be halved. Consider the sorted list in our example with XJC and YYT deleted and arranged as in Fig. 2-3.

In Fig. 2.3. the entries are arranged in ascending order along the bottom. This corresponds to the labeling in the tree structure itself

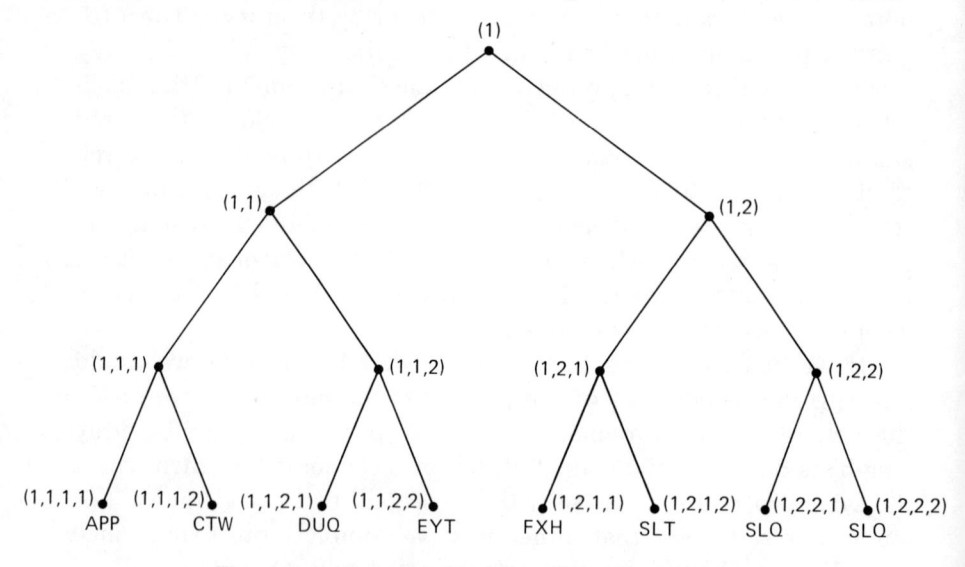

Figure 2-3. Tree diagram of modified list example.

since (1, 1, 1, 1) precedes (1, 1, 1, 2) precedes (1, 1, 2, 1), etc. Now we begin our search at the top of the tree. The branch (1, 1) corresponds to all items beginning with A to E and (1, 2) with items beginning with F to Z. If we are looking for SLQ, then we would go to (1, 2) thereby deleting half of the tree. At (1, 2) we test whether SLQ is less than or equal to SLJ or not. Since SLQ is greater than SLJ, we proceed to test (1, 2, 2). Since both leaf points are the same, we are through. This is an example of a *path search*. Since we display the list in a tree structure and eliminate one-half of the remaining tree at each step, we have a binary tree search.

It should be noted that the tree with all items in the array example can be drawn. It appears in Fig. 2-4 as more ragged than that in Fig. 2-3. The method is still the same, however, although the height of the tree has been increased by one level.

Thus, we again check to see if the item begins with A to E or F to Z and continue the procedure. In programming, each point in the tree would contain two points and the check would be in a binary form so that branching can occur. At the end of the tree the leaf nodes can have pointers with the same direction to indicate the end of the tree.

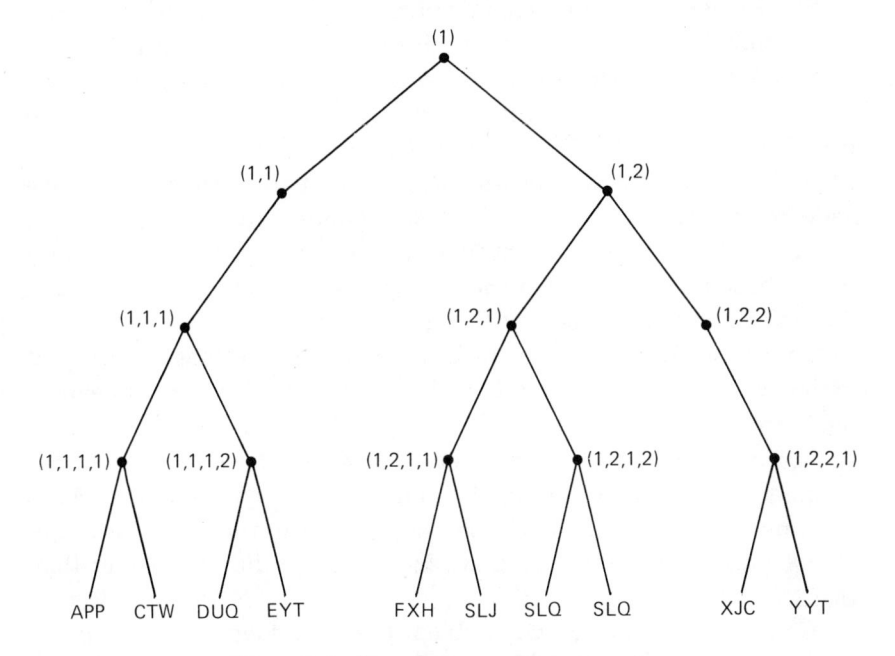

Figure 2-4. Tree diagram of list example.

Another approach is to avoid physically searching through the records. Rather we would construct a method to determine where it belongs. To do this, it is necessary to determine the item position in core. This means keeping a table where items are indicated by a code. An advantage of this method is that entries can be scattered throughout storage. The process is sometimes referred to as *hashing* and the code as a *hash code*. Considerable work has gone into hash codes.

One coding method is to form the product of the item number and a fixed real number (usually irrational, such as $\sqrt{2}$) and extract the last 10 bits in the binary representation of the product. The hope is that the numbers that result are distinct. Another code is to divide the item number by the size of the table of codes (hash table) and use the remainder from the division as the code. Resolution of the situation where items have duplicate codes follows by storing these in a separate list for checking.

One disadvantage of the hashing method is that the size of the hash table must be prespecified. If items are added, this can create problems. Another drawback lies in the difficulty in skipping across the items. The hashing method is effective for large amounts of data, however, and it does replace searching by position locating in a table.

Several searching problems involve the location of an entry with a maximum or minimum value with respect to a given criterion. A method for finding the maximum entry in a file is to begin with the first entry. If the second entry exceeds the first entry in value, the second entry is retained and the first entry is discarded. If the first entry is larger, we continue with it. Thus, at the $K$th step we have made $K$ comparisons and we have the largest entry of the first $K$ items. At the end of a pass through the file, we obtain the maximum value (show this). A similar method holds for finding the minimum of a set of numbers (construct this method).

To see how this could be programmed, suppose that the array of entries was given by (A(J) : $1 \leqslant J \leqslant 50$). One program appears in Fig. 2-5.

We first read in the array and set XMAX equal to the first entry. Statement 9 tests if we are at the end of the array. Statement 10 is the comparison of XMAX and the next entry in the array. We reset XMAX (statement 11) only if we have found a number larger than XMAX.

Consider as a last search problem the first query posed on p. 24. This is complicated in that several conditions are attached. The ve-

```
        DIMENSION A (50)
        READ (1,100) A(I), I =1, 50
100     FORMAT (F10.4)
        XMAX = A(1)
        I =2
9       IF (50-I) 101, 10, 10
10      IF (XMAX- A (I) ) 11, 12, 12
11      XMAX = A (I)
12      I =I +1
        GO TO 9
101     WRITE (5,102) XMAX
102     FORMAT ('MAX IS', 2X, F10.4)
        STOP
        END
```

Figure 2-5. Program to locate the maximum of a set of numbers.

hicle must be made in 1970, be a Chevrolet, and have a Nevada license plate that contains a 9. An alternative to the search methods above is to use an inverted file structure. This structure is a set of vectors. Each vector is keyed to an attribute possible for access. The remaining components of the vector contain pointers which identify record locations which have this attribute. For example, if the file contained information on a collection of automobiles, then possible attributes include car model, year, make, license, engine, and owner. There could be a vector for sedans, coupes, 1954, 1962, Chevrolet, Plymouth, Ford, etc. Looking into the 1970 vector would yield pointers to the records of all 1970 cars.

In a search for a car with a given set of attributes, each vector of this set of attributes is searched and any pointers to common records are detected (why?). This is done prior to going to the main file of cars. All records that have all these attributes are then examined in the main car file in core.

The problem with an inverted file structure lies in part in updating. Each time a record is added, the relevant lists of attributes must be added to. Arrays must be changed. The advantages lie in avoiding a lengthy search through the main file.

### 2.2.3 *Sorting and merging procedures*

Sorting procedures can be related to a search procedure. For example, suppose a list or array is located in storage that we wish to sort in ascending order. The first entry is read into the new list where the sorted information will be stored. The second item is then compared with the first. If the second item exceeds the first, then it is placed after the first entry. Otherwise, the second entry precedes the first entry. The process continues. As a new item is brought in, its location is determined by (say) a linear search of the existing sorted sublist. This procedure continues until the entire list is formed. If there are $M$ items to be sorted and if $N$ items have been sorted already, then it will take on the average $N/2$ moves to find the location. Assuming that the average list length is $M/2$, then the average number of steps is $M/2/2$ (= $M/4$). If we perform this operation $M$ times, the total number of steps is $M^2/4$.

Another sorting procedure based on search is to find the smallest element in the list, remove it from the list, and repeat the procedure. At each point, we are finding the minimum of a smaller number of values. The average number of moves to accomplish this using the reasoning on averages above is $N^2/2$. These averages should be taken seriously but not as final because they assume phenomena are behaving uniformly so that certain events are equally likely to occur.

A second procedure based on maximization is to begin as in the search method when a new maximum value occurs. Then we trade places of the new and old maximum value and continue. At the end, if any changes have been made, the entire process is repeated. An example is given below. Consider the numbers.

$$8, 7, 5, 9, 6, 11, 10$$

On the first pass, 8 is the maximum value until 9 occurs. The 8 is inserted before the 9 to obtain

$$7, 5, 8, 9, 6, 11, 10$$

The 9 drops out due to the presence of the 11 to obtain

$$7, 5, 8, 6, 9, 11, 10$$

The 11 and 10 exchange places and we begin at the start of the array with the 7 since changes occurred in the previous pass. After the second pass, we obtain

$$5, 7, 6, 8, 9, 10, 11$$

The third pass interchanges the 6 and 7. Since there was an exchange, a last pass is run; since then there are no exchanges, we are through.

Sorting can also be done by the hardware sorting device. This device sorts on the value in one column on a standard keypunch card. A given subcollection can then be sorted on another column. The process can be repeated.

A technique to speed up sorting is to construct a table of pointers (one for each item), sort this table, and access.

The third topic we wish to consider here is a generalization of sorting to handle multiple arrays or lists. This operation is called *merging*. Each list to be combined is assumed to be sorted with respect to the same order relationship. Consider the following lists and let $Z(K)$ be the $K$th element of the merged list.

| $X(I)$ | $Y(J)$ |
|--------|--------|
| 1 | 2 |
| 5 | 4 |
| 6 | 7 |
| 8 | 9 |
| 11 | 12 |

We begin at the top and compare $X(1)$ and $Y(1)$. Since $X(1) < Y(1)$, we know $X(1)$ is the first element in the new list (why?). Thus, we define $Z(1) = X(1)$. The element $X(1)$ is now deleted since it has been put in the merged array and we compare $X(2) = 5$ with $Y(1)$. Since $X(2) > Y(1)$, we set $Z(2) = Y(1)$. Next we remove $Y(1)$ and compare $X(2)$ and $Y(2)$. This yields $Z(3) = Y(2) < X(2)$. This process continues until one list is empty. Then the remainder of the other list (nonempty) is included at the bottom of the merged list. The list $Z(k)$ appears as

| Z(1) | Z(2) | Z(3) | Z(4) | Z(5) | Z(6) | Z(7) | Z(8) | Z(9) | Z(10) |
|------|------|------|------|------|------|------|------|------|-------|
| X(1) | Y(1) | Y(2) | X(2) | X(3) | Y(3) | X(4) | Y(4) | X(5) | Y(5) |

The programming of this method is direct in that we begin at the top of the lists, make comparisons, and move down in the table. We should note, however, that in programming this method we would have to check at each stage on whether either list was empty. The merging procedure outlined above can be generalized to more than two lists in a pairwise manner.

## 2.3 File Structures and Selection

This section examines some of the popular file structures in terms of advantages and disadvantages as well as relationship to operations analysis methods. File selection together with the programs that operate on the files constitute the system connected to a data base structure.

There are three general categories of file structure form: sequential, random access, and list. The data base can be designed in either a horizontal or a vertical hierarchy. In a vertical hierarchy, the components are the attributes of the subject (items), the collection of attributes (record), and the collection of records (file). To search through files, indicators are needed for checking. These are called *access keys*.

For a horizontal hierarchy, the data base is structured around the storage device. For data management applications, the most common structures with horizontal hierarchy include sequential, indexed sequential, inverted list, ring, double linked, and multilist.

The most common structure is that of sequential files. Records are stored in locations referencing other records in a specified order and ordered by attribute. An advantage of this method is rapid access if the file is accessed in order of attribute. Ordering reduces the need for identification words and thereby reduces storage space. A disadvantage is that updating may require rewriting of an entire file, another is that search procedure methods such as heuristic network methods must scan the file from the beginning. Dodd[12] indicates that an exception to this is in binary searches with random access files.

The indexed sequential file utilizes a compound file organization technique. Most of the data is stored sequentially in one file while a second file is an index directory with keys to the first file. With random access, search time is less since it takes less time to search an index file than it does to search the main file. This becomes an advantage when the application is nonsequential in structure. However, index addresses require storage and maintenance with file alteration. Flexibility is gained in growth since the main file is position independent.

In the inverted list structure an access key is assigned to each individual record. Thus, a list of accession numbers is assigned to each index term associated with the file. Search is then done through the index file for the access keys. A comparison of accession numbers from each key list will reveal availability and location in the data file. This inverted list is useful when records have a complex combination of keys, however, the key structure must be altered with major changes in the data base. The key lists also require substantial storage.

In the ring or chain structure, each data element serves as a pointer to the next element in the sequence. Data elements then make up a sequential searchable file while the elements are stored randomly in memory. The ring is completed by the last element pointing to the first. With multikeys per record, elements of different attributes can be linked. This removes the need for additional tables since data records provide pointers through the file for a single attribute. The disadvantage lies in the time for housekeeping and storage space for addressing. Chapin[11] indicates this is more severe here then in the previous structures.

The fifth method is a double-linked or multiple double-linked chain (double chain). Here a record points backward in the file as well as forward. The file is then positionally organized in either direction for a given attribute. Double pointers permit two-way searches. Updating is easier since record changes only require the added changes of the parameters of the adjoining records. Two pointers, however, increase storage space.

A multilist structure has a sequential index that contains key values for file indexing. Associated with a given key value is a pointer to the records having this value. Records are stored in fixed-size block (cells) that are referenced through their own address. Further referencing is done within each cell. This form is advantageous with large data files and records easily associated into blocks. In limited main storage a record block can be brought in from tape and then individual records can be accessed. Because of the fixed block structure, difficulties occur when records are added that overflow the fixed block. Also, the association adds another level to the addressing scheme.

The goal in file structure selection and integration for the given system configuration is efficiency constrained by available resources for implementation. An alternative to a single structure is to establish multiple formats so as to be optimal with respect to different mathematical methods that require the same data base. An example would be two operations research methods programmed in distinct languages with different functions for optimization. In addition to the user's needs, two added areas that guide file selection are the data set and device specifications. The former is the size, format, linkage, and index key, while the latter refers to the hardware.

Using these elements, let us attempt to set up a method for file selection for one type of structure as an example. This is based on minimizing cost where cost is a function of the number of I/O operations and the storage required. These costs will now be defined along with a procedure for evaluation.

The cost for storage with either sequential or random access has an associated cost per data item in storage per unit time. Denote this cost by $C_s$.

Access time is the time necessary to obtain a record for output, modification, or processing. We shall associate with it the cost of processing the record in terms of CPU time. Denote this cost by $C_a$.

Each has individual storage and access time properties for a given situation. Most of these are available for testing and have statistics on performance. The objective function for a given structure $\mathscr{S}$ is given by

$$\text{minimize } C(\mathscr{S}) \tag{2.1}$$

where

$$C(\mathscr{S}) = C_s s(\mathscr{S}) + C_a t(\mathscr{S}) \tag{2.2}$$

Here $s(\mathscr{S})$ is the total storage required by $\mathscr{S}$ and $t(\mathscr{S})$ is the average access time for $\mathscr{S}$. Note that this could be generalized to account for time dependence. Also, the advantages of one structure in terms of updating could be accounted for by adding a maintenance or overhead cost in Eq. (2.2). The constraints are the maximum delay time between request and receipt of data and storage size available.

Input for the model comes from the user and data base and device specifications. Some of the parameters for the user include the following lists. It should be remarked that these lists are for example only and are not to be taken as complete. Values of these parameters will be influenced by the operations analysis method used.

The frequency at which the file is updated (e.g., hourly, weekly) as measured in fractions of days (FREQUP).

The frequency at which the file is queried as measured in fractions of days (FREQRY).

The number of access keys to be used, which is important in evaluating the applicability of inverted file and double chains (MULTKY).

The maximum delay time tolerable between request for and receipt of data (RETSPD).

The average number of elements of data needed per query response (AVGITM).

The second list is a partial definition of the computer environment that includes both hardware and operating system software:

The size of the buffer block that can be accessed by the CPU (BLKLNT).

The average access time of the memory device used (ACCTME).

The cost of the memory device per unit time (MEMCST).

The cost of the main frame computer per unit time (CPUCST).

The third list defines the data base to be processed.

The type of updating that will be performed on the file whether it be change only, add only, delete and add, etc. (TYPUDT).

The method of updating, whether it be by batch processing or on-line (MODUDT).

The expected number of records to be stored in the file (RECNUM).

The expected record length (RECSZE).

The format of the record, whether it will be constant (RECFMT) (fixed) or variable in length (RECFMT).

The number of access keys per record (KEYNUM).

The average length of the access keys (KEYSZE).

The lists of properties of hardware, user needs, and data base above reveal the complexity in the situation.

Because the analysis method is similar for each file structure, we shall consider the sequential structure as an example.

Recall that data is stored sequentially per record for a given attribute. Records are stored in order with respect to a key attribute. Efficiency is gained when records are retrieved in order with respect to storage. No memory is needed for keys or tables.

To test applicability of the sequential file, we examine MULTKY. If this exceeds unity, then the number of access keys makes the form inefficient with a large number of records.

Another test for feasibility relates to the query response time. With a data base on tape the average query time is one-half the time needed to read the file. The average query time can be computed as the product of one-half the average access time per record, the number of records, and the buffer density. In the notation above this is given by

$$t_q = \text{ACCTME} * \text{RECSZE} * \text{RECNUM}/2 * \text{BLKLNT} \quad (2.3)$$

If $t_q$ exceeds the maximum delay time, the sequential file is rejected.

The next step, given feasibility at the preceding stages, is to compute costs. For a sequential file the storage needed is the amount required to hold the data file. This is the product of the expected number of records and the expected record length on

$$S(\mathscr{S}) = \text{RECNUM} * \text{RECSZE} \quad (2.4)$$

Processing time is made up of query and updating time.

Updating in a sequential file requires the reading of the entire file, which is given by

$$t_u(\mathscr{S}) = \text{ACCTME} * \text{RECNUM} * \text{RECSZE}/\text{BLKLNT} \quad (2.5)$$

This assumes updating is constrained by the I/O speed of the storage device. Query time is given in Eq. (2.3). If the file is stored on a random access device and a binary search is used, however, then we have from Meadow[8] that

$$t_q = \ln(\text{RECNUM}) + \ln(\text{ACCTME}) \quad (2.6)$$

For the total time period (PERIOD) we can multiply $t_q$ and $t_a$ by their respective frequencies. In our notation the total update time is given by

$$t(\mathscr{S}) = t_u * \text{PERIOD}/\text{FREQUP} + t_q * \text{PERIOD}/\text{FREQRY} \tag{2.7}$$

The cost as defined in Eq. (2.2) can be expressed by

$$\text{COST} = \text{MEMSCT} * s(\mathscr{S}) + \text{CPUCST} * t(\mathscr{S}) \tag{2.8}$$

A similar analysis can be done with the other file structures. The value of some of these quantities could be found by experimental testing or by analysis of programs for similar applications.

## 2.4 Management Information Systems

As indicated earlier, management information systems (MIS) are software systems that apply elements of the data base to solve a specific need or needs. MIS are important since they provide the key for the user to unlock the data base and utilize it effectively.

Several forces are making MIS spread. First, there is the need for more extensive analysis of production, marketing, and society trends. Information available for analysis has grown rapidly. More parts are being labeled and tracked. More sampling of population segments is occurring. A second force is the reduction in the cost of on-line storage per storage bit [Samuelson[9]]. A third force has been the spread and maturation of data handling systems.

MIS is a collection of programs and general operations analysis methods that are sensitive to the data base and its structure. To illustrate the complexity of MIS, we shall consider an example that will be referenced in later chapters. This problem is the assignment of airline crews to flight segments for a given time period such as a month. The MIS for this problem must access a flight schedule and provide interface between program modules and with the user. For our purposes here, we shall view the solution procedure as a black box, based on a mathematical programming method. This method and its surrounding support and control programs form the MIS.

40 / Data Management and Information Systems

The data base is the schedule; crew information; and data on equipment, weather, and other operational factors as well as the various rules and government regulations that affect the operation of the airline. Figure 2-6 gives an overall view of the MIS. It is shown as having operations research and data handling parts. Each of the fingers from the sides is an aggregate of many subprograms. This structure will now be examined in some detail.

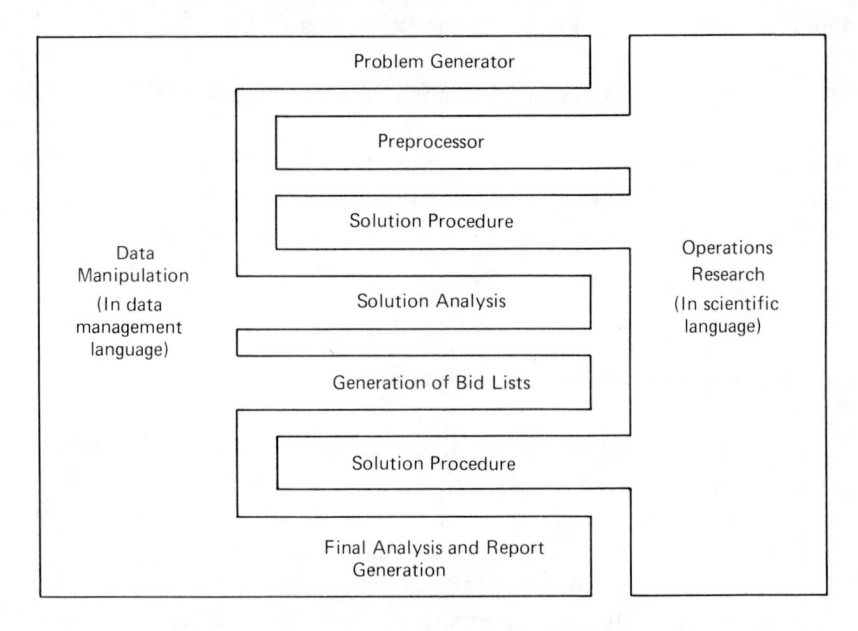

```
                    Problem Generator

                       Preprocessor

                    Solution Procedure
    Data                                              Operations
  Manipulation                                         Research
   (In data          Solution Analysis               (In scientific
  management                                           language)
   language)
                  Generation of Bid Lists

                    Solution Procedure

                Final Analysis and Report
                        Generation
```

Figure 2-6. Overview of MIS for scheduling problem.

The system is written in two languages: one for data handling and one for the operations research method. Two languages are employed because of their capabilities in handling data and in solving mathematical problems, respectively. Many researchers in operations research concern themselves only with this last part. In reality for a realistic use of a MIS oriented toward operations research, an entire system must be considered. Great gains in algorithm efficiency may be erased by inadequate attention to file structure and data handling.

The procedure begins with the MIS accessing the data base to extract a schedule. The first stage in the MIS is to edit and arrange the schedule in proper format to generate the problem. This is in part a set of validity checks and comparisons with rules and regulations to ensure that there is less chance of an error. (An erroneous run may cost several hours of computer time on a large machine.)

The problem generator is a feature employed by mathematical programming methods. It generates legitimate combinations of flight segments that can be flown by a crew. The rows are flight segments and the columns are possible crew assignments. Specifically, a matrix of 0's and 1's is generated where a 1 appears in entry $(i, j)$ of the matrix if crew assignment $j$ flies row $i$. Otherwise, a 0 appears in the $(i, j)$th entry. Generally, this problem like others in scheduling is sparse in the sense that the percentage of 1's in the matrix is small (e.g. 3-5%). Because of this, it is inefficient to store the data in a matrix form. Rather, each column is stored as a record with the entries being the row numbers flown by that column (row numbers where a 1 appears). Pointers then separate columns.

The problem generator is usually a tree or graph-theoretic method with extensive evaluation and costing of each column for the solution procedure. There is no optimization in the mathematical approach except to enumerate possible combinations efficiently. The generator produces the problem but does not solve it.

The next phase preprocesses the data by perhaps altering formats and setting up additional tables to be accessed by the solution method. The output of the solution method are sets of columns. Each set is optimal or near-optimal with respect to a given objective criterion and satisfies the stated operating conditions and constraints.

These solutions are then evaluated economically and operationally by the data handling part of the MIS to be output to the user by the data management system. The user can now select the solution that best fits his needs or he can modify some conditions and restart to find new solutions.

After an operationally usable solution has been selected by the user, the MIS accesses pilot information and prepares admissible bid lists for the entire month (the previous solution was a crew assignment for a week). This is then solved by a solution program. The last step is the actual final performance analysis, bid lists, and economic analysis.

The example above contained two parts of an operations research MIS. We have already referred to the problem generator. The second part is the report generator. For final and even intermediate reports, there may be a number of different analysts, each of whom (because of his position) must view the results of the analysis in a different light. These analysts would include the finance officer, the head of the pilots' organization, the heads of the individual crew bases, and the head of crew training. A MIS to be effective must have the capability of displaying key information in a variety of formats. Graphs and diagrams should be part of this report generation capability.

Report generation was one of the early objectives of data management systems. The goal as pointed out in the preceding paragraph is flexibility. If a firm is attempting to market a MIS or a data management system, the capability to vary formats and displays of information is important. Some computer printouts may be used directly as part of a report to shareholders, management, or technical personnel. Other reports may be in a prescribed format specified by a government agency or in an input format to another MIS. For example, once an airline schedule is fixed, reports must go to compose the Official Airline Guide, the reservation system, flight plans, FAA supplemental reports, and Post Office for mail carriage. Each is in a different format and may contain different information.

Building a report generator involves establishing and storing a data base that will provide information for all reports. Each report is then represented by a separate module that accesses this data base and produces the report.

This complex MIS is not unique but is a good example of what it takes to move operations research theory out in the field to solve real problems. Similar remarks can be made about statistics and numerical analysis. We could, for example, consider a marketing research problem. This is the classical problem of attempting to determine trends and properties of consumers so as to give indications on the products to be sold. An article appeared in *Computer Decisions* by V. F. Free and T. E. Neman.[13] It traces the events in a marketing research problem. These include a successive battery of statistical tests and computations to determine acceptability, appeal of packaging, advertising media, potential market, and sales potential. The statistical methods include correlation, regression, cluster analysis, and factor analysis. Based on the approach in Reference 13, a MIS can be constructed that accesses data concerning survey and questionnaire results and then can control the application of the appropriate statistical method. This could then be phased through each level and tested.

This section has briefly explored several examples of MIS and some of the factors in its composition. As the use of the computer grows, the applications will continue to keep pace. MIS has become important in several fields in decision-making. One reason for this is that it allows the decision maker to ask "what if" questions and to pose hypothetical situations to test his logic and the solution provided by an operations research program. The MIS allows the user to pose such questions easily.

## 2.5 Programs

The existing programs occupy a spectrum from specialized sorting programs to generalized data management systems and management information systems. The selection of a data management system is of vital interest to the organization. If the system is to maintain and be the central source for information on accounts, sales and marketing, and other activities and it malfunctions, serious breaks in the organization flow can occur. Several cases have resulted in lengthy litigation.

A data management system should be flexible enough to permit a variety of query commands. These include requests for statistical comparisons; changes in individual record items; and output of selected records that possess a set of attributes to a printer, tapes, disk, or drum. It should be able to access multiple files and permit the linking of operations research and numerical methods. Ideally a data management system should be able to communicate with the nonprogrammer in natural English. This is in the research stage. One difficulty is the structure of a natural Language with synonyms and varied meanings for a given word. New data management systems are announced in the nontechnical journals listed below.

Some general data management systems appear in the *ICP Quarterly*. Included is a brief description, price, documentation, and compatible machines.

Data management programs for sorting and merging and other specific operations are available through the system support software for a computer system and from the computer user groups. The latter is listed in Table 2-2.

In addition to the utility programs listed in Table 2-2 there are data management systems that combine the operations discussed in this chapter to permit a user to establish files, manipulate data, perform retrieval, and produce reports. These systems include languages for data description and manipulation. Some of these systems and their creators include IMS (IBM), TOTAL (Cincom Systems), System 2000 (MRI Systems), and Mark IV (Informatics).

Table 2-2. COLLECTION OF AVAILABLE DATA MANAGEMENT PROGRAMS

| Program | User Group | Language |
|---|---|---|
| Generalized retrieve and build | RCA | RCA machine |
| Information oriented language—information and retrieve system | Educational information network | CDC FORTRAN |
| Sort/Merge | XDS | Symbol |
| Sort | XDS | FORTRAN II |
| Sort into descending order | Educational information network | FORTRAN IV |
| Integer sort | Common (small IBM computer user group) | FORTRAN |
| Sort | SHARE | FORTRAN |
| Sort program—KWIC | CUBE | COBOL |
| Keyword in context (KWIC) | CUBE | COBOL |

Other programs handle data conversion from one format to another. An example of the system support sorting and merging routines is that described in the manufacturers support manuals (e.g., Reference 15).

Examined in the manuals are the relationship to the operating system, core storage and intermediate requirements, the job control instructions for access and range, and some error analysis. The instructions cover cases of fixed variable length arrays.

Data management systems and related subjects such as library systems, information storage, and retrieval are the subject of much current study. Some of the mathematical oriented journals include

*Communications of ACM*

*Computer Journal (The)*

*Computing Reviews*

*Computing Surveys*

*Fall Joint Computer Conference, Proceedings*

*Spring Joint Computer Conference, Proceedings*

*IBM Systems Journal*
*IEEE Transactions on Computers*
*IFIPS Proceedings*
*Information and Control*
*Journal of Association for Computing Machinery (ACM)*

Papers found in these journals would include new procedures for sorting and merging of data, combinatorics of data structures, and new results in the theory of data management.

Applications would usually appear in the journals oriented toward the particular application field such as logistics, library systems, and industrial engineering; however, there are several computer periodicals oriented toward general applications and usage. Three of these are *Datamation, Computer World,* and *Computer Decisions*. Some articles are interesting here since problems are viewed from the user's standpoint.

The textbooks and other references include the list given on p. 45. Most basic computer science texts contain at least a chapter on data structures. This includes those listed in References. Cuadra[2] is a collection of papers written in the field for a variety of applications. Gruenberger,[4] Meadow,[8] and Wegner[10] are useful data management texts. Maurer[7] discusses programming along with some aspects of data management.

Lyon[6] considers the design of a data base from an intermediate view. The Association for Computing Machinery[1] has issued an excellent analysis of general data management. Two of the best sources for sorting are Flores[3] and Knuth[5].

## REFERENCES

*Textbooks*

1. "Analysis of Generalized Data Base Management Systems," *Association for Computing Machinery*, (1971).
2. CUADRA, C. A. (ed.), *Annual Review of Information Science and Technology*, Vol. I and II. New York: Interscience Publishers, 1966, 1967.
3. FLORES, I., *Computing Sorting*. Englewood Cliffs, N.J.: Prentice-Hall, Inc. 1969.
4. GRUENBERGER, F., *Critical Factors in Data Management*. Englewood Cliffs, N.J.: Prentice-Hall, Inc., 1969.

5. KNUTH, D. E., *The Art of Computer Programming*, Vol. III, *Sorting and Searching*. New York: Addison-Wesley Pub. Co., 1972.
6. LYON, J. K., *An Introduction to Data Base Design*. New York: John Wiley & Sons, Inc., 1971.
7. MAURER, W. D., *Programming: An Introduction to Computer Techniques*. San Francisco, Calif: Holden-Day, Inc., 1972.
8. MEADOW, C. T., *The Analysis of Information Systems*. New York: John Wiley & Sons., Inc., 1967.
9. SAMEULSON, K. (ed.), *Mechanized Information, Storage, Retrieval and Dissemination*. Amsterdam: North Holland Publishing Co., 1968.
10. WEGNER, P., *Programming Languages, Information Structures, and Machine Organization*. New York: McGraw-Hill Book Co., 1968.

*Additional References*

11. CHAPIN, N., "A Comparison of File Organization Techniques," *Proceedings of the 24th Conference of ACM*, 1969.
12. DODD, J. G., "Elements of Data Management Systems," *Computing Surveys*, I, No. 2 (1969).
13. FREE, V. H. and T. E. NEMAN, "Market Research Matches Products to Consumers, *Computer Decisions* (May, 1972), 12–15.
14. WEISSMAN, C., *A LISP 1.5 Primer*. Belmont, Calif.: Dickenson Pub. Co. 1967.
15. "Sort/Merge," *IBM System/360 Operating System*. IBM System Reference Library, File No. 5300-33, 1970.

# PROBLEMS

1. A problem in sorting and arranging file structures is to select the ordering of information that can be sorted efficiently most often. Examine this problem for the following situation. A bank maintains account records on the depositor: social security number, balance in the account, and past history of transactions.

2. Develop a cost model to optimize the amount of information that should be stored on each access device for a management information system. Use the following notation.

    $n$ = average number of calls for data from files
    $i$ = index of access device
    $t_i$ = average time to access one record on device of type $i$
    $m_i$ = number of accesses to type $i$ device
    $c_i$ = cost of storage of one record on device $i$
    $c$ = total funds available for storage of all records
    $x_i$ = amount of records on type $i$ device

3. A production line manager is concerned with maintaining records on the activities of his production workers. Each worker, in an automated system, would enter a code (such as man number) and task that he would be working on as well as the area in which the work is to be performed. The computer could use this information along with schedules to predict completion time, find bottlenecks, and estimate tasks and their times for the next day. Discuss the feasibility of such a system in a factory where
   (a) Many components of the same type are produced.
   (b) Many different types of components are produced in small lot sizes.
4. In the production monitoring system in Problem 3, several alternative configurations are
   (a) Small central processing unit with minicomputers at remote locations on the factory floor.
   (b) Large central processor with memoryless terminals in the production area.
   Contrast these in terms of ability to handle information and compare information structures needed for processing.
5. In a virtual memory computer, programs are allowed to use almost unlimited amounts of core storage. The virtual memory system is structured on the operating system and special disk units. Discuss the benefits and drawbacks to running a general data management system on such a machine.
6. Write a program to do a linear search on the following array. Apply the program to search for 7.8. and 1.1.

   $-1.2, -7.3, -5.4, 1, 1.3, -1.6, 7.5, 6.2, 7.8, -1.32,$
   $0.0078, 0.0987, 7.6, 7.8$

7. Sort by hand the data in Problem 1 and write a binary search program. Apply it to the same values as Problem 1.
8. Two companies have merged their customer records along with their organizations. Discuss how to apply a merge routine and describe any problems that might arise including incompatibility.
9. The following data is available and a binary tree search is to be applied. Write a program and describe how the search would proceed. Assume that the value QXAS is sought.

   XJYT, AXQT, QXAT, QXAS, SQAY, YAST, DGBF, BXQT, BXRS,
   XYZA, ZZAA, ACBD, CAFG, EQRS

10. Repeat Problem 9 except add the entries FFAC and CABD to the data.
11. A shoe company wishes to construct a MIS to control the production and marketing of its product. This will require a number of statistical routines for marketing analysis as well as scheduling methods for producing the shoes. Describe some of the problems and features in considering MIS.
12. For the data in Problem 6, write a program to find the minimum of the numbers.

48 / Data Management and Information Systems

13. Using the program of Fig. 2-5 or the result of Problem 12, write a program that will sort the numbers of Problem 6.
14. The following data is available as a central file:
    (a) DC-9, two engines, short range, McDonnell-Douglas.
    (b) 707 four engines, long range, Boeing.
    (c) 747, four engines, long range, Boeing.
    (d) DC-8, four engines, long range, McDonnell-Douglas.
    (e) DC-10, three engines, long range, McDonnell-Douglas.
    (f) 727, two engines, short range, Boeing.
    (g) FH-227, two engines, short range, Fairchild Hiller.

    Construct an inverted file for this information using the attributes given. Why are these attributes insufficient for isolating specific aircraft types?
15. Using the following data construct an exchange program to sort the data in increasing order.

    $\pi$, 6.22, 7.38, 1.73, 2.09, $-1.63$, $-9.74$, 1.09, 0.087, $-0.24$, 69.24, $-31.73$, 24.62, 4.73, 2.09, 3.11

    Describe the first few steps of the sort.
16. Suppose a polynomial function is given as

    $$p(x) = 5x^4 - 6x^3 + 3x^2 - 7x + 10$$

    Construct a program to evaluate the function for values of $x = 1, 1.5, 2, 2.5, 3, 3.5,$ and 4 and to sort these values as they are computed.
17. A series of tests on biological specimens have produced data on life length, size, and four other characteristics for each specimen. This information is to be evaluated by several statistical methods, each of which sorts on a different characteristic. Discuss how a multilevel sort on characteristics can be used to obtain a data structure for the different statistical methods.

# 3

# MATHEMATICAL PROGRAMMING

## 3.1 Introduction

### 3.1.1 *Overview*

One of the problems faced by governmental agencies and corporations is the allocation of resources to satisfy demands or to produce goods and services. Operations research and management science provide a general roof over such problems. Areas dealing with allocation, routing, and production include mathematical programming and network analysis. In this chapter we take up mathematical programming.

As with any area of applied mathematics, there is an attempt to represent in a mathematical way the conditions of the real-world environment. For example, in scheduling aircraft crews we should take into account the flight schedule, crew base or domicile structure, delay times due to weather, and traffic as well as maintenance and training. Unfortunately, unless some conditions are simplified, problems either become too complex or large for rapid solution. When this is realized, the magic associated with the "optimal solution" begins to fade. In its place for complex problems, we seek several or many near-optimal solutions. The user can then select the solution that best fits the operating conditions. In such a case the goal is to obtain *operationally optimal solutions.* This is not to say, however, that many existing problems cannot be represented and solved mathematically. Generally, we are only allowed to optimize one function or measure of a number of variables or quantities that we can affect. Optimization then is to minimize or maximize this measure. Minimization occurs in response time for communication networks, penalty costs for routing, and mileage for vehicle scheduling. Maximization occurs in production lines and manufacturing, throughput for computing centers, and item availability or reliability of systems. Linear programming problems admit fractional values for quantities being allocated or assigned. The interest in integer programming stems in part from the situation that frequently quantities being assigned are whole numbers or integer-valued. The purchasing of machine tools are in units as is the problem of allocating spare components to enhance system reliability. Problems where there is a mixture of quantities that can assume integer and real-number values are referred to as *mixed integer problems.*

Having discussed some of the objectives in applying and using a new method, we can now consider the evaluation of a new method. For a new approach the questions involve efficiency, programmability, and adaptability. Often with a new method some limited computational results are given. These generally are small problems. Furthermore, the solution times may be based on using a medium-to-large computer. If problems are randomly generated, their internal structure may not correspond to that obtained from the real physical situation. *Randomly generated* means that some or all of the data for the problem are obtained by means of pseudo-random number generator (this is examined in Chapter 6 in detail). Another remark is that the method may be programmed inefficiently so that the speed of the method is not exploited to its maximum. There has been a trend to establish a standard class of test problems so that a new method can be benchmarked against existing techniques.

In this chapter we shall consider the mathematical methods for solving the class of linear and integer programming problems; also we shall give examples that outline the transfer of the real problem into a mathematical form.

For linear problems there is a general optimization method that is examined in Section 3.2. For integer problems there is no such general method. Rather, methods are based on mathematical or heuristic rules. The value of a solution in integer programming depends on the savings over present methods, additional cost of the new method, and usability of the method with respect to solution time and operating conditions. Available programs are examined along with some particular applications.

The general framework of an optimization problem is given by

$$\max_{x_1,\ldots,x_n} (\min) f(x_1, \ldots, x_n) \tag{3.1}$$

subject to

$$g_i(x_1,\ldots,x_n) (\geqslant)(=)(\leqslant) 0 \quad 1 \leqslant i \leqslant k \tag{3.2}$$

Here $x_1, \ldots, x_n$ are the variables, $f(\cdot)$ is the objective function to be maximized or minimized, and Eq. (3.2) indicates the constraints of the problem for which we assume all coefficients are constants. That is, we ignore problems that have "random" elements.* If all of the functions in Eq. (3.1) and (3.2) are linear functions of $x_1, \ldots, x_n$, then the problem is called a *linear programming* problem. The general linear programming problem is given by

$$\max_{x_1,\ldots,x_n} (\min) \sum_{j=1} c_j x_j \tag{3.3}$$

subject to

$$\sum_{j=1}^{n} a_{ij} x_j - b_i (\geqslant)(=)(\leqslant) 0, \quad 1 \leqslant i \leqslant k \tag{3.4}$$

where all coefficients are constants.

If, in addition to the constraints, Eq. (3.4), we require the variables to be integer, then the problem lies in integer programming. The general form of Eq. (3.1) and (3.2) with at least one nonlinear func-

---

*See Chapter 5 for definitions of random variables and probability distribution.

tion in either the objective function or the constraints gives a *nonlinear programming* problem.

Before considering methods for solving Eq. (3.1) and (3.2) the phases that the researcher or analyst must work through for an optimization problem are

1. Constructing a mathematical representation of the problem.
2. Solving the mathematical problem to obtain optimal or near-optimal solutions.
3. Reconciling the solution with the real world situation.

The first and last are learned by practice and working in the actual environment. In this chapter we shall concentrate on the first two topics. Many difficulties associated with reconciliation can be overcome by spending more effort in establishing the problem framework. Several examples in problem formulation will now be considered.

### 3.1.2 *Establishing the mathematical form of the problem*

The translation of problems into a mathematical format is an important task since it defines the relationship between the model representation and the real world. Thus, it directly affects the utility of any and all solutions that are found.

The basic method is first to define the variables of the problem that we can influence by allocation. After this the function we wish to optimize (objective function) can be formulated in terms of these variables. The next step is to delineate all constraints of the problem. Although this last part is easy with completely formulated word problems, it is difficult and frustrating in applications. In many situations the analyst obtains the substance of the problem from members of the operations section. Usually the objectives and variables are clear to these people from practice. The constraints are usually composed of explicit conditions as well as ill-defined, vague constraints that relate to operational experience and knowledge. Straightforward conditions include some government regulations and union rules. But even here there can be vagueness in situations not taken into account when the rules were composed.

**Example 3.1.** An airline must schedule its aircraft fleet on a weekly or monthly basis. A schedule is produced by the marketing organization of the airline. This schedule consists of flight legs or segments that are nonstop flights between sets of two-city pairs at a certain time of day and day of week. The aircraft routing staff must minimize total costs. The constraints of the problem include that of no deadhead plane routing (a routing of a plane outside the schedule) as well as those on the maintenance of the aircraft.

The flight legs can be viewed as rows of a matrix. The columns would be possible assignments for a particular aircraft. The $(i, j)$th entry of the matrix is a 1 if column $j$ assignment flies flight leg $i$. Otherwise, a 0 appears. This matrix of 1's and 0's is sparse in the sense that the percentage of 1's to total matrix entries is small. Each column has a cost associated with flying that assignment. A sample matrix with penalties is given in Fig. 3-1.

| Row/Column | 1 | 2 | 3 | 4 | 5 |
|---|---|---|---|---|---|
| 1 | 1 | 0 | 1 | 0 | 1 |
| 2 | 0 | 0 | 0 | 1 | 0 |
| 3 | 1 | 1 | 0 | 1 | 0 |
| 4 | 0 | 1 | 1 | 1 | 0 |
| 5 | 0 | 0 | 1 | 0 | 1 |
| Penalty | 11 | 9 | 5 | 12 | 7 |

Figure 3-1. Sample aircraft routing matrix.

Suppose column $j$ has penalty $c_j$. Let an arbitrary assignment (collection of column indices), be denoted by $a$. Let $x_{ij}$ be the $(i, j)$th entry of the matrix. Then the objective function is given by

$$\sum_{j \in a} c_j x_j \qquad (3.5)$$

The constraints on deadheading and covering are given by

$$\sum_{j \in a} x_{ij} = 1 \quad 1 \leq i \leq m \qquad (3.6)$$

and

$$x_{ij} = 0 \text{ or } 1 \quad 1 \leq i \leq m, 1 \leq j \leq n \qquad (3.7)$$

The constraints of Eq. (3.6) insure that each flight leg is flown by exactly one aircraft. There may be other constraints that are more difficult to handle. These might include operational constraints on collections of columns and conditions of maintenance stations.

Although the constraints of Eq. (3.7) make the problem an integer programming problem by requiring $x_{ij}$ to be 0 or 1, this restriction is often replaced by $0 \leqslant x_{ij} \leqslant 1$ in a planning context.

**Example 3.2.** This sample deals with the blending of raw materials. In this problem ingredients such as unrefined resources are combined to yield amounts of finished products. For a unit of each finished product a certain known quantity of each of the raw resources is needed. The goal is to maximize the gain, which may be sales or profits. The constraints relate to the quantities of raw materials available. The blending problem occurs, for example, in refining gasoline and other petroleum products from oil and additives. Suppose there are $k$ raw resources and $n$ products. Let the variable $y_{ij}$ denote the amount of raw material $i$ devoted to product $j$. The variables $\{y_{ij}\}$ will then determine the profit or gain from production. Suppose the gain per unit for product $j$ is $p_j$, then the total gain is given by

$$\sum_{j=1}^{n} p_j \sum_{i=1}^{k} y_{ij}$$

Now to determine the objective function, the cost of the resources and production would have to be subtracted from this summation. Suppose a unit of resource $i$ costs $c_i$. Then the objective is to maximize

$$\sum_{j=1}^{n} p_j \sum_{i=1}^{k} y_{ij} - \sum_{i=1}^{k} c_i \sum_{j=1}^{n} y_{ij}$$

A major constraint is the limitation on the available quantities of each resource. Suppose resource $i$ is limited to $d_i$. Then the availability limitations are given by

$$\sum_{j=1}^{n} y_{ij} \leqslant d_i \qquad 1 \leqslant i \leqslant k$$

Since the amounts of raw materials are nonnegative, we must have

$$y_{ij} \geqslant 0 \qquad 1 \leqslant i \leqslant k, 1 \leqslant j \leqslant n$$

For each product there are constraints on the percentages of compositions for each raw material. These are of the form

$$y_{ij} \leqslant a_{ij} \sum_{\ell=1}^{k} y_{i\ell} \quad 1 \leqslant i \leqslant k, 1 \leqslant j \leqslant n$$

The constraints here are easier to formulate if there is a simple percentage restriction. If there are dependencies between mixtures of raw materials, however, the situation becomes more complex. Petroleum blending has been one of the most important applications of linear programming and has been a source for much of the theoretical results in the field.

**Example 3.3.** A gambler can choose to play several games of chance over some time period. Analogously, an investor can choose between a number of investment alternatives. Usually the time period or horizon is broken into discrete intervals with each interval representing a 3-month, 6-month, or a 1-year period. There is a fixed amount of capital $C_0$ at the beginning of the horizon. The goal is to maximize total gain over the time period with the given initial amount of capital $C_0$. The variables are then the amounts that can be invested at each of these time intervals in the various possible games or investment possibilities. To be fully realistic this problem would have to be nondeterministic with random elements associated with possible payoffs. This will be simplified here and then discussed.

Suppose at any time there are $n$ possible investments or games and that there are $m$ times at which investments can be made. This is in itself a simplification since not all investments may be available at each time. Similarly, all blackjack playing positions may be taken at a given casino so that blackjack cannot be played at certain times. Continuing, let $x_{ij}$ be the amount invested at time $i$ in investment $j$. Now between time $i$ and $i + 1$ a unit invested in $j$ will earn a certain expected payoff $g_{ij}$. We can now formulate the objective function as

$$\sum_{i=1}^{m} \sum_{j=1}^{n} g_{ij} x_{ij}$$

If there were no constraints except for the initial capital $C_0$, we would do best to invest all our money in the investment with the best gain for each time interval. In investments, however, this is almost never the case since there are often additional conditions. There may be minimal time periods during which an investment may not be changed. There may be penalties for early withdrawals as well as minimum required investment levels. In gambling, each game has a certain expected payoff. If this is constant, then under certain conditions the best strategy will be to play the game with highest payoff.[*]

The constraints to the problem in an investment situation relate also to the total amount available for reallocation. At time $i + 1$ this is given by

$$\sum_{j=1}^{n} g_{ij} x_{ij}$$

The constraint is then

$$\sum_{j=1}^{n} x_{i+1,j} \leq \sum_{j=1}^{n} g_{ij} x_{ij} \quad 1 \leq i \leq m - 1$$

and for $i = 0$

$$\sum_{j=1}^{n} x_{0j} \leq C_0$$

As in the example,

$$\sum_{j=1}^{n} x_{ij} \leq C_0$$

Additional examples appear in the problem section.

## 3.2 Definitions and Basic Methods of Linear Programming

### 3.2.1 *Basic problem and geometry*

Suppose that the mathematical form of the problem has been developed for a particular situation. Then the problem is

$$\max_{x_j} (\min_{x_j}) \sum_{j=1}^{n} a_j x_j \qquad (3.8)$$

---

[*]The actual strategy would depend on the underlying probability distributions.

subject to

$$\sum_{j=1}^{n} a_{ij} x_j \, (\geqslant) \, (=) \, (\leqslant) \, b_i, \quad 1 \leqslant i \leqslant k \qquad (3.9)$$

and

$$x_j \geqslant 0, \quad 1 \leqslant j \leqslant n \qquad (3.10)$$

From the previous section we note that all examples use nonnegative variables. This is due to the fact that allocation usually involves giving, buying, or trading commodities or resources. The result is the nonnegativity conditions in Eq. (3.10).

With a proper formulation of the problem, the operationally optimal solution should satisfy the constraints in Eq. (3.9) and (3.10). A collection of variables $x_1, \ldots, x_n$ can be considered as a vector $(x_1, \ldots, x_n)$. The set of vectors $(x_1, \ldots, x_n)$ satisfying Eq. (3.9) and (3.10) is called the *set of feasible solutions*.

The set of feasible solutions has a number of properties deriving from Eq. (3.9) and (3.10). Consider the following simple example:

$$\max 3x_1 + 2x_2$$

subject to

$$2x_1 + x_2 \leqslant 5$$
$$x_1 + x_2 \leqslant 3$$
$$x_1, x_2 \geqslant 0$$

Graphically, we can find the set of feasible solutions. These are given in Fig. 3-2. This example will be used throughout this section. Moreover, the discussion will be in the context of maximization; analogous steps can be followed for minimization.

The set of feasible solutions is shown in the shaded region. We note that every point on the perimeter of the region is a feasible solution (why?). Because all linear programming problems have this property, the set of feasible solutions is said to be *closed*.

Next we see that if we join any two points in the set of feasible solutions with a straight line segment, any point lying on the line is a

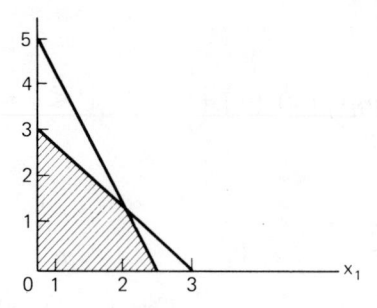

**Figure 3-2.** Set of feasible solutions for example problem.

feasible solution. A set in which this occurs for any two points is called a *convex set*. Formally, a set $A$ is convex if for any two points $x_1$ and $x_2$ in $A$ the point $\alpha x_1 + (1 - \alpha)x_2$ lies in $A$ for $0 < \alpha < 1$.

The theoretical proofs of the properties of being closed and convex follow from examining the constraints. Each straight line constraint divides the space into two regions or half planes. For each line, a half plane satisfies the constraint. This half plane is closed and convex. Suppose each half plane where each point satisfies the inequality is represented by a different colored transparent plastic sheet. If we have many constraints, we shall obtain a region in which all colors appear to give a black effect. This region is formed by the intersection of all colored sheets. Since it is the intersection of a collection of closed and convex sets, it too is closed and convex. This simplified view is not a formal proof but rather an indication of how the properties are derived.

The constraints can sometimes be reduced if there is redundancy. Let $C_i = \{\underline{x}: \Sigma\ a_{ij}x_j\ (\leqslant, \geqslant, =)\ b_i\}$ so that $C_i$ is the set of points satisfying the $i$th constraint. The set of feasible solutions is

$$\bigcap_{i=1}^{k} C_i$$

Constraint $j$ can be removed if

$$\bigcap_{\substack{i=j \\ i \neq j}}^{k} C_i \subset C_j$$

because then

$$\bigcap_{\substack{i=1\\i\neq j}}^{k} C_i = \bigcap_{i=1}^{k} C_i$$

We have just described the set of feasible solutions as a closed, convex set with straight line segments as edges. The vertices of this figure are the points on the boundary of the set of feasible solutions that are the intersection of lines corresponding to constraints. In Fig. 3-2 the vectices are $(0, 0)$, $(0, 3)$ $(\frac{5}{2}, 0)$, and $(2, 1)$. Now we can generate all edges using lines connecting these points to obtain the boundary. Also, it can be shown that any point inside the region can be written as a linear combination of the vertices. Because of this we say that the set of feasible solutions is the *convex hull* of the vertices.

Heretofore, we have restricted attention to the set of feasible solutions independent of the objective function. The objective function is a straight line that we wish to pass over the set of feasible solutions. In a simple case this would amount to passing a ruler (slanted to reflect the slope of the line) over the feasible region to find the optimal solutions. Because this problem is linear in both objective and constraint functions, the optimal solution lies on the boundary of the feasible region. This is proved formally by showing that, for any point in the region, we can do no worse in terms of the objective function by using some point on the boundary.

Given that the optimal point is on the boundary, the next result is that the location of the optimal point can be refined by showing that the following statements hold.

Either there is none, one, or an infinite number of optimal solutions. If there is no solution, the problem is said to be infeasible.

If there is one solution, that solution is a vertex point.

If there is an infinite number of solutions, the objective function has the same slope as one of the constraints and so any point on the corresponding edge in the boundary is optimal.

In this example problem we first note that there are points in the feasible region. Hence, there is at least one solution. The problem is not infeasible. Also, the slope of $y = 3x_1 + 2x_2$ is not parallel to an edge so that there is a unique optimal solution and it is a vertex. The values of the objective function at the vertices are given by

$$(0, 0) \quad 0$$
$$(0, 3) \quad 6$$
$$(\tfrac{5}{2}, 0) \quad \tfrac{15}{2} = 7\tfrac{1}{2}$$
$$(2, 1) \quad 8$$

The optimal solution is 8 and occurs at the point (2, 1).

It was easy in this example of two variables to find the set of vertices and then determine the point that maximizes the objective function. The situation above grows rapidly in complexity as the number of vertices grows. The number of vertices is affected by the number of variables. For each variable a dimension is added. If constraints are added and are not capable of elimination, then the feasible region is reduced in size and the number of edges increased. What is needed, then, is a method which will reduce some of the computations and which improves, or least does not reduce, the value of the objective function at each iteration.

### 3.2.2 Simplex method

The major computation technique that has been developed to solve linear problems is the simplex method, which we shall describe in terms of the example used in this section. The method is outlined here stepwise.

*Step 1.* Formulation of inequality constraints as equalities. A constraint of the form

$$\sum_{j=1}^{n} a_{ij}x_j \leqslant b_i$$

is changed to an equality by adding a new variable $x_{n+i}$ by defining

$$x_{n+i} = b_i - \sum_{j=1}^{n} a_{ij}x_j$$

so that the constraint becomes

$$a_{i1}x_{j1} + \cdots + a_{in}x_n + x_{n+i} = b_i$$

The new variable, like $\{x_i\}_{i=1}^n$, is nonnegative by definition from the constraint. With $\leq$, the new variable is called a *slack variable* in that it takes up the slack in a specific resource. Using this method, all constraints that are inequalities become equalities. If the $i$th constraint is an equality, set $x_{n+i} = 0$. In our example, define $x_3$ and $x_4$ by

$$x_3 = 5 - 2x_1 - x_2$$

and

$$x_4 = 3 - x_1 - x_2$$

so that the problem is then

$$\max_{(x_1, x_2)} 3x_1 + 2x_2$$

subject to

$$2x_1 + x_2 + x_3 = 5,$$

$$x_1 + x_2 + x_4 = 3,$$

and

$$x_1, x_2, x_3, x_4 \geq 0$$

Note that $x_3$ and $x_4$ do not enter the objective function. The general space is now $E^4$ and not $E^2$, however, because of the addition of the variables $x_3$ and $x_4$.*

Before proceeding to Step 2, we first define a basic feasible solution as a feasible solution $(x_i, \ldots, x_n, x_{n+1}, \ldots, x_{n+k})$ in

---

*$E^2$ and $E^4$ are defined in Appendix A.

which $k$ variables are solved using the constraints with the remaining variables set equal to zero. These $k$ variables are called basic variables. This step involves solving a set of $k$ simultaneous linear equation in $k$ variables and is explored in Chapter 7.

*Step 2.* Finding an initial or starting basic feasible solution. To find an initial basic feasible solution, we can set $x_i = 0, 1 \leq i \leq n$, and solve the constraint equations by Step 1 to obtain $x_{n+1}, \ldots, x_{n+k}$. The solution $(0, \ldots, 0, x_{n+1}, \ldots, x_{n+k})$ is then feasible and gives a value of the objective function of zero. In the example, $x_3 = 5$ and $x_4 = 3$. The first basic feasible solution is then $(0, 0, 5, 3)$.

We must now find a method to improve on the initial solution if this is possible. Since any vertex is a basic feasible solution, we should keep in mind that if any additional variables are made basic, some variable must be removed from the set of basic variables (why?). This leads to the next step.

*Step 3.* Improvement of objective function by the addition and deletion of a variable. In this step, we wish to enter one variable and then remove another variable from the set of basic variables. The selection of the entering variable should be sensitive to the objective function. The exact procedure is to make basic the variable that yields the largest per unit gain in the objective function. For minimization we would select the variable with smallest rise per unit. This is a heuristic in that it does not guarantee an increase in value of the objective function. In the case of ties for entering variables, a choice can be made arbitrarily.

In the example, the candidates for the entering variable are $x_1$ and $x_2$. Since $x_1$ has a coefficient of 3 and $x_2$ has a coefficient of 2, we should enter $x_1$.

The next decision is to select the leaving or exiting variable. As the entering variable is increased from value zero, the constraints act to reduce the value of some or all of the candidates for the leaving variable. The rule is to extract the variable that is first forced to zero as the entering variable increases.

For the example the candidates are $x_3$ and $x_4$ since the variable $x_1$ is the entering variable and $x_2$ is still zero, the constraints become

$$2x_1 + x_3 = 5$$
$$x_1 + x_4 = 3$$
$$x_1, x_3, x_4 \geq 0$$

Now as $x_1$ increases to $2\frac{1}{2}$, $x_3$ is forced to 0 and $x_1$ is forced to $\frac{1}{2}$ (show this). Thus, $x_3$ will reach zero first as $x_1$ increases and so becomes the exiting variable. The new basic variables are $x_1$ and $x_4$. Solving for these from

$$2x_1 = 5$$
$$x_1 + x_4 = 3$$

we obtain as the next solution $(2\frac{1}{2}, 0, 0, \frac{1}{2})$, which has a value of $7\frac{1}{2}$.

Step 3 constitutes one iteration or point. We repeatedly go through this step until the objective function cannot be improved further. Thus, at the next step, $x_2$ would be entered and $x_4$ exited to obtain the optimal solution (2, 1, 0, 0) with a value of 8.

The procedure above will lead to an improvement of the objective function at each iteration and finally to the optimal solution. Because the process is usually carried out on a digital computer, however, there are limitations and potential pitfalls. For example, in a large problem with many variables there may be roundoff errors in solving the simultaneous equations. As these errors build up, we may lose feasibility. Alternatively we might cycle and become locked in some part of the feasible region, unable to get out because of roundoff error. Physical available core storage may be limited so that part of the data must be stored peripherally on disk or tape. The number of I/O operations may then increase substantially.

Additionally, there are special cases for the problem that must be considered. With a constraint of the form

$$\sum_{j=1}^{n} a_{ij} x_j \geqslant b_i \ (\geqslant 0)$$

we first introduce a *surplus variable* $x_{n+i}$ to obtain

$$- \sum_{j=1}^{n} a_{ij} x_j + x_{n+i} = -b_i$$

Since $-b_i$ is negative, Step 3 will fail here. A method to avoid this is to insert another variable $x_{n+m+i}$ so that

$$\sum a_{ij} x_j - x_{n+i} + x_{n+m+i} = b_i$$

Another correction is needed to guarantee correspondence between the optimal solution in the revised problem and the original problem. We insert a term $-M_i x_{n+m+i}$ into the objective function to obtain

$$\sum_{j=1}^{n} c_j x_j - M_i x_{n+m+i}$$

Here $M_i$ is an arbitrarily large number. The justification for this can be found in references [2] and [3] of this chapter.

A basic feasible solution is degenerate if a basic variable has the value zero. In the event of a tie between two candidates for the exiting variable, arbitrarily selecting a variable may not lead to a solution. This can occur in large scheduling problems. One way around this is to consider the dual of the problem, which is discussed later in this section. This potential problem again points to the importance of a proper formulation of the problem and selection of the method for solution.

An important development in linear programming theory has been in the area of solving the dual version of a linear programming problem. For the problem in Eq. (3.8) to (3.10) with $\leq$ constraints, the dual version is obtained from the original problem or primal by the following steps.

Step 1. Set $d_{ij} = a_{ji}$ for $1 \leq i \leq k, 1 \leq j \leq n$.

Step 2. Replace $\leq b_i$ by $\geq c_i$ for $1 \leq i \leq k$.

Step 3. Replace the variables $\{x_1, \ldots, x_n\}$ by $\{z_1, \ldots, z_k\}$ and the set $\{c_i\}$ by $\{b_i\}$.

The problem is then to minimize

$$\sum_{j=1}^{k} b_j z_j \qquad (3.11)$$

subject to

$$\sum_{j=1}^{k} d_{ij} z_j \geq c_i, \quad 1 \leq i \leq n \qquad (3.12)$$

and

$$z_j \geqslant 0, \quad 1 \leqslant j \leqslant k \qquad (3.13)$$

The value in considering this problem is that the optimal solutions for both versions are identical. Also, the optimal value of the variables in the dual problem correspond to the values of the slack variables in the original version. In our example, the dual version of the problem is

$$\min \; 5z_1 + 3z_2$$

subject to

$$2z_1 + z_2 \geqslant 3,$$
$$z_1 + z_2 \geqslant 2,$$

and

$$z_1, z_2 \geqslant 0.$$

A simplex method can be used to solve Eq. (3.11) to (3.13). The value of working with the dual is in problems where the number of variables far exceeds the number of constraints. The dual will then have few variables and many constraints.

### 3.2.3 Computational methods

Here we wish to consider methods for implementing the simplex method for obtaining solutions rapidly. The data used and obtained by iterations of the simplex methods can be stored in a table called a *simplex tableau*, given in Table 3.1 for the example used in this section. In this table the second column is the basic variable at each iteration. The third column is the unit gain in the objective function for the corresponding variable. Columns 4 to 8 include the coefficients of the variables as each iteration is followed. The eighth column contains a summation of the rows. The last column computes a ratio to determine which variable to exit by dividing the solution by the objective function coefficient of the new basic variable.

We begin with the basic feasible solution. In row 1, $x_3$ is entered with its gain (0). Also entered in this row are the coefficients of the

## 66 / Mathematical Programming

Table 3.1. EXAMPLE OF A SIMPLEX TABLEAU

| (1) No. Row | (2) Basic Variables | (3) Unit Gain | (4) $x_1$ | (5) $x_2$ | (6) $x_3$ | (7) $x_4$ | (8) $b_i$ | (9) Row Summation | (10) Entering Ratio |
|---|---|---|---|---|---|---|---|---|---|
| 1 | $x_3$ | 0 | 2 | 1 | 1 | 0 | 5 | 9 | $\frac{5}{2}$ |
| 2 | $x_4$ | 0 | 1 | 1 | 0 | 1 | 3 | 6 | 3 |
| 3 |  |  | 3 | 2 | 0 | 0 | 0 | 5 |  |
| 4 | $x_1$ | 3 | 1 | $\frac{1}{2}$ | $\frac{1}{2}$ | 0 | $\frac{5}{2}$ | $\frac{9}{2}$ | 5 |
| 5 | $x_4$ | 0 | 0 | $\frac{1}{2}$ | $-\frac{1}{2}$ | 1 | $\frac{1}{2}$ | $\frac{3}{2}$ | 3 |
| 6 |  | 0 | 0 | $\frac{1}{2}$ | $-\frac{3}{2}$ | 0 | $-\frac{15}{2}$ | $-\frac{17}{2}$ |  |
| 7 | $x_1$ | 3 | 1 | 0 | 1 | $-1$ | 2 | 3 |  |
| 8 | $x_2$ | 2 | 0 | 1 | $-1$ | 2 | 1 | 3 |  |
| 9 |  |  | 0 | 0 | $-1$ | $-1$ | $-8$ | $-10$ |  |

equation $2x_1 + x_2 + x_3 = 5$. The row summation is then obtained ($9 = 2 + 1 + 1 + 5$) along with the ratio (5/2). In row 2, the other basic variable $x_4$ is given along with its unit gain; coefficients of $x_1$, $x_2$, $x_3$, and $b_i$; row summation; and entering ratio [3/1 (= 3)].

In row 3, the coefficients of the objective function are given along with the row sum. Now the largest element in row 3, columns 4 to 8, is 3 and occurs in the column for $x_1$. Thus, $x_1$ is the entering variable. The exiting variable is the basic variable in column 10 with the smallest value ($x_3$ with a 5/2 ratio).

Row 4 reflects the new variable $x_1$, which has replaced $x_3$. Columns 4 to 8 are obtained by manipulating row 1 to obtain a 1 in the fourth-column entry. This is done by dividing the coefficients in row 1 by $\frac{1}{2}$. Columns 4 to 8 of row 5 are obtained by subtracting a factor times row 4 from row 2 to obtain a 0 in the fourth column of row 5. A similar procedure is followed for row 6. The largest entry in row 6 in columns 4 to 8 is in column 5 ($x_2$). Hence, $x_2$ is the entering variable and the existing variable is $x_4$ since its ratio (3) is the smaller.

The next iteration turns out to be the last. To find row 7, we seek to annihilate the term in the fifth column by subtracting a multiple of row 5 from row 4. Row 8 entries are based on a multiple of row 5 to obtain a 1 in the fifth column. Row 9 is found by subtracting from row 6 a multiple of row 5 to obtain a 0 in column 5. The iterations cease when all coefficients in the last row of an iteration are nonpositive in columns 4 to 7. Since this is the case, we are through.

At each iteration the value of the objective function is the negative of the element in column 8 of the row above the double line. Thus the solution after the first iteration is $-(-\frac{15}{2}) = \frac{15}{2}$. The row summations in column 9 are used as a check on the arithmetic. Operations performed on the rows in columns 4 to 8 are performed on column 9. This is then checked by adding the elements in the new row. Only nonnegative ratios are recorded in column 10. Negative ratios indicate the variable is not constrained by the equation.

The tableau method formalizes the simplex procedure. The same steps can be followed for other linear programming problems as for this example. Each iteration produces a new set of coefficients based on substitution of a new variable for one that is basic. The zeroing of certain elements is based on an elimination method.

For large problems, the computational problems are centered on solving simultaneous equations and rules for pivoting or starting iterations. For sparse matrices of coefficients it is convenient to save storage by using one-dimensional lists with indicators to indicate rows as a representation of a matrix. Much of the present research in linear programming is centered on computational problems for classes of linear programming problems. There are a number of existing codes some of which we examine later in this chapter.

It can be observed that the simplex method is one that includes the manipulation and solution of linear equations. It can be shown that this is equivalent to the method of Gaussian elimination for solving linear equations, which is a numerical analysis method and is discussed in Chapter 7.


## 3.3 Methods in Integer Programming

Integer programming methods can be divided into two groups. One is the group of mathematical methods and the other is that of heuristic methods. This section is concerned with the first group. References to heuristic methods are (28) and (29). We shall first review several of these methods and then consider some recent results and future new directions of research.

Generally, the mathematical methods require a problem to be at least partially generated. That is, some possible solutions and variables have been obtained and costed out economically and operationally. For a large problem, the generation time may be very consuming. This is especially true if many mathematical solutions are enumerated or listed. To circumvent this problem for large-scale situations, the problem can be partitioned and decomposed so that each part can be generated and solved separately. Then hopefully the parts can be brought together in some fashion to obtain an overall solution.

Great care must be exercised in decomposing a problem. First, the decomposition should have some justification in terms of the true physical situation. One example in vehicle routing is to perform routing by decomposing the problem so that each subproblem is based on an individual depot of vehicles. This could be justified if there was little overlap or intersection in the service areas served by adjacent depots.

The second, and perhaps more important, consideration in decomposition is that of loss of optimality. If the decomposition produces subproblems that are very small, then the solution method may not be used to its maximum advantage. In fact, a faulty decomposition may produce subproblems that are infeasible. Even with larger subproblems the solution method may not be able to improve significantly over existing methods.

Let us consider the problem of assigning aircraft to the route structure of an airline carrier. For a given week of operations, each flight segment (a nonstop flight between two cities) could be represented as a row heading in a matrix. Columns could be possible assignments of aircraft to these flight segments. Now the airline staff itself decomposes this problem by considering subproblems in which each subproblem represents the scheduling of the fleet of a particular type of plane. Thus, there could be 707, 727, DC-9, DC-10, 747, and L-1011 problems. Aircraft that fly the same type of flights in terms of range and passengers could be grouped together; however, even this decomposition may not yield manageable-sized subproblems. A fleet of medium range aircraft for a large carrier could consist of over a hundred aircraft. Thus, the problem must be decomposed further. One possible method would be to divide the problem by geographic zones or by aircraft bases. In matrix form, this would appear as in Fig. 3-3.

Here there are three bases: I, II, and III. The rows or flight segments assigned to group I is the subset $A$. For group II (III), it is $B$ ($C$). Without decomposition we would have to generate all blocks

Methods in Integer Programming / 69

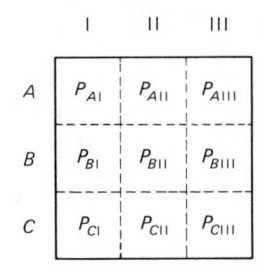

|   | I | II | III |
|---|---|----|-----|
| A | $P_{AI}$ | $P_{AII}$ | $P_{AIII}$ |
| B | $P_{BI}$ | $P_{BII}$ | $P_{BIII}$ |
| C | $P_{CI}$ | $P_{CII}$ | $P_{CIII}$ |

Figure 3-3. Decomposition of aircraft routing problem.

in this matrix. Because of the rules of decomposition, here we only generate the blocks along the diagonal. That is, we generate $P_{AI}$, $P_{BII}$, and $P_{CIII}$.

The next step would be to solve each of the subproblems and then combine the results to obtain a general solution. Difficulties may be encountered if a flight segment is assigned to a base where the costs are high to fly the segment. The general solution procedure must then have the capability of resolving such situations. True mathematical optimality may be lost because the off-diagonal blocks of the matrix in Fig. 3-3 are not considered.

Several observations can be made from examining problems such as the preceding examples. First, the concept of a solution procedure should be viewed in a context larger than solving a specific subproblem. This is only one piece of the problem and may lose significance when compared to attacking the general problem. A general solution method must employ rules and procedures to decompose as well as to control generation, solution procedure of subproblems, resolution of infeasibilities, and completion of an entire solution. A general diagram appears in Fig. 3-4.

The controller unit is the brain of the system so to speak. It creates the decomposition and passes the subproblems onward for generation and solution. After these are solved, the controller then must resolve and integrate the solutions to find a general solution. This could involve solving additional subprograms.

The advance of computer technology has aided in the solution of large-scale problems in two ways. First, larger memories and rapid access peripheral equipment such as magnetic disk and drum units may enable some problems to be solved economically without decomposition. Of course, over time the size of the problem may grow. This was the case in air travel during the last 2 decades, for example.

70 / Mathematical Programming

```
              Data
               ↓
          ┌──────────┐
          │Controller│◄──────┐
          └──────────┘       │
     Decomposition Problems  │
               ↓             │
          ┌──────────┐       │
          │Generator │       │
          └──────────┘       │
               ↓             │
        ┌───────────────┐    │
        │Solution Method│    │
        └───────────────┘    │
       Subproblems Solutions │
               ↓             │
      ┌─────────────────────┐│
      │Resolution of Solutions│◄┘
      └─────────────────────┘
               ↓
         Complete Solution
```

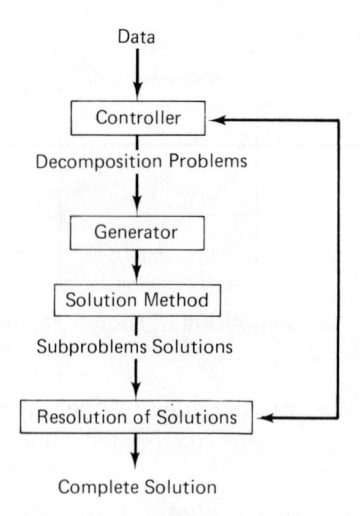

**Figure 3-4.** General solution procedure using decomposition.

A second advance is the development of machinery to parallel process the generation and solution of several subproblems simultaneously. The ILLIAC machine is an example of a parallel processing machine.

Another observation is that the decomposition procedure should be heavily dependent on the nature and conditions of the environment of the problem itself. Thus, an effective decomposition procedure will require the interaction of both scientists and operations personnel. This has the benefit of assistance in producing operationally usable solutions and provides a tie to the operations system.

It should be emphasized that this decomposition is not the one commonly referred to in the research literature. Usually decomposition is viewed as part of the solution procedure for handling a particular problem. Decomposition is often performed on a mathematical basis rather than operationally partitioning the problem. We resort to operational decomposition only when the problem is too large for either effective generation or solution as an entire unit. A further difference in the decompositions involves the relationship between subproblem solutions. For an operational decomposition, the solutions are independent in that one solution cannot be used in a separate subprogram. For a mathematical decomposition, the solutions may be different solutions to the same problem. We shall now examine the mathematical methods and explore this in more detail.

Consider a problem denoted by $P$. A mathematical subproblem $P_\alpha$ satisfies the property that every feasible solution of $P_\alpha$ is a feasible solution of $P$. Furthermore, if $\{P_\alpha\}$ is the collection of subproblems, then a feasible solution of $P$ is a feasible solution of at least one $P_\alpha$. For example, suppose $P$ involves 10 variables with which we shall optimize. Now if one variable is fixed in value in its range of feasible values, then this is a subproblem of $P$.

Generally, we attempt to solve $P$. If we are able to, we are through. If not, we create by some means, a list of subproblems that must be considered. This could, for example, be done by fixing values of variables in $P$ or a feasible region formed by splitting up constraints. We then attempt to solve a subproblem chosen from the list of subproblems. If we can solve it, then we compare its value with the best solution obtained so far. If we have no previous solution or if the new solution represents an improvement, then we keep the solution, select a new subproblem, and continue. If the new solution is not an improvement, we discard it and return to the list for a new problem. At certain points we may create new subproblems from old ones so that the length of the list of subproblems is variable. After exhausting the list, if we have not found a solution that is feasible, then the original parent problem $P$ is infeasible. On the other hand, several possibilities occur if there are solutions to some of the subproblems. If we know we have a solution known to be within a small $\epsilon\%$ of the optimal and this value is sufficient for our needs, then we can stop looking at subproblems in the list. Here $\epsilon$ is the preassigned tolerance level as before. An alternative is to exhaust the list to obtain the exact optimal solution to $P$.

A question that arises is how a bound on the solution can be obtained so that we shall know that we are within $\epsilon\%$ of the optimal solution. The main method to obtain bounds on solution is to eliminate or *relax* a single constraint or a collection of constraints in the original problem. The most common relaxation is to do away with some or all of the integer constraints and then apply a linear programming method. One reason for doing this is that, in terms of structure, the integer constraints complicate the situation. Another reason is that the linear programming method may be very fast so that bounds are obtained rapidly. This relaxation may be applied to subproblems as well as to the original problem.

Several results can occur where a more general, relaxed problem $R$ of a problem $P$ is solved. If $R$ is found to be infeasible, then $P$ will be infeasible (why?). If we are attempting to, say, minimize an objective function, then if the solution to $R$ is better than the best solution found so far, we should go on and consider $P$. If, on the other hand, $R$ is not better than the best solution to date, we do not have to consider $P$ (why?).

The mathematical approaches in integer programming can be placed in the context above. Basically a method can be classified by the way it selects the subproblem, solves the subproblem, and adds the list of subproblems.

One general class of methods is based on relaxation by linear programming and by considering implications of the constraints. This class includes branch and bound and implicit enumeration methods. In a branch and bound method, we represent the set of solutions as a tree. Each path from a root point to a leaf point represents a solution. Each time a new level in the tree is reached, the value of a given variable has been determined or its possible range reduced. Suppose there are two variables with possible values given by $x_1 = 0, 1, 2$ and $x_2 = 1, 2$. The tree of possible solutions is given in Fig. 3-5. A node here represents a specific value in the figure. In this figure, there is an artificial root point for convenience.

Any path or potential solution may be infeasible. If a path is feasible in that the solution is feasible, then there is a value of the path in terms of the objective function. If we are partway along a path, then we have a partial solution with a partial cost. Thus, in Fig. 3-5, the node $x_1 = 1$ has a partial cost. In a larger problem, we would select the variable to "branch" on at each level. To see if we would elect to explore this part of the tree further and plummet down to the next level, we would attempt to estimate the cost of complet-

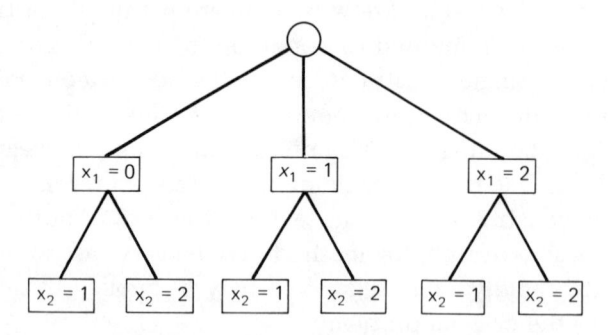

Figure 3-5. Tree of possible solutions for two variables.

ing the problem from this point. By relaxation, we can apply a linear programming method to bound the solution. Thus, we can "bound" the branch. We could cost project for each subbranch emanating from the given node. If no improved solutions were possible from the bounding, then we could move to the next node in the same level of the tree and continue. If several subbranches had bounds that indicated improvement, we would select the subbranch with the lowest (highest) bound if minimization (maximization) was to be done. After we explore this subbranch, we would back up the tree and explore another branch. Suppose now in Fig. 3-5 that this was only a portion of the tree. If we were at $x_1 = 1$ and obtained estimates for the branches $x_1 = 1$, $x_2 = 1$ and $x_1 = 1$, $x_2 = 2$, then we could compare the bounds. If the branch $x_1 = 1$, $x_2 = 2$ was preferred, then we would go down this branch first. Later we would back up to the same level and compare the value of the projected cost and partial cost with the value of the best solution to date.

In terms of the general framework of subproblems, the list of subproblems is added to with each new level being attained. When a subproblem is extracted from the tree, then we are projecting the cost from a given node for a branch.

It is not necessary for each level to be the specific value of a given variable. We could have restricted ranges for several variables such as $0 \leq x_1 \leq 1$, $5 \leq x_2 \leq 7$ and $0 \leq x_1 \leq 1$, $7 \leq x_2 = 9$ thereby dividing the feasible region to the problem. The only requirement is that the branches be disjoint in that the space of variable values are disjoint for each branch.

The elimination of branches and bounding can also be achieved by constructing new constraints from existing constraints. These new conditions follow logically from the old conditions. For example, suppose $x_1 + x_2 = 1$, $x_2 + x_3 = 1$, and $x_3 = 1$ were some conditions obtained from the original constraints or from branching. Suppose that all variables must be either 0 or 1. Then $x_3 = 1$ implies $x_2 = 0$, and $x_1 = 1$ (why?). The problem with this is that the logical implications must be programmed and completely detailed. Hammer and Rudeanu[16] explore this in some detail.

In the bounding operation we are estimating the cost of completing a partial solution. We are not enumerating directly the paths in the branch. For this reason, we are implicitly enumerating the solutions.

## 74 / Mathematical Programming

As an example of branch and bound, consider the problem

$$\min\ 4x_1 + 3x_2 + 2x_3$$

subject to

$$3x_1 + 4x_2 \geq 15$$
$$x_1 + x_2 + x_3 \geq 10$$
$$x_1, x_2, x_3 \geq 0,\ \text{integer}$$

Since $x_3$ has the smallest coefficient in the objective function, we could establish branches for ranges of values of $x_3$, say, $x_3 \leq C$ and $x_3 \geq C + 1$. Then $x_1 + x_2 \geq 10 - C$ for the branch $x_3 \leq C$ (why?). The procedure continues. Later levels could further define the value of $x_3$ or ranges for other variables. For the cost projection for the branches $x_3 \leq C$ and $x_3 \geq C + 1$, we can apply linear programming to solve the problems.

$$\min\ 4x_1 + 3x_2 + 2x_3$$

subject to

$$3x_1 + 4x_2 \leq 15$$
$$x_1 + x_2 + x_3 \leq 10$$
$$x_3 \leq C$$
$$x_1, x_2, x_3 \geq 0,\ \text{integer}$$

and

$$\min\ 4x_1 + 3x_2 + 2x_3$$

subject to

$$3x_1 + 4x_2 \leq 15$$
$$x_1 + x_2 + x_3 \leq 10$$
$$x_3 \geq C + 1$$
$$x_1, x_2, x_3 \geq 0,\ \text{integer}$$

If the solution value of the first subproblem is smaller than that of the second, we would explore that branch further. The selection of the next problem in the list is based on the tree structure and the values of the cost projection added to the value of the partial solution. In the problems above, we have bounds for the partial solution, namely, $2C$ and $2C + 2$, respectively.

An integer solution is obtained either through the linear solution to a subprogram being integer or through the enumeration of an integer solution by the branching operation. In terms of implementation a branch and bound method could be programmed in two parts. The first section would be composed of the input, output, and integer programming code. This section would access the linear programming code as a subroutine. Several advantages of this approach are that various linear programming codes could be tested and existing codes accessed as library routines. Care would have to be exercised in the format of the data so that file structures in the integer programming part would be compatible with the form required by the linear programming subroutine. The method would appear as shown in Fig. 3-6. To improve running efficiency, the linear programming method could be called upon less frequently. The computation time is weighed heavily on the side of the linear programming subroutine since it is there that most of the arithmetic operations are being done. The integer code serves to set up subproblems and to eliminate subproblems from the list. The efficiency would be accomplished by creating a large number of subproblems initially using the branching operation. The linear programming code then would act to bound the solutions of the subproblems in the list. The result of this procedure in some cases would be fewer overall linear programs to solve.

Another aid is to employ the linear solution of a larger subproblem to the present subproblem where it is optimal. This will occur since with any branching the branches are mutually exclusive and exhaustive of all integer solutions in the branch.

The branching code could consist of a graph theory enumeration approach. Once all subproblems in a list have been bounded by the linear program, the subproblems can be sorted on the basis of the bounds so that the next subproblem to consider is that with the best bound. For minimization the best subproblem would be that with the lowest value of the bound.

Elimination of branches or pruning could be accomplished by comparing the bound with the best integer solution found if

76 / Mathematical Programming

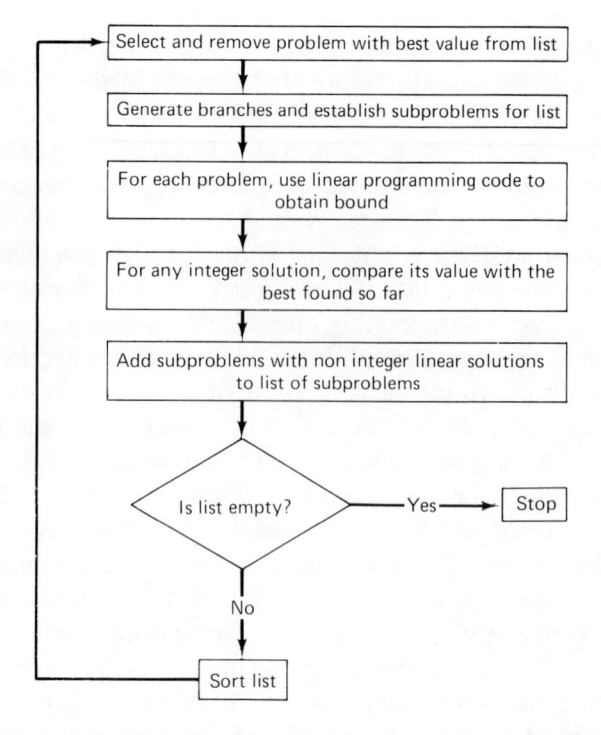

```
┌──▶ Select and remove problem with best value from list
│         ↓
│    Generate branches and establish subproblems for list
│         ↓
│    For each problem, use linear programming code to
│                    obtain bound
│         ↓
│    For any integer solution, compare its value with the
│                    best found so far
│         ↓
│    Add subproblems with non integer linear solutions
│              to list of subproblems
│         ↓
│      ◇ Is list empty? ──Yes──▶ Stop
│         │
│         No
│         ↓
└──── Sort list
```

Figure 3-6. Flow diagram of integer programming method.

the bound indicated that there is no solution better than that found so far.

Another method is that of cutting planes; it is due to Gomory and appears in several of his papers. The basic approach is to start with a linear programming solution. At each iteration, a linear constraint is added that makes the optimal noninteger solution infeasible in the new problem; however, the new problem must have the same set of integer solutions as the first problem. These constraint additions or cuts continue until the optimal integer solution is obtained. Consider the following problem.

$$\min 1x_1 + 3x_2$$

subject to

$$3x_1 - \leq_2 = 5$$

$$x_1, x_2 \geq 0, \text{integer}$$

The optimal linear solution is $x_1 = \frac{5}{3}$, $x_2 = 0$. Because $x_1$ and $x_2$ are integer valued, we have from the first constraint that $x_1 \leq 1$. Since $\frac{5}{3} > 1$, we can introduce the constraint $x_1 \leq 1$ as a cut. We then wish to solve the problem

$$\max\ 1x_1 + 3x_2$$

subject to

$$3x_1 + x_2 \leq 5,$$
$$0 \leq x_1 \leq 1,$$

and

$$x_2 \geq 0$$

The linear programming solution is then $x_1 = 1$ and $x_2 = 2$ and we are through. The cutting plane method will yield an optimal integer solution at the end. No solutions will come out in the interim, however. The problem is to find the added constraints. Suppose that a general constraint (after changing to equality form) is given by

$$\sum_{j=1}^{n} a_{ij} x_j = b_i. \tag{3.14}$$

Because of the integer constraints, we can show that this implies

$$\sum [a_{ij}] x_j \leq [b_i]$$

where $[t]$ is the greatest integer not exceeding $t$. (e.g. $[1] = 1$, $[2.5] = 2$, $[-1.2] = -2$) To make this an equality, we can add a new slack variable $y$ to obtain

$$\sum_{j=1}^{n} [a_{ij}] x_j + y = [b_i] \tag{3.15}$$

Subtracting Eq. (3.15) from Eq. (3.14) we obtain

$$\sum_{j=1}^{n} (a_{ij} - [a_{ij}]) x_j - y = (b_i - [b_i])$$

This constraint is then used in the new linear programming problem. To select the constraint to work with, we first pick a noninteger-valued basic variable and a constraint equation in which it appears with respect to the linear programming solution.

A cutting plane program could be implemented around a linear programming code. The additional program section would be a mechanism for adding the new constraint along with input, output, and stopping. Stopping is done by a check on any linear solution to determine if it is an integer solution.

There are two methods that have been developed over the past few years. One is commonly referred to as Bender's decomposition and is described in Bender.[25] The other approach is based on group theory and is due to Gomory.[26]

Unfortunately, each of the methods has several serious shortcomings. The cutting plane method guarantees a solution, but it may take too long. Cuts may become decreasingly effective. If we stop before the end is reached, we do not have a solution. Only one solution is obtained. With the group theory approach, the problem occurs when the size of the problem is large and so the order of the group is large. Enumeration methods may only slowly converge to a solution. With large problems, computational errors in roundoff may build up and so lead to erroneous branching. These methods have received the most attention in recent times; Geoffrion and Marsten[22] and Gorry and Shapiro[27] consider the approach of combining several methods.

Recent advances have been made on the implementation side. Some of these are reviewed by Beale.[24] Attempts have been made to obtain good solutions quickly. Total computer time is 3 to 5 times greater than the time required to solve the linear programming version. With third-generation machinery, disk and drum units, the number of files that can be employed in information transfer between the sections of a program is large. Thus, separate programs can be run as a unit.

Exploration has been carried out into the selection of subproblems from a list. One method is to select the subproblem that would generate the fewest descendent subproblems. This procedure, however, does not look for an early good solution. The importance in obtaining a good solution lies in part in the need to reduce the size of the list so as not to overflow storage capacity. Beale[24] explores the last in, first out selection rule for subproblems.

## 3.4 Applications

In the previous sections several examples of mathematical programming were considered, including assignment and investment. This section will be concerned with more detailed examples.

In certain situations a nonlinear programming problem can be transformed into a linear programming problem. An example of this was given by Hord[32] in the context of electro-optical systems design. A camera system is being designed that will function in the maximum altitude above the earth in a vertical direction. The first constraint involves the illuminance at the image of an extended object. This quantity can be shown to be of the form

$$H = \left(\frac{KD^2}{f^2}\right) e^{-kR}$$

where $f$ is the lens focal length, $D$ is the lens diameter, $K$ is a function of invariant factors, $R$ is the altitude, and $k$ is a constant. The constraint is that

$$\frac{KD^2 e^{-kR}}{f^2} \geq b_0$$

Because there is a lowest possible altitude,

$$R \geq b_1.$$

Other constraints due to weight, dimension, and similar factors are

$$D \leq b_2,$$

$$b_3 \leq \frac{f}{D} \leq b_4,$$

and

$$\frac{f}{D} \geq \frac{b_4}{b_2}.$$

To transform these nonlinear constraints logarithms are taken. For $H$ we have

$$\ln H = 2 \ln D + \ln k - 2 \ln f - kR$$

80 / Mathematical Programming

Define a set of new variables by

$$y_1 = \ln H$$
$$y_2 = \ln D$$
$$y_3 = R$$
$$y_4 = \ln f$$

Then the constraints above become, respectively,

$$y_1 \geqslant \ln b_0$$
$$y_3 \geqslant b_1$$
$$y_2 \leqslant \ln b_2$$
$$\ln b_3 \leqslant y_4 \leqslant \ln b_4$$
$$y_4 - y_2 \geqslant \ln b_4 - \ln b_2$$

The objective function is $y_3$ since the altitude is to be maximized. It should be noted that Hord[32] also considers additional constraints and computational results. (Construct an example of values and transform into the linear form.)

The second application involves a container company that manufactures corrugated boxes. The production phases are described in Fig. 3-7.

The roll stock has as its main characteristic the basic weight in pounds per thousand square feet and is of two types, $A$ and $B$, each of which requires a different percentage of raw materials. Corrugated sheets are made in Step 2 with three layers composed of two paper liners ($C$) and one medium paper ($D$). At Step 3 the sheets are slotted

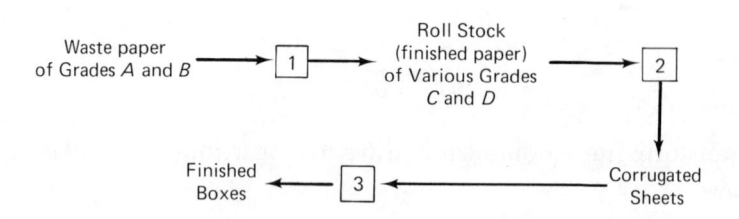

**Figure 3-7.** Container line schematic.

for folding and printed and then folded and closed. The percentage of each raw material required for the linear and medium is given by

|   | A  | B  |
|---|----|----|
| C | 80 | 20 |
| D | 50 | 50 |

This problem can be given a linear programming interpretation but care must be taken because the process has several stages between the raw materials and finished boxes. Wastage at intermediate steps must be taken into account. The approach taken by Russell[33] is to apply a conversion vector to handle intermediate steps. This vector has as components

$V_1$ — type $A$ material to make $V_3$ and $V_4$
$V_2$ — type $B$ material to make $V_3$ and $V_4$
$V_3$ — type $C$ manufactured to make $V_5$
$V_4$ — type $D$ manufactured to make $V_5$
$V_5$ — corrugated sheet manufactured to make $V_6$
$V_6$ — boxes manufactured.

The vector can be determined by working from one box and accounting for wastage. The actual factory must be studied to determine the unit costs and availability of supplies and labor. The variables are

$Q_1$ — purchase of $A$
$Q_2$ — purchase of $B$
$Q_3$ — manufacture of $C$
$Q_4$ — manufacture of $D$
$Q_5$ — manufacture of corrugated sheet
$Q_6$ — construction of boxes

The quantity that describes the process is then

$$\sum_{i=1}^{6} V_i Q_i.$$

Suppose $x_i$ is the amount of $Q_i$ done so that, $x_1$ is then the amount of $A$ purchased. Constraints enter in line balancing. Thus,

$$x_3 Q_3 - x_5 Q_5 = 0$$

To obtain a linear programming model let $y_i$ be the matrix of amount of production at the $i$th stage with corresponding profit matrix $C_i$, $i = 0, 1, 2, 3$. The objective is to maximize

$$\sum_{i=0}^{3} C_i y_i$$

The constraints relate to balancing as well as to incrementally moving from one stage to another. Let $T_j$ be the matrix for converting from the $(j-1)$st to the $j$th level; let $R_j$ be the input availability matrix for the $j$th manufacturing level; and let $a_j$ be the constraint on capacity for the $j$th level. Then the constraints are

$$R_i Y_i \leq a_i \qquad i = 0, 1, 2$$
$$R_3 Y_2 = a_3$$
$$Y_i = T_{i+1} Y_{i+1} \qquad i = 0, 1, 2$$
$$Y_i \geq 0 \qquad i = 0, 1, 2, 3$$

This example illustrates an approach for handling multiphase production with linear programming.

Another application of linear programming has been in estimating recreation tours in a transportation network in a national forest. The application is due to Sullivan[34] and is briefly described here. The linear program formulation is to estimate future volume on a network wherein trips in the network may not have defined termination points. Particular sites are assumed not to influence the decisions on traveling greatly. The model will be formulated and then steps to obtain coefficient values discussed.

The object is to minimize the difference between traffic volume based on estimated tourist potential and that computed at various facilities. Define $R_{ij}(r_{ij})$ as the estimated potential traffic (computed traffic) from location $i$ to location $j$. Then define $A_{ij}$ and $B_{ij}$ by

$$A_{ij} = \left(\frac{r_{ij} - R_{ij}}{R_{ij}}\right) \quad \text{if } r_{ij} \geq R_{ij}$$

$$B_{ij} = \left(\frac{R_{ij} - r_{ij}}{R_{ij}}\right) \quad \text{otherwise if } R_{ij} \geq r_{ij}$$

$$0 \quad \text{otherwise}$$

The pair $(i, j)$ can be used to denote the one-way path in the highway system. Let the set of all such pairs be denoted by $P$. The objective function is

$$\min \sum_{(i,j) \in P} (A_{ij} + B_{ij})$$

Let the travel time between $i$ and $j$ be given by $D_{ij}$. One constraint of the model is that average travel time for all tours is the same. This is given by

$$\sum_{(i,j) \in P'} D_{ij} r_{ij} = A$$

Here $P'$ is the set of all links in the transportation network and $A$ is the average tour length. There are also constraints relating to the flow of traffic. The total flow into each location must equal that exiting. The flow must continue through the location without a reverse in direction. These are given by the equations

$$r_{ij} = r_{jk}$$

and

$$r_{kj} = r_{ji}$$

for all $i, j, k$. These constraints refer to a conservation of flow in the physical sense. There are other similar constraints relating to locations that generate traffic for the system. If node $j$ generates $P_j$ in flow as a percentage of total generated flow, then the total flow into a location $i$ plus the generated flow equals the exiting flow. If $j$ is connected to $i$ and $k$, then

$$r_{ji} + r_{jk} - r_{ij} - r_{kj} = 2P_j$$

84 / Mathematical Programming

The factor of 2 is due to assuming half the generated flow goes to $i$ or $k$ and the remainder flows into $j$ from $i$ and $k$. Constraints of a like type are needed for other locations.

The solution of this problem minimizes the total discrepancy between $(r_{ij})$ and $(R_{ij})$ to obtain estimates of future traffic volume across the highway system.

As Sullivan[34] points out, this is an approach to use mathematical programming as a vehicle for estimating future flow. With actual data it can be used to refine the estimates of potential traffic. This is an example of the interplay between mathematical programming, network analysis, and statistics and is not unusual when approaching many problems.

In reliability a common problem is to allocate spare components to maximize the reliability of the system subject to constraints on cost, weight, volume, or other physical conditions. Consider the structure in Fig. 3-8. There are $n$ components connected in series so that if any component fails, then the system fails. The components are assumed to work independently. Component $X_i$ has a probability $P_i$ of functioning. Each component is assumed to either work or fail. Then the reliability of the system is

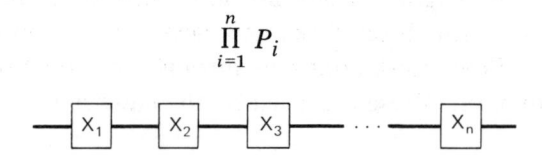

$$\prod_{i=1}^{n} P_i$$

Figure 3-8. All in series structure.

By redundancy we wish to install duplicate components in parallel at various points in the system to enhance the reliability of the system. An example appears in Fig. 3-9.

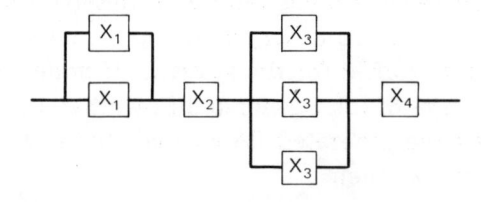

Figure 3-9. Redundant elements in all in series structure.

In this situation all components are assumed to function independently. The system will work if any of the $X_1$ components work, if the $X_2$ and $X_4$ components work, and if any of the $X_3$ components function.

To compute the reliability of this system we first compute the reliability of a given type of component. Suppose $k_i$ components of type $i$ component exist in parallel. Then the reliability is

$$1 - (1 - P_i)^{k_i}$$

which is the complementary (one minus the) probability of the event that all $k_i$ of the type $i$ components fail. Then the reliability of the general system is

$$\prod_{i=1}^{n} [1 - (1 - P_i)^{k_i}]$$

The general problem of component allocation is expressed by

$$\max \prod_{i=1}^{n} [1 - (1 - P_i)^{m_i+1}] \quad (3.16)$$

subject to

$$\sum_{i=1}^{n} C_{ir} m_i \leq C_r, \quad 1 \leq r \leq u \quad (3.17)$$

and

$$m_i \geq 0, \text{ integer} \quad (3.18)$$

Here $m_i$ is the number of components inserted in parallel to the original type $i$ component. A solution is a vector of the form $(m_1, ..., m_n)$. Although this problem requires the determination of integer quantities, the objective function is nonlinear. We shall now transform the problem into an integer programming format. Taking the natural logarithm of the objective function we have

$$\sum_{i=1}^{n} \ln [1 - (1 - P_i)^{m_i+1}].$$

Now set

$$d_{ik} = \ln [1 - (1 - P_i)^{k+1} - 1 - (1 - P_i)^k]$$

and

$$b_r = C_r - \sum_{i=1}^{n} C_{ir}$$

Define $x_{ik}$ as the placing of the $k$th component of type $i$ in parallel so that

$$m_i = \sum_{k=0}^{\infty} x_{ik}$$

and $x_{ik} = 0$ or 1. Furthermore, if we do not place the $k$th component, we cannot place the $(k + 1)$st component of type $i$. Thus, a condition is that $x_{ik} = 0$ implies $x_{ik+1} = 0$ for all $i$ and $k$.

With the notation above, we can show that Eq. (3.16) to (3.18) is equivalent to the following formulation.

$$\max \sum_{i=1}^{n} \sum_{j=1}^{\infty} d_{ij} x_{ij} \qquad (3.19)$$

subject to

$$\sum_{i=1}^{n} \sum_{j=1}^{\infty} c_{ir} x_{ij} = b_r \quad , \quad 1 \leq r \leq u \qquad (3.20)$$

$$x_{ij} = 0 \text{ or } 1 \qquad (3.21)$$

$$x_{ij} = 0 \text{ implies } x_{ij+1} = 0 \qquad (3.22)$$

The upper bound on the summation is not really infinite. Define $Q_i$ by

$$Q_i = \min_{r} \left[\frac{b_r}{c_{ir}}\right]$$

and set

$$Q = \sum_{i=1}^{n} Q_i$$

Then $Q$ can replace the infinite bound in Eq. (3.19) and (3.20).

There have been a number of approaches to the allocation problem. These are summarized in Lientz[29],[30]. Approaches include dynamic programming, branch and bound, network analysis, and heuristic assignment.

Suppose, for example, that there are three component types in series in a structure. The cost and reliability is given by the following table.

| Component Type | Reliability | Cost |
|---|---|---|
| 1 | 0.8 | $2.50 |
| 2 | 0.9 | 3.00 |
| 3 | 0.7 | 1.50 |

We wish to assign redundant components so as to maximize reliability subject to the constraint that we cannot spend more than $10.00. The problem can be formulated as

$$\max \, [1 - (0.2)^{m_1+1}][1 - (0.1)^{m_2+1}][1 - (0.3)^{m_3+1}]$$

subject to

$$2.50 m_1 + 3 m_2 + 1.50 m_3 \leq 10$$

and

$$m_1, m_2, m_3 \geq 0$$

Reformulating we define $(d_{ik})$ and $(b_r)$ to obtain the format of Eq. (3.19) to (3.22). If we were to carry out this computationally on a computer, Eq. (3.19) to (3.22) would be the preferred formulation since it would be a standard integer programming format. Let us apply a branch and bound approach with the nonlinear objective function. First, the constraint in cost implies

$$m_1 = 0, 1, 2, 3, 4$$
$$m_2 = 0, 1, 2, 3$$
$$m_3 = 0, 1, 2, 3, 4, 5, 6$$

(Give reasons for this.) Because $m_2$ can branch on only four values, we shall construct four subproblems based on $m_2$. This is shown in Fig. 3.10. Attached to each branch is the value of the partial solution. This is given in parentheses by each branch. (Compute and verify these.) The best value is 0.5599 and is an entire feasible solution since we cannot add any additional components of any type (why?). This

88 / Mathematical Programming

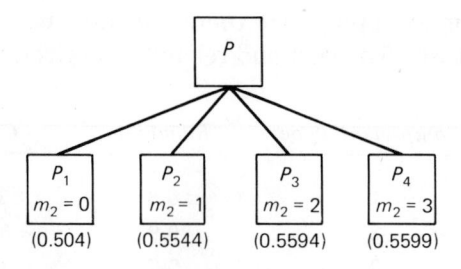

**Figure 3-10.**

subproblem is removed from the list and we go to the next best in value.

The second highest partial value is 0.5594. It has a partial cost of 6, which would allow the following values of $m_1$ and $m_3$:

$$m_1 = 0, 1$$
$$m_3 = 0, 1, 2$$

Suppose for convenience that each solution is a vector $(m_1, m_2, m_3)$. Then the following relationships follow immediately (show this).

$$(0, 2, 0) < (1, 2, 0) < (1, 2, 1)$$
$$(0, 2, 0) < (0, 2, 1) < (0, 2, 2)$$

Here $(a, b, c) < (d, e, f)$ means $(d, e, f)$ has a higher value than $(a, b, c)$ in terms of the objective function. Thus, we have only to compare $(1, 2, 1)$ and $(0, 2, 2)$ to find the best integer solution in this branch. These values are, respectively, 0.8727 and 0.7776. We now remove $P_3$ from the list and $(1, 2, 1)$ becomes the best current integer solution with a value of 0.8727. All other solutions previously obtained are discarded.

The next subproblem is $P_2$. With $m_2 = 1$ we have a partial cost of 3. The feasible value of $m_1$ and $m_3$ are $m_1 = 0, 1, 2$ and $m_3 = 0, 1, 2, 3, 4$. As before, we can order some solutions to obtain

$$(0, 1, 0) < (1, 1, 0) < (2, 1, 0) < (2, 1, 1)$$
$$(0, 1, 1) < (0, 1, 2) < (0, 1, 3) < (0, 1, 4)$$
$$(1, 1, 0) < (1, 1, 1) < (1, 1, 2) < (1, 1, 3)$$

$(2, 1, 1)$, $(0, 1, 4)$, and $(1, 1, 3)$ have values 0.8937, 0.7901, and 0.9426, respectively. Comparing these with the best solution so far, we retain (1, 1, 3) and its value 0.9426 and consider the branch $P_1$, which gives $m_1$ = 0, 1, 2, 3, 4 and $m_3$ = 0, 1, 2, 3, 4, 5, 6.

Next we remove $P_1$ and form five new subproblems based on the value of $m_1$. This is shown in Fig. 3-11. With components 1 and 2 fixed, we can expend the remainder of funds in type 3 components. The best solutions appear as vectors below each branch.

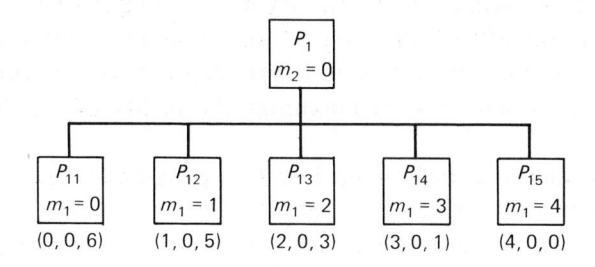

Figure 3-11

Computing the value of the objective function for each branch yields the following values.

$$
\begin{array}{ll}
(0, 0, 6) & 0.7199 \\
(1, 0, 5) & 0.8633 \\
(2, 0, 3) & 0.8856 \\
(3, 0, 1) & 0.8177 \\
(4, 0, 0) & 0.6298
\end{array}
$$

Comparing these to the best solution found to date we see that $m_1 = 1$, $m_2 = 1$, $m_3 = 3$ is the best solution at 0.9426. It is optimal since we have exhausted our list.

This example demonstrates the branch and bound method with bounds obtained by a dominance relationship. With a larger problem we would want to bound with linear programming and use the linear formulation of the problem.

Another application of integer programming involves the selection of warehouse sites to serve depot locations. The problem here is to minimize cost by selecting the best locations. This problem is somewhat specialized with each occurrence. There are usually only a limited number of warehouse sites possible. Furthermore, each site has a certain tax structure, neighborhood, relation to transportation system, and similar factors. Different sites may not be in the same city and so are subject to different tax rates. These conditions are sometimes difficult to quantify. What is the "goodness" of service of the railroad or trucking system? What routes between depots and warehouse sites should be used in the problem? The list can be continued. Because of these factors that are difficult to quantify, it might be preferable to employ a heuristic method and then vary parameters to examine the sensitivity of selecting the sites. This will also have the benefit of allowing for multiple and conflicting objectives. Possible goals would be to minimize fleet size, minimize warehouse and servicing costs, or maximize the utility of existing vehicle fleets.

The problem can be framed in a 0-1 programming context. Let $x_{ij} = 1$ depot $i$ is assigned to warehouse $j$ and set $x_{ij} = 0$ otherwise. The commitment of depot $i$ to warehouse $j$ will carry with it a cost $c_{ij}$ in terms of a specified objective function. The objective function is then

$$\sum_i \sum_j c_{ij} x_{ij}$$

Constraints would be related to inadmissible assignments, minimum and maximum number of depots capable of being served by a warehouse, and similar factors.

Suppose three warehouses are available for assignment to four depots. Each depot can only be assigned to one warehouse. No warehouse can serve more than two depots. The distances between warehouses and depots are given by the following matrix:

|   | 1   | 2   | 3   |
|---|-----|-----|-----|
| 1 | 1.2 | 1.0 | 1.1 |
| 2 | 2.3 | 2.4 | 2.6 |
| 3 | 1.1 | 1.3 | 1.0 |
| 4 | 7.6 | 7.2 | 6.8 |

The objective function is then

$$\min \sum_{i=1}^{y} \sum_{j=1}^{z} c_{ij} x_{ij}$$

where $c_{ij}$ is the $(i,j)$th entry in the matrix. The constraints are

$$\sum_{j=1}^{z} x_{ij} = 1 \quad \text{for all } i$$

$$\sum_{j=1}^{y} x_{ij} = 2 \quad \text{for all } j$$

and

$$x_{ij} = 0 \text{ or } 1 \quad \text{for all } i \text{ and } j$$

To solve this problem we could apply one of the integer programming methods. With cutting planes we would first insert slack variables and we could use the equality constraints to reduce the size of the problem. If we eliminate $(x_{i3})$, we obtain

$$\min 11.5 + 0.1x_{11} - 0.1x_{12} - 3x_{21} - 0.2x_{222}$$
$$+ 0.1x_{31} + 0.3x_{32} + 0.8x_{41}$$

subject to

$$4 = \sum_{i=1}^{y} \sum_{j=1}^{z} (x_{ij}) - y_3$$

$$\sum_{i=1}^{y} x_{ij} + y_i = 2, j = 1, 2$$

$$x_{ij} = 0 \text{ or } 1$$

and

$$y_i \text{ is integer}$$

We first find the optimal linear solution. Since its variables are not integer valued, we add a new constraint. The final integer solution is to assign depot 1 to warehouse 2, 2 to 1, 3 to 3, and 4 to 3. The minimum distance is 11.1. This is obvious by inspecting the matrix. We went through the steps, however, to show the benefit in using equality constraints to reduce the dimensionality of the space of variables.

In previous chapters reference was made to the problem of assigning flight crews to flight segments so as to minimize costs. Because of the size of this problem in integer programming, most methods employ a decomposition method. After decomposition, several approaches that have been employed include cutting planes, heuristics, and branch and bound. Successful methods have usually been reliant on the internal structure of the particular airline's network.

The preceding three applications are only representative of many. Other applications are mentioned in the References, including O'Neil.[31]

## 3.5 Programs

Linear programming was started during and after World War II. The basic simplex method was developed by George B. Dantzig. Later attention has been focused on improved methods for special classes of problems as well as efficient coding and programming procedures for digital computation. The texts by Dantzig[2] and Hadley[3] deal in detail with linear programming theory and some applications. Texts by Hillier and Lieberman[4] and Wagner[5] have chapters devoted to the theory and methods of linear and integer programming.

Daellenbach and Bell[6] assume a user or application oriented approach where the basic methods are discussed along with examples, data format, and common traits among existing software. Fraser[7] and Gass[8] are earlier texts in a similar vein. Gass[8] gives a listing of available codes and features as of 1963. Charnes and Cooper[1] cover both theory and industrial applications.

The programming codes that will be discussed here are sophisticated in the sense that they rely on numerical analysis methods to reduce the accumulation of error and to reduce the number of pivots and computation time. Thus, it should be kept in mind that although the basic structure of pivoting and solution is similar to that outlined in Subsection 3.2.3, the programs themselves are more complex. The use of existing codes is governed in part by the way in which the problem at hand fits into the computational capabilities of the existing programs in terms of problem size and characteristics of the hardware and software support systems. The use of the code must also be cost-justified in terms of setting up the programs and data as well as the computer time itself. Many times, however, using an existing program is cheaper than building an entire system. Thus, one effect of available software is to make the technique available to a wider class of potential users.

A number of user manuals exists for some of the available linear programs. These include References 9 to 11 for the IBM programs and References 12 and 13 for the Control Data Corporation method.

A number of computer programs for mathematical programming are available from the user groups mentioned in Chapter 1. There is a gradient projection method for nonlinear problems (SHARE). Some linear programming codes, the library source, and language are listed below:

| Title | User Grp. | Language |
|---|---|---|
| Dual symmetric linear programming | RCA-CUA | FORTRAN |
| Linear programming | FOCUS | FORTRAN |
| ICES/360 Optech I | SHARE | ICES |
| Computer program for parameter optimization | COSMIC | FORTRAN |
| Linear programming | EIN | FORTRAN |
| Linear programming | PAL | MACHINE |
| Linear programming simplex | SHARE | FORTRAN |

There are numerous linear programming codes that rely on modifications to a simplex-type method for computation time reduction. Treated in this section are programs available from two computer manufacturers. These are not discussed here because of particular efficiency or preference; rather, they are representative because of their wide availability and general usage.

Two central features of any linear programming package that must be evaluated prior to selection and commitment to wide use are usage and accuracy. By usage is meant the ease and degree of utility of the program; this includes the format of data inputs. If the coefficients or bounds of certain constraints are being varied to obtain some measure of sensitivity, then the input should be capable of being either easily charged or arranged in a hierachical structure. Intermediate output during pivoting operations may also be helpful to save computer time, especially if numerical errors appear to be dominant. In a large problem it would be desirable to have a capability of stopping and then restarting without repeating previous steps.

By accuracy we mean not only reliability of the programs in terms of working, but also the size of problems that have been tackled successfully in previous experience. Included here are the type of machine, available storage, and number of I/O operations if disk or tape storage is required. Numerical accuracy is significant because feasibility may be lost through roundoff error. The amount of roundoff error is affected by such things as hardware and the means by which arithmetic operations are performed.

IBM has two basic program modules for linear programming: MPS and MPS-X. MPS was constructed first and is widely available. MPS-X is an extended version of MPS and is available for use from IBM at some cost. We consider here MPS since it is available at no purchase or lease cost. The basic description of MPS is contained in the *Mathematical Programming System 360 Users Manual*.[10],[11] As in using many software packages, a control subprogram activates the program to be used. Tapes may be required to be mounted or a tape read or copied and modified in certain parameters. In Reference 11 the job control cards are specified.

Control Data Corproation (CDC) has developed a number of mathematical programming codes. Two of these are PDQ/LP and OPHELIE II. PDQ/LP[17] is a linear programming code written mainly in FORTRAN designed for up to moderate-sized problems. The method uses a standard simplex method. Data format is eased by allowing insertion of inequality constraints of either $\leqslant$ or $\geqslant$. One technique PDQ/LP employs is a routine to find a starting basis different from the origin for the original variables. This saves time by getting a better initial value of a starting solution. The method outputs a line per iteration, which permits diagnostic checking to be done easily. The format followed is of a general simplex type. The linear program matrix may have any size as long as the following inequality holds:

$$6M + 10N + MN \leqslant 116{,}000$$

Here $M$ is two more than the number of constraint rows and $N$ is the number of nonslack and right-hand side columns. This would be a limitation for a problem with a small percentage of nonzero coefficients. Data formats are specified and an example is given in Reference 12. There is also a forcing capability that allows various criteria for selecting an entering variable into the basis. There are also modification capabilities in PDQ/LP.

OPHELIE II[12] contains methods for linear programming as well as problem generation in a matrix form. The OPHELIE II control program operates in a language oriented to linear programming usage. Inequality constraints may be specified. Data format is through the MPS or SHARE format. In Reference 12 it states that OPHELIE can solve problems of up to 10,000 constraints with the number of variables unlimited. The basic technique includes methods for rapidly generating an initial basis. OPHELIE II uses a revised simplex method. Correction procedures exist when the method is blocked. Round-off error is lessened by using the 60-bit word on the CDC 6600. OPHELIE II can move from a continuous linear program solution to one in which certain variables have integer solutions. Some types of sensitivity analyses are permitted.

Sources of existing programs in integer and mixed integer programming are either the method developers themselves or the hardware manufacturers. Most of these methods are enumerative in nature. OPHELIE-Mixed is available from Control Data and runs on a CDC 6600. IBM offers MPS-X-MIP for use on Model 360 and 370 computers. These methods are aimed at general classes of problems. Thus, for a given specific problem, some efficiency is lost in the storage and perhaps steps in the solution procedure not necessary for a given application. Given that these may be in assembly code, however, changes to specialize code may be time consuming and unwarranted. Two other programs developed by researchers are RIP30C and UMPIRE. Geoffrion created RIP30C, an integer programming code based on enumeration. Beale and Tomlin developed UMPIRE.

A method touched on briefly in Section 3.3 was Bender's decomposition. There are at least three programs using this approach including MIDAS-2, FMPS-MIP, and IPE. Geoffrion and Marsten[22] review the programs mentioned here in detail and examine the comparative results in problem solving.

There are a number of journals that publish results in integer programming. Some of these are listed below. These journals publish theoretical results with some limited applications.

*Journal of Optimization Theory & Applications*

*Operations Research*

*Management Science*

*Mathematical Programming*

*Operational Research Quarterly*

*Econometrica*

*Australian Computer Journal*

*Naval Research Logistics Quarterly*

*Computers and Operations Research*

In addition to these journals, there are proceedings of regularly held symposiums in mathematical programming. One example is the proceedings of the NATO Advanced Institute on Mathematical Programming.

The textbooks in integer programming are very limited, due in part to the newness and expansion of the field. Hu[16] is an advanced level text giving many algorithms in integer programming and network flows up to 1969. Muth and Thompson[18] consider integer programming in an industrial engineering context. Hammer and Rudeanu[15] explore integer programming problems for the case of 0-1 variables. Lasdon[17] considers general large-scale problems with some reference to integer programming. New results appear in the proceedings of specialized conferences. Two of these are Abadie[13] and Graves and Wolfe.[14]

To maintain the status of state-of-the-art up to date, several excellent survey articles have appeared since 1960. Balinski[19] Balinski and Spielberg,[20] and Beale,[21] are three of these. Trauth and Woolsey[23] review computational experience. An excellent recent review paper is Geoffrion and Marsten.[22] This paper not only reviews the literature but also unifies the methods into a general framework and discusses efficiency in applications.

## REFERENCES

*Linear Programming*

*Theoretical and Methodological*

1. CHARNES, A. AND W. W. COOPER, *Management Models and Industrial Applications of Linear Programming*, 2 vol. New York: John Wiley & Sons, Inc., 1960.
2. DANTZIG, G. B., *Linear Programming and Extensions*. Princeton, N. J.: Princeton University Press, 1961.
3. HADLEY, G., *Linear Programming*. Reading, Mass.: Addison-Wesley Pub. Co., 1962.
4. HILLIER, F. S. AND C. J. LIEBERMAN, *Introduction to Operations Research*. San Francisco, Calif.: Holden-Day, Inc., 1967.
5. WAGNER, H. M., *Principles of Operations Research*. Englewood Cliffs, N. J.: Prentice-Hall, Inc., 1969.

*Application Oriented Textbooks and Manuals*

6. DAELLENBACH, H. G. AND E. J. BELL, *User's Guide to Linear Programming*. Englewood Cliffs, N. J.: Prentice-Hall, Inc., 1970.
7. FRASER, J. P., *Applied Linear Programming*. Englewood Cliffs, N. J.: Prentice-Hall, Inc., 1968.
8. GASS, S. I., *Linear Programming*, 2nd ed. New York: McGraw-Hill Book Co., 1964.
9. ———, *An Introduction to Linear Programming*. IBM, Technical Publications Department, White Plains, N. Y.: IBM Data Processing Division, 1964.

10. \_\_\_\_, *Mathematical Programming System/360 (360A-C)-14X) Version 2, Control Language User's Manual.* IBM Corp., H20-0290-3, White Plains, N. Y.: IBM Data Processing Division, 1966.
11. \_\_\_\_, *MPS/360 Linear and Separable Programming User's Manual.* IBM Corp., Technical Publications Department, H20-0476-1, White Plains, N. Y.: IBM Data Processing Division, 1966.
12. \_\_\_\_, *OPHELIE II General Information Manual.* Control Data Corporation, Document, Pub. No. D0001507001, May, 1970.

*Integer Programming*

*Textbooks*

13. ABADIE, J. (ed.), *Integer & Non Linear Programming.* Amsterdam: North Holland Pub. Co., 1970.
14. GRAVES, R. L. AND P. WOLFE (ed.), *Recent Advances in Mathematical Programming.* New York: McGraw Hill Book Co., 1963.
15. HAMMER, P. L. AND S. RUDEANU, *Boolean Methods in Operations Research and Related Areas.* Berlin: Springer-Verlag, 1968.
16. HU, T. C., *Integer Programming and Network Flows.* Reading, Mass.: Addison-Wesley Pub. Co., 1969.
17. LASDON, L. S., *Optimization Theory for Large Systems.* New York: The MacMillan Co., 1970.
18. MUTH, J. F. AND E. L. THOMPSON (ed.), *Industrial Scheduling.* Englewood Cliffs, N. J.: Prentice-Hall, Inc., 1963.

*Survey Articles*

19. BALINSKI, M. L., "Methods, Uses and Computation," *Mgmt. Science*, XII, (Nov., 1965), 253-313.
20. BALINSKI, M. L. AND K. SPIELBERG, "Methods for Integer Programming: Algebraic, Combinatorial, and Enumerative," in J. S. Aronofsky (ed.), *Progress in Operations Research*, III. New York: John Wiley & Sons, Inc., 1969.
21. BEALE, E. M. L., "Survey of Integer Programming," *Operational Research Quarterly*, XVI (June, 1965), 219-228.
22. GEOFFRION, A. M. AND R. E. MARSTEN, "Integer Programming Algorithms: A Framework and State of the Art Survey," *Mgmt. Science*, XVIII (May, 1972), 465-491.
23. TRAUTH, C. A. AND R. E. WOOLSEY, "Integer Linear Programming: A Study in Computational Efficiency," *Mgmt. Science*, XV (May, 1969), 481-493.

*Additional References*

24. BEALE, E. M. L., "The Significance of Recent Developments in Mathematical Programming Systems," *Proc. NATO Advanced Study Institute*, University of Coimbra, Portugal, 1972.

25. BENDERS, J. F., "Partitioning Procedures for Solving Mixed Integer Variables Programming Problems," *Numerische Mathematik*, IV (1962), 238-252.
26. GOMORY, R. E., "On the Relation Between Integer and Non Integer Solutions to Linear Programs," *Proc. Nat. Acad. Sci.*, LIII (1965), 260-265.
27. GORRY, G. A. AND J. F. SHAPIRO, "An Adaptive Group Theoretic Algorithm for Integer Programming Problems," *Mgmt. Science*, XVII, No. 5 (Jan., 1971), 285-306.
28. GRAVES, G. AND A. WHINSTON, "An Algorithm for the Quadratic Assignment Problem," *Mgmt. Science*, XVII (1970), 453-471.
29. LIENTZ, B. P., "Allocation of Components to Maximize Reliability Using an Implicit Method," *IEEE Trans. on Reliab.*, (June, 1974).
30. ———, "Stochastic Allocation of Spare Components," *Optimizing Methods in Statistics*, (J. Rustagi, ed.), New York: Academic Press, Inc., 1971.
31. O'NEIL, B. F., "Evaluating Heuristics for Vehicle Scheduling," *Technical Report*, University of Miami, Miami, Fla., 1971.
32. HORD, R. M., "Using Linear Programming in Optimal Systems Design," presented at 40th National Conference of the Operations Research Society of America, Anaheim, Calif., 1971.
33. RUSSELL, E., "Lessons in Structuring Large LP Models," *Industrial Engineering*, 9 (March, 1970) 12-18.
34. SULLIVAN, EDWARD C., "An LP Model for Estimating Recreation Tours on a National Forest Transportation Network," presented at 40th National Conference of the Operations Research Society of America, Anaheim, Calif., 1971.

## PROBLEMS

In Problems 1 to 3, formulate the problem as a linear programming problem.

1. Three types of programs $X$, $Y$, $Z$ can be run on each of two machines $A$ and $B$. The cost in minutes required to run one program on a machine is given by

|   | $A$  | $B$  |
|---|------|------|
| $X$ | 0.06 | 0.08 |
| $Y$ | 0.07 | 0.09 |
| $Z$ | 0.09 | 0.15 |

$500 is available for production. To get $1.00 of time takes 0.20 minutes for machine $A$ and 0.15 for machine $B$. There is a minimum requirement of two runs per program. The goal is to maximize the number of runs.

2. A local radio station wishes to allocate time during an 8-hour period in a "rational" way to maximize profits using linear programming. The cost of news is $300 per minute. Commercials bring in $500 per minute. Music cost is $200 per minute. Because of policy there must be at least 5 minutes of news, and the total of news and music time should be $3\frac{1}{2}$ times greater than time for commercials.

3. A used car dealer wishes to stock up his lot to maximize his profit. He can select cars $A$, $B$, and $C$, which are valued wholesale at $500, $700, and $800, respectively. These can be sold at $600, $850, and $1050, respectively. For each car type, the probabilities of sale are

| Type of Car | Probability of Sale in 90 Days |
|---|---|
| A | 0.7 |
| B | 0.8 |
| C | 0.6 |

For every two cars of $B$, he must buy one car of type $A$ or $C$. If he has $10,000 to invest, what should he buy to maximize his expected gain?

4. Solve Problem 1.
5. Solve Problem 2.
6. Solve Problem 3.
7. Find the set of feasible solutions graphically and the optimal solutions to the following problems.

(a.) max $3x_1 + 7x_2$
   subject to
   $$x_1 + x_2 \leq 7$$
   $$2x_1 + x_2 \leq 8$$
   $$x_1, x_2 \geq 0$$

(b.) min $5x_1 - 2x_2$
   subject to
   $$2x_1 + 3x_2 \geq 1$$
   $$x_1, x_2 \geq 0$$

(c.) min $4x_1^2 + 7x_2^2$
   subject to
   $$3x_1^2 + x_2^2 \geq 4$$
   $$10x_1^2 + 3x_2^2 \geq 3$$

8. Write a program to find all vertices of the region defined by the following inequalities.

$$2x_1 + x_2 \geq 2$$
$$2x_2 - x_1 \leq 6$$
$$x_2 - x_1 \geq -3$$
$$x_2 - 2x_1 \geq -7$$
$$3x_2 + x_1 \leq 14$$
$$x_1, x_2 \geq 0$$

9. Solve the following problems using the simplex method, both manually and by computer.

(a.) max $2x_1 + 3x_2 + 5x_3$
subject to
$$x_1 + 2x_2 + 3x_3 \leq 7$$
$$5x_2 + x_3 \leq 6$$
$$x_1, x_2, x_3 \geq 0$$

(b.) max $7x_1 + 11x_2 + 18x_3$
subject to
$$3x_1 + 6x_2 + 6x_3 \leq 14$$
$$x_1 + x_2 - x_3 \leq 6$$
$$x_1, x_2, x_3 \geq 0$$

(c.) max $2x_1 + 5x_2 + 7x_3$
subject to
$$3x_1 + 7x_2 - x_3 = 12$$
$$5x_1 + 13x_2 + x_3 \leq 15$$
$$x_1, x_2, x_3 \geq 0$$

10. Find the dual version of parts a to c listed in Problem 9.

11. Show that the problems given in Eq. (3.16) to (3.18) and Eq. (3.19) to (3.22) yield equivalent solutions. Hence, show that there is a one-to-one correspondence between the set of feasible solutions and then the set of optimal solutions.

In Problems 12 to 15, formulate the problem in an integer programming context and discuss possible approaches in solution.

12. In industrial engineering, a common problem is plant layout. A plant is partitioned into 100 work areas. Each of the areas is to be selected for 1 of the 100 production tasks. When pairings are made between 2 work sites $a$ and $b$ and 2 tasks $A$ and $B$, the cost $C_{a,b,AB}$ is incurred. This occurs for any two combinations. The goal is to minimize costs associated with assigning tasks to work areas.

13. A production line can sometimes be viewed as a modified all-in-series system. Items are worked on for different times by certain processing steps. The total time to complete production of all items is to be minimized.

14. A railroad is attempting to assign empty railroad cars to demand points with each car. There is an associated travel time to a demand point. There are two objectives. The first is to minimize total travel time and the second is to maximize the number of cars assigned.

15. A plan is being constructed to assign house blocks to fallout shelter locations. The objective is to minimize total distance.

Solve Problems 16 to 18 by (i) branch and bound and (ii) cutting planes.

16. max $4x_1 + 2x_2$

    subject to

    $2X_1 + 7x_2 \leq 23$

    $2X_1 + 5x_2 \leq 15$

    $x_1 - x_2 \leq 3$

    $x_1, x_2 \geq 0$, integer

17. max $3x_1 + 2x_2 + 5x_3$

    subject to

    $5x_1 + 3x_2 + 7x_3 \leq 28$

    $4x_1 + 5x_2 + 5x_3 \leq 30$

    $x_1, x_2, x_3 \geq 0$, integer

18. max $27x_1 + 22x_2 + 28x_3$

    subject to

    $5x_1 + 4.25x_2 + 2.5x_3 \leq 22$

    $x_1 + 3x_2 + 5x_3 \leq 14$

    $x_1, x_2, x_3 \geq 0$, integer

19. Suppose, in the assignment of crews to flight segments, a heuristic method was being used where conditions could be used to eliminate some otherwise feasible solutions. Explain how the following factors could be taken into account.

    (a.) Weather delays.

    (b.) Short turnaround times between flights.

    (c.) Leveling of flight hours for balancing.

20. Formulate the problem of routing messages in a computer network. The total mileage of message traffic is to be minimized.

# 4

# NETWORK ANALYSIS

## 4.1 Formulation of Networks Definition

In Appendix B some properties of trees and general network structure are considered. This chapter concentrates on the application of graph-theoretic methods to problems capable of being formulated in a network framework.

Network oriented situations have been explored in such diverse areas as communications, transportation, circuit theory, information flow, power systems, production, and planning for large projects represented as a network of nodes and links. For the moment some objectives and questions can be formed. How much of a commodity (or commodities) can be transferred across the network over some time period? What is the shortest path or route between two nodes? How should the links be built so as to minimize cost? What path should be followed to visit all nodes while minimizing travel time? Some of these questions will be approached in Sections 4.2 and 4.3.

Table 4-1 presents four examples of networks. Included here are the definitions of nodes and links for the situation along with possible objectives. The appliance serving problem is that of constructing routes for servicemen and their vehicles. Customer requests for service received on one weekday would be processed and sorted that day. Vehicles would then be loaded at night and routes prepared. When the servicemen arrive for work the next weekday, routing slips would be distributed and servicing done.

Table 4-1. NETWORK FORMULATIONS

| Application | Appliance Servicing | Project Planning | Computer Network | Pipeline |
|---|---|---|---|---|
| Nodes | Customers Plant yards | Program tasks | Computers | Pumping stations |
| Links | Roads | Logical relationships | Communication lines | Pipes |
| Objective | Minimize total miles | Critical path load leveling | Minimize response time or maximize throughput | Maximize flow |

Project planning and computer networks will be examined in Section 4.4. One of the early applications of network analysis was in the design and layout of pipelines for petroleum supplies. From a supply point, which could be the oil field or a tanker offshore, oil is pumped through a network whose links are the pipes themselves. The goal could be to maximize the flow of oil from a supply point to reservoirs for refining and processing. In a design phase the network structure could be determined.

Caution should be used when deciding to attack a problem in a network context. Some problems can be tackled more easily if put into a mathematical programming setting. Also, some problems relating to general situations such as multicommodity flow in a network are still unsolved.

Before exploring some algorithms for solving particular problems, several additional definitions are necessary. These are mainly to bring the general, theoretical networks as described in Appendix B into a physical situation. For each link there may be associated a distance, time measure, or both. For a pipeline or freeway there is also the concept of capacity. Capacity here means the amount of a quantity that can be loaded upon the link without oversaturation.

A supply point, such as a stockpile, warehouse, or plant yard is commonly called a *source*, while a demand point, where goods or services are needed, is a *sink*. It is not necessary, however, for a network to have nodes formally labeled as sources and sinks. Also, it can occur that only a subset of the nodes are either sources or sinks. For the appliance servicing example, plant yards are supply points or sources, and customers needing service are demands or sinks. Intermediate nodes could be city blocks or intersections and would be neither supply or demand nodes. For the pipeline, an offshore tanker would be a source, while refinery tanks would be sinks.

Consider the sample networks drawn in Fig. 4-1. If we delete or remove any node or link in Fig. 4-1(a), there is still a path from any remaining node to any other remaining node. In Fig. 4-1(b), however, if node 3, node 4, or link (3, 4) is removed, then no traffic can go from nodes 1 and 2 to nodes 5 and 6. Then the network is broken into two disjoint parts. In Fig. 4.1(a) we would have to remove two links or nodes to produce such a break. The breaking of a network into at least two parts is called a *cut*. The set of links that produce this cut is a *cut-set*. Cuts can occur due to jamming, saturation, or a variety of conditions depending on the setting. The minimum number of nodes (or links) that must be broken to split the network into at least two disjoint parts is defined as the *articulation level*. Thus, in Fig. 4-1(a), the articulation level is 2 and the cut-set is (1, 2), (2, 4) (or any other two links). For Fig. 4-1(b) link (3, 4) is a cut-set and the network has articulation level 1.

For several applications including communications, it is important that the network not be so vulnerable as to cut off service between two centers with the destruction of one node or link. Similar remarks hold for certain types of pipelines. In the sense of the network topology or configuration, articulation level is related to the vulner-

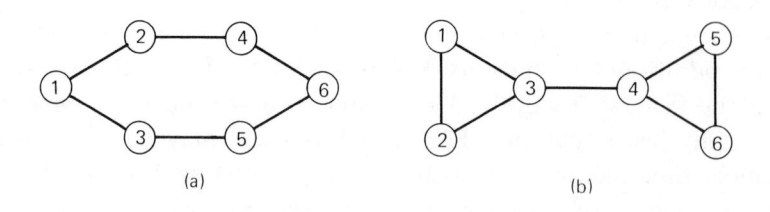

Figure 4-1. Sample networks.

ability of a network. By incorporating probabilities or likelihoods of failure, we can determine the likelihood of a break. An example would be a power blackout in a network where demands exceed capacity. The problem is to estimate the likelihood of a power reduction or shortage.

There are several basic classes of problems considered in network analysis. First, there is the maximal flow problem. This is examined in Section 4.2. The problem of finding the shortest route is considered in Section 4.3. Several applications including project planning and evaluation appear in Section 4.4. The applications are in terms of the general management information system as described in Chapter 2.

### 4.2 Maximal Flow in a Network

One of the problems faced by command and communication systems, pipelines, or traffic is that of maximizing the throughput or flow of messages, petroleum, or traffic, respectively, through the network. A network is specified with capacities given as labels for all links. One or more nodes are labeled as sinks and sources. Several cases are possible. First, there can be a single source and sink. After this case is examined, we shall develop a method for transforming the general source and sink problem into the single sink case. Consider the network in Fig. 4-2. The technique we shall follow here for determining maximal flow appears in Hillier and Lieberman.[8] This network has dual capacities on each link. The source is node 1 and the sink is node 6. The link label closest to a node is the capacity of that link emanating from the node. For example, there is a capacity of 3 from node 1 to node 2 and capacity 2 from node 2 to node 1. Some capacities can be very large so that for practical purposes are infinite. This is the case with the capacity from node 2 to node 3.

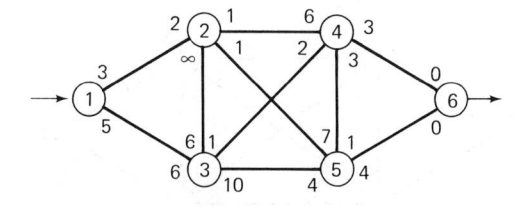

Figure 4-2. Network for maximizing flow.

106 / Network Analysis

The solution method works as follows. At any given stage we look for a path from the source to the sink that has positive flow. That is, at least some material can be moved along a path from source to sink. The amount of material that can be moved is governed by the bottleneck that is the link with smallest capacity. When the path goes from node $i$ for link $(i, j)$, we consider as capacity the label at node $i$ for link $(i, j)$.

The next step of the process, after finding the path, is to decrease the capacities along the path by the smallest capacity in the path. Also, each time we decrease capacity on a link by $k$ units, we add $k$ units of capacity in the opposite direction.

The steps above constitute one iteration of the method. The method continues until no path of positive flow can be found. Then we are finished and the theory behind the method is that this is optimal in the sense of maximizing the flow from source to sink.

Considering our example in Fig. 4-2, we see that 4 units of flow can be assigned along the path given by $1 \rightarrow 3 \rightarrow 5 \rightarrow 6$, where 1, 3, 5, and 6 are nodes and arrows indicate direction of flow. The flow limit is 4 because the smallest capacity along the path is from 5 to 6 and is 4. Using our procedure we must delete 4 units of flow from each capacity and also add 4 units of flow in the opposite direction along the path. The result is the network shown in Fig. 4-3. The capacity along the link from 5 to 6 is 0, which is correct since this is the smallest capacity. Looking at the preceding network we note that a flow of 1 is possible along the path $1 \rightarrow 2 \rightarrow 4 \rightarrow 6$ (why only 1?). Following the same procedure we obtain the network shown in Fig. 4-4. A flow of 1 is possible along the path $1 \rightarrow 3 \rightarrow 4 \rightarrow 6$ and yields the network shown in Fig. 4-5. Available capacity from 1 to 6 is decreasing as flows are assigned. Some links cannot be traversed from left to right due to their capacity being reached. It is still possible, however, to assign a flow of 1 along the path $1 \rightarrow 2 \rightarrow 5 \rightarrow 4 \rightarrow 6$, which gives the network shown in Fig. 4-6.

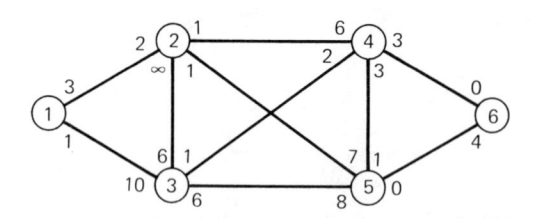

Figure 4-3. Network after 1 flow assignment.

Maximal Flow in a Network / 107

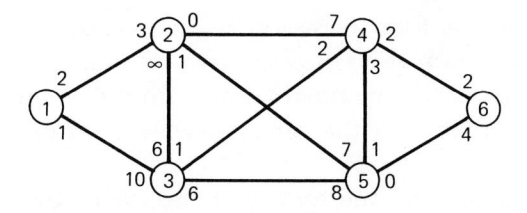

Figure 4-4. Network after 2 flow assignments.

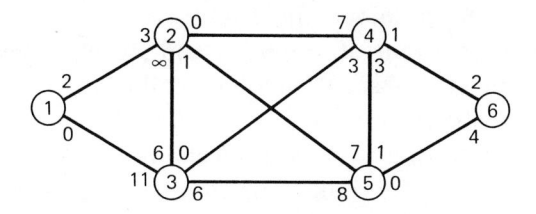

Figure 4-5. Network after 3 flow assignments.

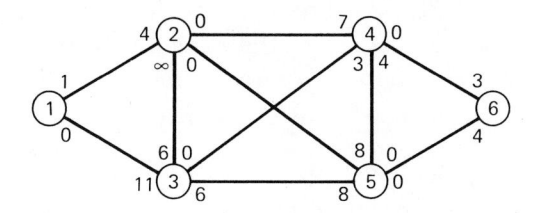

Figure 4-6. Network after 4 flow assignments.

We continue to look for a path since there is still a unit of flow from node 1. The capacities of the links connecting 6 have been used up, however, so that the procedure ends. No additional flow assignments are possible. The summary of the flows is as follows:

| Flow | Path |
|---|---|
| 4 | 1 → 3 → 5 → 6 |
| 1 | 1 → 2 → 4 → 6 |
| 1 | 1 → 3 → 4 → 6 |
| 1 | 1 → 2 → 5 → 6 |

Thus, the maximal flow is 7.

On examining our procedure we found that at least several possible distinct paths with different flows could be found from source to sink. Since our goal is to maximize flow, and since the network is given, we can select any path with positive flow at any iteration.

Completion of an iteration increases the assigned flow.

The flows in the reverse direction are introduced to ensure that the procedure gives the maximal flow. Other procedures involve a labeling process that is in the same vein [see, for example, Hu[10] and Wagner[15]].

In constructing a program for finding maximal flow or for solving another problem by a network method, the programmer must take great care in the data format preparation. This is due to the sensitivity of the method's speed to the file structure. An efficient program will minimize the amount of searching and sorting necessary to extract information on links. With each method in this chapter we shall consider the structure.

For the maximization of flow for each link, we have the capacity in each direction along the link. Suppose this is given in general by $(i, j, C_{ij}, C_{ji})$. An infinite number can be replaced by a very large number. These vectors should now be arranged in order of levels from source to sink. This will reduce time from searching through a nonarranged list of vectors. For the example in Fig. 4-2 we could arrange the vectors to obtain the following list.

$$(1, 2, 3, \quad 2) \quad (3, 4, 1, \quad 2)$$
$$(1, 3, 5, \quad 6) \quad (3, 5, 10, 4)$$
$$(2, 3, 500, 6) \quad (4, 5, 3, \quad 1)$$
$$(2, 4, 1, \quad 6) \quad (4, 6, 3, \quad 0)$$
$$(2, 5, 1, \quad 7) \quad (5, 6, 4, \quad 0)$$

The method now examines the list to see if flow is possible from node 1 to node 6. At the first step it sees that a flow of 3 can go from 1 to 2. The program then would examine vectors beginning with 2 and see that flow was possible from 2 to 3. It would continue with node 3 and find a flow of 1 was possible to node 4. At any step the program must have available the smallest flow along the path up to that point. In this case the flow is 1 (= min (500, 1, 3)) up to node 5. The last step detects that a flow of 1 is possible from 5 to 6. The program recognizes that 6 is the last node and it now adjusts all vectors along the path by decrementing flow along the path by 1 unit and incrementing it by 1 in the opposite direction.

The program flow would appear as shown in Fig. 4-7. The difficult part of the program is the search procedure for a path. To reduce, storage, define $C(I, J)$ as the capacity from node I to node J; let

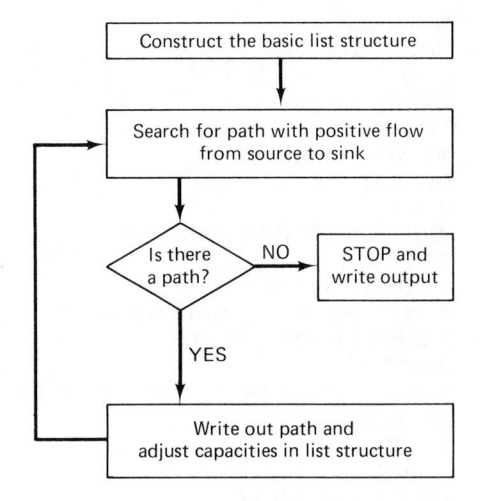

```
┌─────────────────────────────────────┐
│ Construct the basic list structure  │
└─────────────────────────────────────┘
                  │
                  ▼
┌─────────────────────────────────────┐
│ Search for path with positive flow  │◄──┐
│        from source to sink          │   │
└─────────────────────────────────────┘   │
                  │                       │
                  ▼                       │
           ╱ Is there ╲   NO    ┌──────────────────┐
           ╲ a path?  ╱────────▶│ STOP and         │
                                │ write output     │
                                └──────────────────┘
                  │
                 YES
                  ▼
┌─────────────────────────────────────┐
│        Write out path and           │──┘
│  adjust capacities in list structure│
└─────────────────────────────────────┘
```

Figure 4-7. Flowchart for maximizing flow.

XMIN be the minimum capacity at a given step; let N(I) be the number of nodes connected to I but either parallel to I in terms of the source or one step closer to the sink node. Now node I connects to nodes M(I, 1), M(I, 2), ..., M(I, N(I)). Let $P(k)$ be an indicator for the node that is the $k$th node in the path. The nodes where no capacity exists between one node I and the next level are given by BAD(I, −). With this notation the search part of the program could be written as shown in Fig. 4-8. For large problems the subscripting could be eliminated by coding the subscript as a unique one-dimensional number. Another method would be to store the table of capacities in part of a disk or a tape.

Suppose now that a multisource and/or multisink network is given. Figure 4-9 has two sources and three sinks. We can transform this into a single source and single sink problem by inserting dummy nodes at either end of the network shown in dotted lines and then assigning infinite capacity for each added link, in both directions. Then we are still looking for a path with positive flow from one end to the other.

For a large network several questions arise. One of these is the search method to detect paths with positive flow. Here we can employ a graph theory enumeration and generate, in effect, a tree from the source. When a leaf point is the sink, we have found a path of positive capacity.

```
C           INITIALIZATION
            XMIN = 100
            I = 1
            K = 1
            P (1) = 1
            DO 30 I = 1, NN
      30    BAD (I,1) = 0
            M = 1
C           LOOK FOR POSITIVE CAPACITY
      10    DO 11 J = 1, N (I)
            DO 20 MA = 1, M
      20    IF (M(I,J).EQ.BAD (I-1,MA) ) GO TO 11
            IF (C(I,M I,J) ).GT.0) GO TO 12
      11    CONTINUE
C           THERE IS NO CAPACITY LEFT - BACK UP
            BAD (I-1,M) = I
            M + M =1
            I = I +1
            IF (I.EQ.0) GO TO 17
C           COMPARE C(I,J) WITH SMALLEST CAPACITY SO FAR
      12    IF (C(I,M(I,J) ) -XMIN) 13, 14,14
      13    XMIN = C (I,M(I,J) )
      14    I = J
            P(K +1) = J
            K = K +1
C           TEST IF AT SINK NODE
            IF (ENDN.EQ.J) GO TO 15
            GO TO 10
C           HAVE FOUND A PATH - NOW UPDATE
      15    DO 16 I = 1, K-1
            C(P(I I ), P(I +1) ) = C(P(I), P(I +1) ) -XMIN
            C(P(I +1), P(I) ) = C(P(I +1, P(I) ) + XMIN
      16    CONTINUE
C           WOULD NOW WRITE OUTPUT
C           THERE ARE NO PATHS-WRITE OUTPUT
      17    WRITE ( ) —
```

Figure 4-8. Partial program for flow maximization.

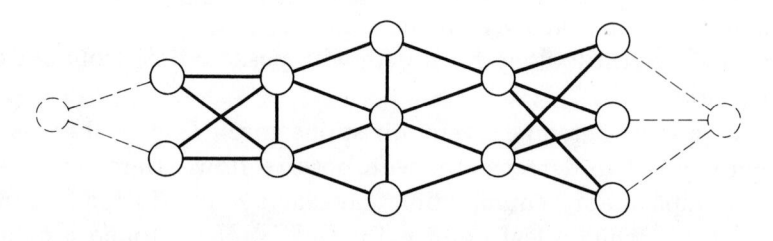

Figure 4-9. Sample multisource and multisink network.

A second question is whether or not it is possible to determine the maximal flow so that when we use the procedure outlined above we can stop looking for paths at the time maximal flow is attained. The basic theorem here is that the maximal flow equals the value of the minimal cut (max flow-min cut). It follows from this result that all cuts are upper bounds (why?). Consider Fig. 4-2 again in Fig. 4-10 with some of the capacities removed. Several cuts are revealed in dotted lines. The cut value is the sum of the capacities of the links that intersect the cut. The cuts in Fig. 4-10 have values as follows:

| Cut | Value |
| --- | --- |
| $C_1$ | $8 = 3 + 5$ |
| $C_2$ | $\infty$ |
| $C_3$ | $13 = 10 + 1 + 1 + 1$ |
| $C_4$ | $7 = 3 + 4$ |

Thus, we know the maximal flow cannot exceed 7. In fact, we could show that further cuts cannot be less than 7; thus, 7 is the value of the minimal cut and the maximal flow.

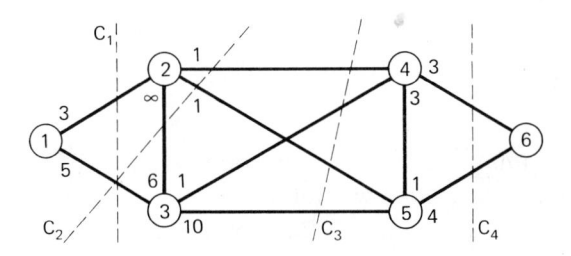

Figure 4-10. Sample cuts.

One method of implementation is to enumerate all cuts and maintain the value of the lowest cut at a given time. Since a cut removes certain links, we could utilize the setup used in the maximal flow program earlier. Link removal could be done by reading the list structure and setting all capacities on deleted links equal to zero. The original list would be kept intact. With the new list the search method would be employed to find a path from source to sink. If a path was found, it would not be a cut and the next link combination would be considered with a cut; its value would be computed and compared with the best found to that time. If the new cut value was lower, it would replace the old best value. The next link combination would be considered.

Link combinations could be generated in the first stage by a straightforward enumeration of combinations. These combinations would then be stored and accessed sequentially before using the search method procedure.

In the previous section it was pointed out that many network problems can be treated as mathematical programming problems. As an example we shall formulate the maximal flow problem in this way.

An assignment or solution is a set of values given to every link in the network. For a given link it is the amount of capacity that is used by the assignment. A constraint is then that the flow assigned to the link $(j, k)$ (say, $F_{jk}$) does not exceed the capacity $C_{jk}$ or

$$0 \leq F_{jk} \leq C_{jk}.$$

Another constraint that is more subtle is that of conservation of flow. For a given node $k$ the flow into $k$ from all nodes must equal the flow out from $k$. This is given by

$$\sum_i F_{ik} = \sum_i F_{ki}$$

where the summations are over all nodes. (Except for the preceding and following nodes, these will all be zero.)

The objective function of flow maximization can be viewed in one of two ways. This can be to maximize the flow from a source. Alternatively, it can be to maximize the flow into a sink. In the case of single source and sink because of flow conservation these objectives are the same and become.

$$\max \sum_i F_{1i} = \max \sum_i F_{iN}$$

where 1 is the source node and $N$ is the sink node.

The multicommodity flow problem has been only partially solved. It is of interest because in some situations different commodities share the same pipeline. This is true of trucks, buses, and automobiles on freeways and various priority level messages in communications systems. Frank and Frisch[6] and Hu[10] explore some of these available methods.

## 4.3 Shortest Path

Recall from Section 4.1 that links can have several labels other than capacity. Two of these include distance and travel time between nodes. Either of these can be employed in the shortest route problem. This problem is to determine the shortest path between two specified nodes in distance or time. There are no labels for capacity. An example of a network is given in Fig. 4-11. Suppose we wish to go from node 1 to node 12 to minimize distance. The information given in Fig. 4-11 can be displayed equivalently in a series of tables as follows:

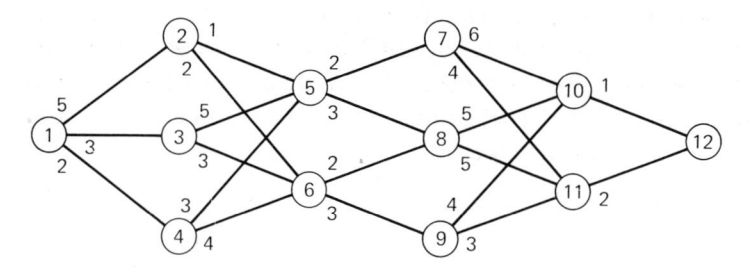

**Figure 4-11.** Distance- or time-related network.

|   | 2 | 3 | 4 |
|---|---|---|---|
| 1 | 5 | 3 | 2 |

|   | 5 | 6 |
|---|---|---|
| 2 | 1 | 2 |
| 3 | 5 | 3 |
| 4 | 3 | 4 |

|   | 7 | 8 | 9 |
|---|---|---|---|
| 5 | 2 | 3 | — |
| 6 | — | 2 | 3 |

|   | 10 | 11 |
|---|----|----|
| 7 | 6  | 4  |
| 8 | 5  | 5  |
| 9 | 4  | 3  |

|    | 12 |
|----|----|
| 10 | 1  |
| 11 | 2  |

In a given table the $(i, j)$th entry is the distance between nodes $i$ and $j$. The rows of a table are the nodes preceding those given in the column headings. The dashed entries in the third table indicate feasible links or the absence of links. The network can be constructed from the five tables.

The solution procedure is to begin at the destination node (12) and work back to the beginning node (1) so that when we reach node 1, the optimal solution will be found.

114 / Network Analysis

A node $n_1$ is said to be *k-removed* from another node $n_2$ if the node $n_2$ can be reached by the first node $n_1$ in a minimum of $k$ steps. We begin by considering the nodes that are 1-removed from the destination (10, 11). At the $k$th iteration we consider the nodes that are $k$-removed from the destination. For each node that is $k$-removed we find the optimal, minimal distance route to the destination node. The procedure continues until the starting node 1 is attained.

Computationally, we need to know how to reach the destination from a given node in the network. If this node is $k$-removed, then by our method we shall know the optimal routing and its value for all nodes that are $(k-1)$-removed from the destination node. To find the optimal routing we add the cost in distance from getting from the $k$-removed node to all nodes [which are linked to this node and are $(k-1)$-removed] to the optimal value from the $(k-1)$-removed node (for reaching the destination node). By finding the minimum of such sums we have found the value of the minimal path and the actual minimal path from this node to the destination node.

This procedure can be applied to our example using the tables. At the first step we have no problem since nodes 10 and 11 are connected directly to 12 (destination node). However, the following table is always constructed.

|    | 12 | Best | Best Route to Destination |
|----|----|----|----|
| 10 | 1  | 1  | 10 → 12 |
| 11 | 2  | 2  | 11 → 12 |

The arrows in the rightmost column indicate the connection. The first column is the list of nodes that are $k$-removed. The second and succeeding columns up to that labeled *Best* are the nodes that are $(k-1)$-removed. The $(i, j)$ entry in this part of the table is the cost of first going from node $i$ to node $j$ and then proceeding along the minimal path to the destination. For a given row the column labeled *best* is the minimum value of the values in this row. The final column is then the best route to the destination.

We proceed now to the nodes that are 2-removed and construct a similar table.

|   | 10 | 11 | Best | Best Path to 1-Removed |
|---|----|----|----|----|
| 7 | $7 = 6 + 1$ | $6 = 4 + 2$ | 6 | 7 → 11 |
| 8 | $6 = 5 + 1$ | $7 = 5 + 2$ | 6 | 8 → 10 |
| 9 | $5 = 4 + 1$ | $5 = 3 + 2$ | 5 | 9 → 10, 9 → 11 |

The (7, 10) entry is computed by adding the distance from 7 to 10 to the optimal distance from node 10 to 12 given in the second to last column of the previous table. In this case there are two "best" routes for getting from node 9 to 12, and we can save either or both of these. To find the entire route from 9 to 12 we could tie the results of the two tables. For node 7 this would be combining 7 → 11 and 11 → 12 to obtain 7 → 11 → 12.

Next we consider the 3-removed nodes. The table is given below with lines to indicate impossible paths due to the absence of links.

|   | 7 | 8 | 9 | Best | Best Route to 2-Removed |
|---|---|---|---|------|-------------------------|
| 5 | 8 = 2 + 6 | 9 = 3 + 6 | — | 8 | 5 → 7 |
| 6 | — | 8 = 2 + 6 | 8 = 3 + 5 | 8 | 6 → 8, 6 → 9 |

The final two steps and tables are given below.

|   | 5 | 6 | Best | Best Route to 3-Removed |
|---|---|---|------|-------------------------|
| 2 | 9 = 1 + 8 | 10 = 2 + 8 | 9 | 2 → 5 |
| 3 | 13 = 5 + 8 | 11 = 3 + 8 | 11 | 3 → 5 |
| 4 | 11 = 3 + 8 | 12 = 4 + 8 | 11 | 4 → 5 |

|   | 2 | 3 | 4 | Best | Best Route to 4-Removed |
|---|---|---|---|------|-------------------------|
| 1 | 14 = 5 + 9 | 14 = 3 + 11 | 11 = 2 + 11 | 13 | 1 → 4 |

We now have the optimal solution, namely 13. The path that yields this value is

$$1 \to 4 \to 5 \to 7 \to 11 \to 12$$

The procedure outlined above is called *dynamic programming*. Dynamic programming can solve a class of problems that have certain properties relating to the problem's discreteness and cost structure. In general, the problem must be decomposable into a finite number of discrete stages or levels as in a tree structure with a finite number of nodes at each stage. Second, we must be able to construct a cost formula that is recursive in the sense that the cost for traversing from the $k$th removed level (or $k$th stage) to the destination can be split into the cost from the $k$- to $(k - 1)$st-removed level and the cost from the $(k - 1)$st level to the destination node. Denote the cost of the optimal solution from state $s$ with $j$ levels to go to the beginning node by $C_j(s)$. We then want $C_0(1)$, which is the optimal cost from node 1 to the end with no levels to go. Let the cost of going from $s$ to node $n_k$ and then to the terminal node with $j$ levels to go be $C_j(s, n_k)$. The transition cost from node $s$ to $n_k$ is given by $TC(s, n_k)$. Using our procedure and sample problem we see that the value $C_j(s)$ can be obtained from the following expression.

$$C_j(s) = \min_k \left[ TC(s, n_k) + C_{j-1}(s, n_k) \right] \qquad (4.1)$$

Formula (4.1) is the sought after recursive expression. The minimum is over the nodes which are linked to nodes and which are $(N - j - 1)$-removed. Here $N$ is the total number of stages or levels. Another assumption of the method is that, given some location in the network, the optimal route can be determined independently of previous policy.

Implementing a dynamic programming method requires attention to the table structure as well as to storage available. Since dynamic programming functions incrementally, a table would be read in and the computations done for this stage. After finding the best partial paths at this stage, the next table would be read in and computations begun. At a given stage the computations required are to compute the sum of the incremental cost and the best cost to complete. After this the best cost would be computed for each row. The program to find a minimum value could be used as in Chapter 2. The best path from a given node to the end could be stored then peripherally.

Some remarks can be made on the program structure. For small problems it may be possible to keep all tables in storage simultaneously. Secondly, the original data input could be in the form of a distance list where an entry is the distance between two nodes that are connected by a link. Tables would be constructed using this list and another list of the best distance to completion from nodes at an earlier stage. The table would be constructed by finding the sum of two numbers in the tables.

There are some difficulties in using dynamic programming. First, for a large problem the amount of storage needed for the method (paths, connections, etc.) may be large. Sometimes this can be overcome by storing data in secondary storage. This would apply, for example, to the optimal route from a given point. After the beginning node has been reached, the solution could be obtained by a table search. A second problem is that of efficiently formulating the situation in a dynamic programming context. For continuous time problems we can subdivide the time interval into subintervals. Other parts of a problem, such as division of a level into a finite number of nodes, may not be so easy. Sources in dynamic programming, some of which include applications, appear in Section 4.5.

Other methods exist for finding the shortest route between two nodes. Some of these are explored in Frank and Frisch[6] and Hu.[10] One such method is to enumerate paths and to find the shortest distance to the node. This method is particularly desirable when each node is sending commodities to each of the other nodes; an example would be a communications network where messages are likely to be sent between any two nodes.

Another problem in the same class as minimal distance is that wherein the nodes and their locations are specified. The goal is to find the branches with the minimal total distance and allow a path between any two nodes. This is called a *minimal spanning tree* since a tree structure is the result. As an example, consider Fig. 4-12.

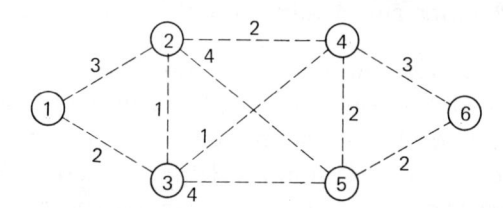

Figure 4-12. Nodes without link structure.

The dotted lines in Fig. 4-12 indicate possible links and the labels are the distances of the links.

The procedure begins at any given node, say, 1. The next step is to proceed to the node nearest this node. At any given step we link the node closest to any node in the partly constructed tree. Ties are connected simultaneously.

In the situation of Fig. 4-11, if we start with node 1, we first connect nodes 1 and 3. We then find the nodes closest to 1 and 3. We see that there are two nodes, namely, 2 and 4. The result is shown in Fig. 4-13. The only remaining nodes to be tied to the tree are nodes 5 and 6. We see node 5 is closest to the partial tree by connecting it to node 4. Node 5 is then closest to node 6. The final

118 / Network Analysis

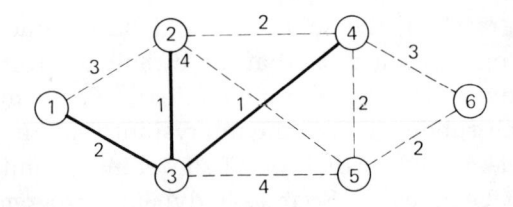

Figure 4-13. First iteration of minimal spanning tree method.

tree can then be drawn in a number of ways, several of which are shown in Fig. 4-14. We note that we could have begun the tree at any point. Minimal spanning tree problems can be found in such areas as pipeline construction. For large problems, a table of possible links could be maintained on disk and scanned.

After a node is added to the tree, possible links with other nodes in the tree can be eliminated from the table so as to reduce storage. When the problem is sufficiently reduced, all tables can be brought into core.

## 4.4 Program Planning and Applications

In the late 1950s', network methods began to be applied to problems in scheduling projects and tasks in a program. An early example was that of Polaris submarine construction. The Program Evaluation and Review Technique (PERT) methodology was developed for this project. This was expanded and a number of programs and methods have been built to solve particular problems in scheduling. One of these is to find the path(s) such that if any step in the path(s) is delayed, the final completion date of the project is delayed. This is called the critical path(s) and the techniques used to find the critical paths are referred to as Critical Path Methods (CPM).

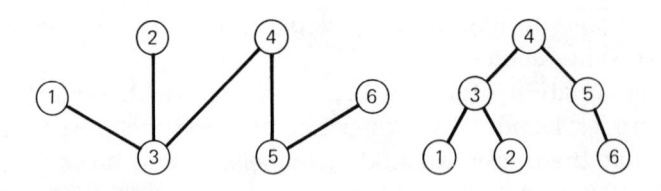

Figure 4-14. Equivalent representations of minimal spanning tree.

PERT and CPM are employed in problems where resource allocation and usage are of less concern than time and completing a project as soon as possible. Three areas of resource oriented problems are trade offs between time and cost, resource load leveling, and resource allocation. The tradeoffs between time and cost are to find the most cost-effective way to add additional resources to hasten the completion of a project. Leveling is based on the problem of completing a project in a given time but not to overtax any resource during a given time interval. It can also be used to obtain more uniform usage of resources such as personnel. With a fixed cost structure the purpose of resource allocation is to find the optimal mixture of resources to procure.

PERT methods have been employed with some success on a variety of governmental and private projects. The results have been mixed. One factor that has contributed to their success has been a careful construction of a project network and its parameters. Here a node can be thought of as an event in a project. Events can be the completion of a final or interim report, the finishing of a subassembly of a rocket, or the completion preprocessing and debugging of a computer program. A link could then be considered to be an activity such as performing analysis, drilling, packaging, or checking.

Consider the sample project in Fig. 4-15. In this example, events 2 and 3 must be completed prior to a start on the activities that take the project from event 4 to events 5, 6, or 7. Node 1 (8) is project start (finish). Networks can be scaled over time so that one horizontal inch could represent, say, one month. We remark in passing that we could also consider nodes as activities and links as events.

To formulate an industrial problem in this context requires that the activities can be defined and estimated correctly in sufficient detail so that the program can be evaluated. There can be only one source and one sink. There can be no multiple links between nodes, for this would convey the impression that some activities are not

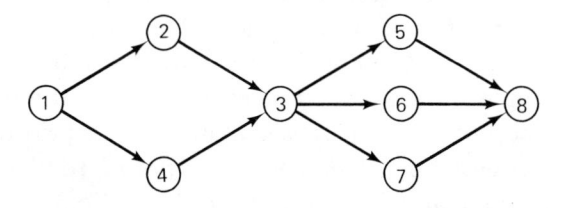

Figure 4-15. Sample project diagram.

needed (why?). Although this occurs in some real programs, we do not permit it in PERT-analysis. There can be no lags since the program progresses over time and as a step is completed the next logical activities are begun.

Problems that can arise in applying PERT methods include the occurrence of emergencies or variation in specifications requiring fewer or more steps to be taken. These deviations in large projects may be complex and involve subcontractors' operations.

The time to perform a task is not fixed but is random and can vary depending on many factors. Some terms in project planning include the earliest time of an event, which is the first time the event can occur if the preceding activities began as soon as possible. The latest time for an event is the last time at which an event can happen without delaying the completion of the program. If the latest and earliest times are the same for an event, then there is no room for delay. We say the slack is zero. More generally, the *slack* of an event is defined as the difference between the latest and earliest time for the event. If we connect all events that have no slack, the critical path is obtained. Statistics are employed to estimate the variation in slack for given sets of events.

The critical path is really the longest path in the network from source to sink. We can modify some of the shortest path methods to find the longest path. The distance here is the expected elapse time for an activity. Thus, instead of finding the minimum path from a node to a destination, we find the maximal path to the destination. The critical path helps to determine the potential bottlenecks.

A PERT-type program allows the user to input the activities, events, and data on resource availability and deadlines. The program then may find the critical and subcritical path and display the analysis results in a GANTT chart, shown in Fig. 4-16. Tasks are shown over time as bands. In this case task 1 begins and is nearly completed when tasks 2 and 4 begin. After these are completed, task 3 can start. In a network task 1 could be divided into the sections of the part preceding the inception of tasks 2 and 4 and that carried out concurrently. The program may allow activities to be rescheduled to level off resource utilization. For each resource the program may reveal when and how much it is used along with its priority.

Resource oriented problems have often been formulated as integer programming problems. Variables are then functions of the start and completion times of various tasks. The objective function can be to

Tasks

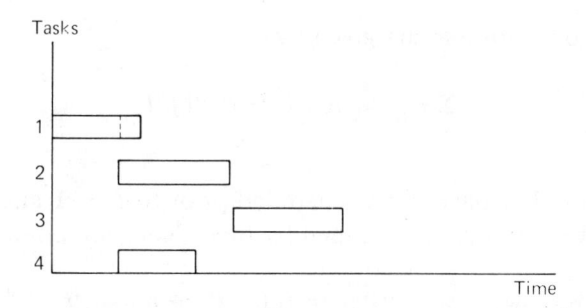

Figure 4-16. Sample GANTT chart.

minimize project duration, cost, or some utility function. Constraints are of several types. One type is imposed by the maximum level of a resource assignable during a given time interval and overall across the project. A second type is based upon the dependence of occurrence between certain tasks.

As an example, suppose there are 14 time intervals for a project to be started and completed. There are five tasks with durations and precedence relationships given here.

| Task | Duration | Precedence (task must be completed before other task begun) |
|---|---|---|
| 1 | 1 | 2, 4 |
| 2 | 2 | 3 |
| 3 | 3 | 5 |
| 4 | 4 | 5 |
| 5 | 2 | |

Suppose now that task $i$ consumes $r_{ijt}$ of resource $j$ during time interval $t$ and that during this interval $R_{jt}$ of the $j$th resource is available.

Define $x_{it}$ as 1 if task $i$ is begun in time interval $t$ and as 0 otherwise. Then to obtain the number of variables we need to find the number of possible start times. For example, task 1 can be started in intervals 1, 2, ..., 7. Task 5 can be started in intervals 7, 8, ..., 13.

If the objective is to minimize project duration, then this would be the equivalent to minimizing the start time of the fifth task (why?). Thus, the objective is

$$\min_t \quad x_{5t}$$

Constraints on resources are given by

$$\sum_i r_{ijt} \leq R_{jt} \quad \text{for all } j, t$$

and for all $i$ that have been scheduled prior to $t + 1$ and are being done in $t$. Constraints determined by precedence are given by

$$x_{R,t} = 1 \text{ implies } x_{2,t'} = x_{4,t'} = 0 \text{ for } t' = t' \leq t + 1$$
$$x_{2,t} = 1 \text{ implies } x_{3,t'} = 0 \text{ for } t' \leq t + 2$$
$$x_{3,t} = 1, x_{4,t} = 1 \text{ implies } x_{5,t''} = 0 \text{ for } t'' \leq \max(t + 3, t' + 4)$$

Similar formulations can be obtained for other resource oriented problems. For small problems with only a few tasks and time intervals, the integer programming approach is reasonable computationally. As the number of tasks and intervals increases, however, the number of variables increases rapidly. This is due to the possible number of start times being increased. Approaches that have been successful on larger problems have in general taken advantage of the structure of the specific problem. A review of some of the approaches used is given in Herroelen.[18] The remainder of this section will consider applications of network methods.

As an application of shortest path we can consider a large-scale simulation and management information system aimed at analyzing computer networks. Recall that the nodes are computer centers and the links are communication lines. One part of the system is to simulate message routine in the network by network analysis. The goal of the routing is to find the shortest path between two computer centers. The outline of this system is given in Fig. 4-17.

In the schematic, the network configuration, traffic loads between two centers, and processing characteristics are specified. The shortest path routing algorithm then determines the best path between every pair of nodes. As the computer network program begins to execute, messages are routed over time by means of the results of the shortest path method. In Chapter 6 we shall consider simulation and this model in more detail. For now we note that this system is an example of a simulation model that is dependent on network analysis. As the model progresses through time, messages are processed and results must be routed to the origination point. The routing influences the performance measures. For example, response time is the time necessary to transmit a message, process the data, and have the results returned. Nonoptimal routing procedures could lead to messages being queued up for a time at intermediate nodes because lines are saturated. Throughput of the nodes is the processing rate in terms of messages processed per day. If intermediate nodes become bottlenecks and saturated, throughput of some computers may be affected because of the lack of processing demands.

This system is one example of how networks methods may be incorporated into a larger simulation or analysis tool to evaluate a complex system. Other examples occur in the simulation of pipeline and refinery operations that are spread over a wide area.

## 4.5 Programs

The programs available are oriented toward PERT-type or routing problems. Some of these are given in Table 4-2.

Table 4-2

|  | *Program* | *User Group* | *Language* |
|---|---|---|---|
| PERT | Computer Assisted PERT Simulation | RCA-CUA | Machine |
|  | ICES/300 Project-I | SHARE | ICETRAN, CDL |
|  | MPCS-Modified Project Computer System | Common | FORTRAN (1130) |
|  | Busk Critical Path Method | XDS | FORTRAN II |
|  | Critical Path Schedule | DECUS | FORTRAN IV |
|  | Critical Path Summary | EIN | FORTRAN IV |
| Minimum Path | MIT-Increment Traffic | SHARE | FORTRAN II |

In addition, some of the hardware manufacturers and software firms offer as products or services programs using network methods. An example is IBM's VSP-X, which produces at least near-optimal solutions to vehicle routing problems. Some programs are also available from time-sharing vendors.

For a long-term application tied in intimately with a management information system that has an existing structure, it may be

124 / Network Analysis

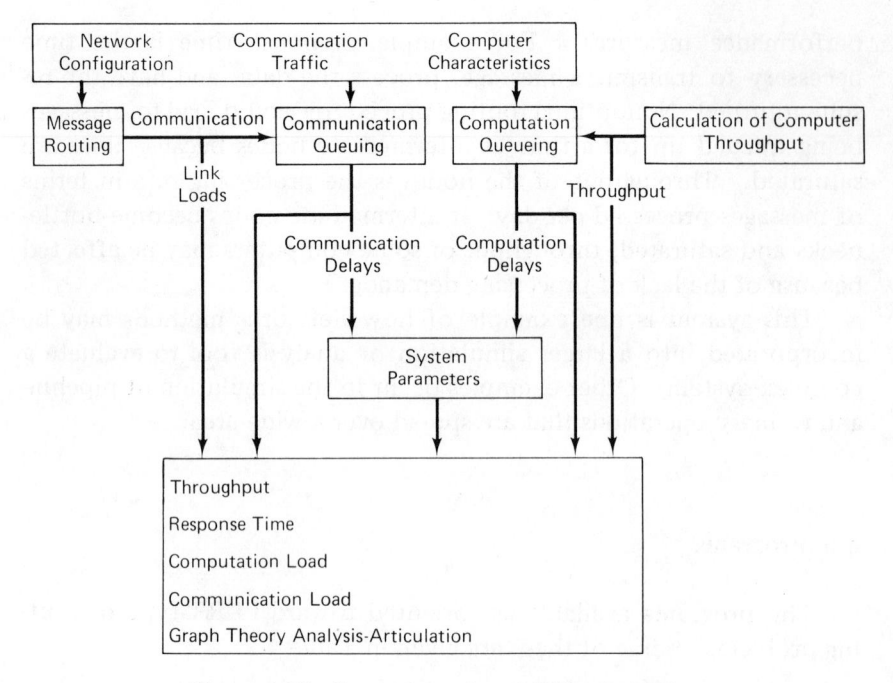

Figure 4-17. Computer network MIS schematic.

necessary to modify the tables and lists of one of the standard methods for access by the network method.

The journals and proceedings that publish papers regularly on network analysis and its applications include the following list. *Management Science* and *Operations Research* tend to publish theoretical results as do the *Communications of the ACM* and the *IEEE Transactions*.

*AFIPS Conference Proceedings*
*Bell System Technical Journal*
*Bulletin of Mathematical Biophysics*
*Communications of the ACM*
*IEEE Transactions on Circuit Theory*
*IEEE Transactions on Communications Technology*
*Management Science*
*Naval Research Logistics Quarterly*
*Networks*

*Operations Research*

*Transportation Research*

*Transportation Science*

The books on network analysis range over theory and application. Ford and Fulkerson[5] is the original text in the area. Frank and Frisch[6] explore networks with application in communication. Benes,[3] Kim and Chien[11] and Kleinrock[12] examine communication networks. Dennis[4] considers electrical networks. Hu[10] presents results and the theory of integer programming and network analysis. A series of excellent review papers appeared in *Management Science* [Elmaghraby.[16],[17]] The original text in dynamic programming was Bellman.[1] Later texts include Bellman and Dreyfus,[2] Hadley,[7] Howard,[9] and Nemhauser.[14] An interesting book on PERT and CPM with applications is Moder and Phillips.[13]

## REFERENCES

*Textbooks*

1. BELLMAN, R., *Dynamic Programming*. New York: John Wiley & Sons, Inc., 1967.
2. BELLMAN, R. AND S. R. DREYFUS, *Applications of Dynamic Programming*. Princeton, N. J.: Princeton University Press, 1962.
3. BENES, V. E., *Mathematical Theory of Connected Networks and Telephone Traffic*. New York: Academic Press, 1965.
4. DENNIS, J. B., *Mathematical Programming and Electrical Networks*. New York: John Wiley & Sons, Inc., 1959.
5. FORD, JR., L. R. AND D. R. FULKERSON, *Flows in Networks*. Princeton, N. J.: Princeton University Press, 1962.
6. FRANK, H. AND I. T. FRISCH, *Communication, Transmission, and Transportation Networks*. Reading, Mass.: Addison-Wesley Pub. Co., Inc., 1971.
7. HADLEY, G., *Nonlinear and Dynamic Programming*. Reading, Mass.: Addison-Wesley Publishing Company, Inc., 1964.
8. HILLIER, F. S. AND C. J. LIEBERMANN, *Introduction to Operations Research*. San Francisco, Calif.: Holden-Day Publishing Company, 1967.
9. HOWARD, R., *Dynamic Programming and Markov Processes*. Cambridge, Mass.: MIT Press, 1959.
10. HU, T. C., *Integer Programming and Network Flows*. Reading, Mass.: Addison-Wesley Pub. Co., 1969.

11. KIM, W. H. AND R. T. CHIEN, *Topological Analysis and Synthesis of Communication Networks*. New York: Columbia University Press, 1962.
12. KLEINROCK, L., *Communication Networks—Stochastic Message Flow and Delay*. New York: McGraw Hill Book Co., 1964.
13. MODER, J. J. AND C. R. PHILLIPS, *Project Management with CPM and PERT*. New York: Reinhold Publishing Co., 1964.
14. NEMHAUSER, G., *Dynamic Programming*. New York: John Wiley & Sons, Inc., 1967.
15. WAGNER, H., *Principles of Operations Research*. Englewood Cliffs, N. J.: Prentice-Hall, Inc., 1969.

*Articles*

16. ELMAGHRABY, S., "Theory of Networks and Management Science—I," *Management Science*, 17 (Sept., 1970) 1-34.
17. ———, "Theory of Networks and Management Science—II," *Management Science*, 17 (Oct., 1970) B54-B71.
18. HERROELEN, W. S., "Resource-Constrained Project Scheling—The State of the Art," *Operational Res. Quarterly*, 23 (Sept., 1972) 261-275.

## PROBLEMS

For Problems 1 to 3, construct a network structure defining nodes, links, capacities and/or distances and what could be optimized.

1. A drunk is on the middle of a pier. For every forward step he takes two steps back. Each step is to the next board in the pier. Eventually he will fall into the bay, leave the pier, or drop asleep on the pier.
2. An airplane terminal.
3. An office building.

For Problems 4 to 7, find the articulation level and the minimal cut.

4.

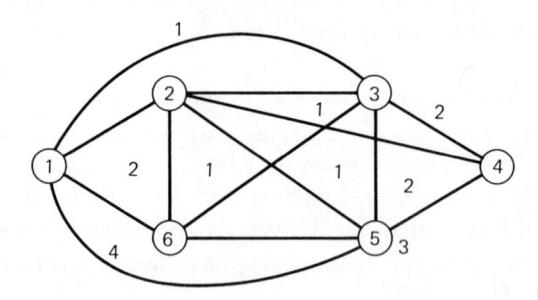

Figure P4-4

5.

Figure P4-5

6.

Figure P4-6

7.

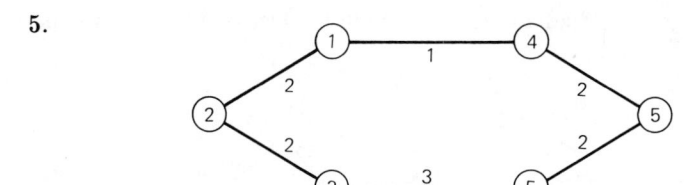

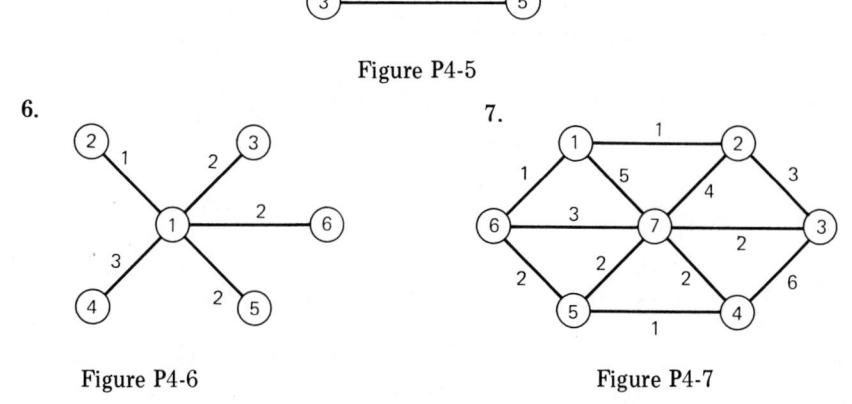

Figure P4-7

8. A bus company wishes to install programs that can access a large file and find the best paths from a customer's house to a bus stop. The method must be dependent on the time of day, travel time, and bus schedule. Develop a network analysis approach and consider the appropriate file structure.

9. A commercial agency is responsible for expediting the flow of documents and requisitions in an overseas commercial management structure. The problem involves lost and missent documents. No optimization is involved. Design a network model of the management structure and information flow of the documents. Describe how computer processing can be employed to monitor and update the flow of documents.

10. Write a program to find the maximal flow and paths of flow for Fig. P4-10.

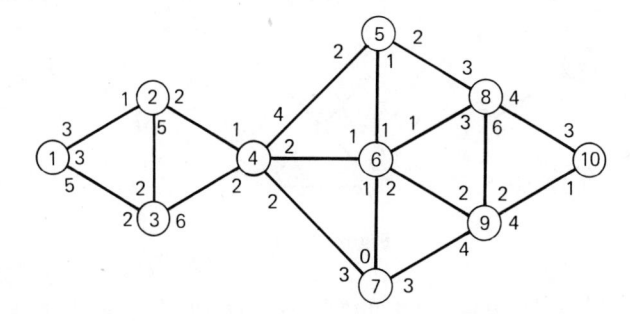

Figure P4-10

## 128 / Network Analysis

11. Write a program to find the shortest route for Fig. P4-11. Find the path from 1 and 2 to 8.

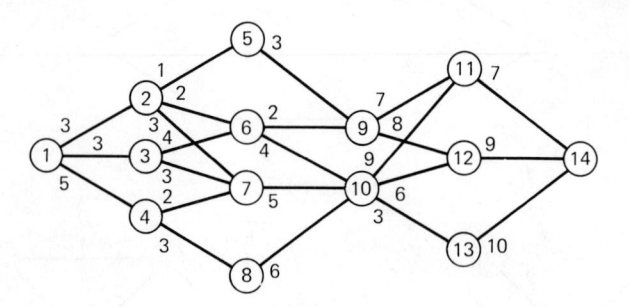

**Figure P4-11**

12. Write a program to find the shortest route for Fig. P4-12.

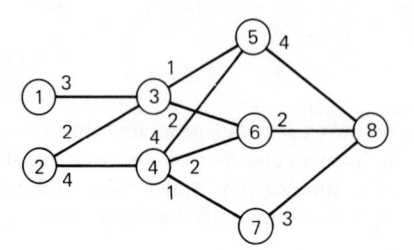

**Figure P4-12**

13. For the following network, find the shortest path from node 1 to node 20 going by way of node 12.

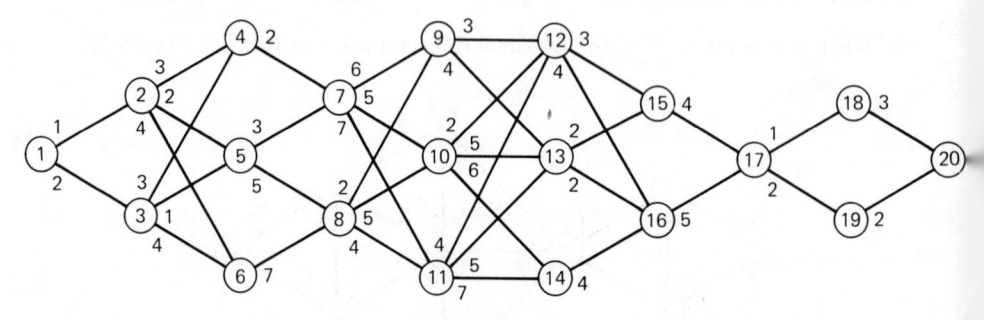

**Figure P4-13**

In Problems 14 to 16, find the minimal spanning tree for the given set of nodes and distances.

14.

| Node | Node | Distance | Node | Node | Distance |
|---|---|---|---|---|---|
| 1 | 2 | 5 | 4 | 5 | 3 |
| 1 | 3 | 6 | 6 | 7 | 7 |
| 2 | 3 | 3 | 6 | 8 | 4 |
| 2 | 4 | 2 | 7 | 8 | 5 |
| 3 | 4 | 4 | 3 | 5 | 3 |
| 1 | 4 | 6 | | | |
| 4 | 6 | 1 | | | |
| 5 | 6 | 3 | | | |
| 4 | 7 | 2 | | | |
| 5 | 7 | 1 | | | |

15.

| Node | Node | Distance | Node | Node | Distance |
|---|---|---|---|---|---|
| 1 | 2 | 4 | 2 | 4 | 1 |
| 1 | 3 | 4 | 2 | 6 | 3 |
| 1 | 4 | 2 | 2 | 7 | 3 |
| 1 | 9 | 3 | 2 | 8 | 4 |
| 2 | 3 | 2 | 2 | 9 | 2 |

Other possible links are inadmissible.

16. Network design is sometimes performed for multiple cities. Construct a program that will take as input and latitude and longitude of cities in the United States and will construct a minimal spanning tree. Verify the program by manual checking. Use the following cities.

| | | |
|---|---|---|
| New York | Denver | Houston |
| Chicago | St. Louis | Philadelphia |
| Los Angeles | Miami | |
| Seattle | Atlanta | |
| Boston | New Orleans | |

In Problems 17 to 19, construct a network for the projects or programs given.

17. Construction of a FORTRAN sorting program.
18. Assembly and printing of a textbook.
19. Construction of a house.
20. In Problem 8, compute the critical path.

## 130 / Network Analysis

21. Find the critical path in Fig. P4-21.

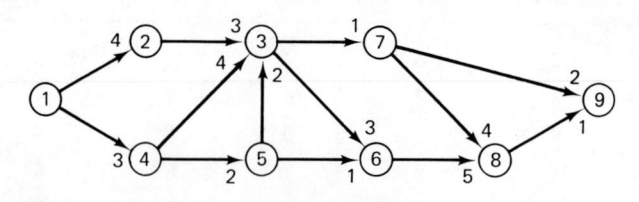

**Figure P4-21**

# 5

# STATISTICS

## 5.1 Overview of Probability and Statistics

### 5.1.1 *Probability*

This section reviews the basic definitions of probability and statistics. Later sections examine particular application areas in the context of statistical methods. Included are regression analysis, goodness-of-fit, analysis of variance, and nonparametric statistics.

Suppose a coin is tossed or a die is thrown. This is viewed as an experiment. An experiment also occurs when stress is applied to a material, a drug is tested among animal subjects, or traffic volume is measured along a given section of roadway. Each experiment described above has an associated set of events. For a simple experiment, such as a coin toss, the collection of all events can be considered as set unions of elementary events. For a coin, elementary events are *head* and *tail*. For a die, the elementary events are 1, 2, 3, 4, 5, and 6. Elementary events have no elements in common and so are disjoint from each other. Furthermore, when all elementary events are joined by union, the set is obtained from which all events can be found as subsets. This inclusive set is called the *set of events* or *sample space*. Consider a test of stress in which the time to failure of a material is to be estimated. Suppose the number of times the material is stressed is between 30 and 60 times. Then the set of events is the interval (30, 60). A simple event is any integer point in this interval. For this set of outcomes in an experiment a *probability* or measure of likelihood of occurrence of an event can be obtained. If $\Omega$ denotes the set of events, then probability is a function from $\Omega$ to the interval [0,1], denoted by $P; \Omega \to [0,1]$, with the following properties:

$$P(\Omega) = 1,$$

$$P(\phi) = 0, \quad P(A) \leq P(B) \quad \text{if } A \subset B,$$

$$P(\bigcup_{i=1}^{n} A_i) = \sum_{i=1}^{n} P(A_i) \quad \text{for } \{A_i\} \text{ events}$$

with $A_i \cap A_j = \phi$ for $i \neq j$

From these properties it follows $P(A) + P(A') = 1$ for any event $A$ (why?). The first equality states that the probability that something happens is unity. The second states that the probability of an event is at least as great as that of a subset of the same event. The third gives the additive relationship between disjoint events. If a coin is fair, then obtaining a head or tail is equally likely so that $P(\text{head}) = P(\text{tail}) = \frac{1}{2}$. Similarly, for a fair die, $P(2, 4, \text{ or } 6) = \frac{1}{2}$.

Associated with the set of events may be a payoff function. Suppose in the coin experiment 1 is lost with a head and won with a tail. This can be represented by a function $X:\Omega \to (-\infty, +\infty)$ with $X(\text{head}) = -1$ and $X(\text{tail}) = 1$. Any function $X$ from $\Omega$ to $E^1 = (-\infty, +\infty)$ such that $\Omega$ has a probability $P$ is called a random variable (r.v.). The probability and random variable functions can be shown as in Fig. 5-1. The functions $P$ and $X$ can be linked by considering the composition $P(X^{-1}):(-\infty, +\infty) \to (0, 1)$. Define a new function $F$ by

$$F(x) = P(X^{-1}(-\infty, x)) = P(\{w: w \in \Omega \text{ and } X(w) \leq x\})$$

Overview of Probability and Statistics / 133

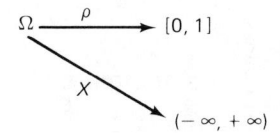

$$\Omega \xrightarrow{p} [0, 1]$$
$$X \searrow$$
$$(-\infty, +\infty)$$

Figure 5-1. Probability and random variable functions.

The function $F$ is known as the *distribution function* for $X$ with respect to $P$. The function provides the link between $P$ and $X$ and has the following properties:

$$\lim_{x \to \infty} F(x) = F(\infty) = 1$$

$$F(x) \leqslant F(y) \quad \text{whenever } x \leqslant y$$

$$\lim_{x \to -\infty} F(x) = F(-\infty) = 0$$

These follow from the definition of $F$ and $P$.

If $F$ is differentiable with derivative $f$, then $f$ is referred to as the *density function* of $X$ with respect to $P$. The region where $F$ takes values more than 0 and less than 1 is the *range*. Because $F$ is nondecreasing, $f$ takes on the value 0 outside the range. If $F$ takes discrete steps at a finite set of points $\{a_i : 1 \leqslant i \leqslant m\}$ and is constant between each step, then the function $p$ can be defined by $p(a_i) = P(X = a_i)$. The function $p$ is the *mass function* of $X$ with respect to $P$.

Some common distributions that are encountered are given in Table 5-1. Densities along with ranges are given in the second column. The quantities that affect the shape, scale, and locations of the densities are called *parameters* and listed in the third column of the table. The sixth column gives cases where the distribution is employed. In some instances the case provided the motivation for deriving the distribution.

By integrating certain functions with respect to $F$, properties of $X$ can be obtained. For a r.v. $X$ with distribution function $F$, the *mean* or *expectation* of $X$ is defined as

$$E(X) = \int_{-\infty}^{+\infty} x \, dF(x)$$

**Table 5-1.** DENSITY AND MASS FUNCTIONS OF COMMON DISTRIBUTION

| Distribution | Density Function | Parameter | Mean | Variable | Cases where Distributions Use |
|---|---|---|---|---|---|
| Bernoulli $B(1:p)$ | $P[X=1] = p; P[X=0] = 1-p$ | $p;\ 0 \leq p \leq 1$ | $p$ | $p(1-p)$ | Any two-outcome experiment |
| Binomial $B(n:p)$ | $P[X=k] = \binom{n}{k} p^k (1-p)^{n-k}$ $k = 0, 1, 2, \ldots, n$ | $p;\ 0 \leq p \leq 1$ | $np$ | $np(1-p)$ | No. of successes in series of Bernoulli trials |
| Geometric $G(p)$ | $P[X=k] = p(1-p)^{k-1} \quad k = 0, 1, 2, \ldots$ | $p;\ 0 \leq p \leq 1$ | $\dfrac{1}{p}$ | $\dfrac{1-p}{p^2}$ | No. of trials until first failure |
| Poisson $P(\lambda)$ | $P[X=k] = e^{-\lambda} \dfrac{\lambda^k}{k!} \quad k = 0, 1, 2, \ldots$ | $\lambda;\ \lambda > 0$ | $\lambda$ | $\lambda$ | Random failure of machine output |
| Uniform $u(a, b)$ | $\dfrac{1}{b-a} \quad a \leq x \leq b$ | $a, b;\ a < b$ | $\dfrac{a+b}{2}$ | $\dfrac{(b-a)^2}{12}$ | Waiting times, simulation |
| Normal $N(\mu, \sigma^2)$ | $(1/\sqrt{2\pi}\,\sigma) e^{-(x-\mu)^2/2\sigma^2} \quad -\infty \leq x \leq \infty$ | $\mu, \sigma$ | $\mu$ | $\sigma^2$ | Approximation to other distributions |
| Exponential $\epsilon(\lambda)$ | $\lambda e^{-\lambda x} \quad x \geq 0$ | $\lambda > 0$ | $\dfrac{1}{\lambda}$ | $\dfrac{1}{\lambda^2}$ | Life length of light bulbs |
| Gamma $G(\lambda, \alpha)$ | $\dfrac{\lambda^\alpha x^{\alpha-1} e^{-\lambda x}}{\Gamma(\alpha)},\ x > 0$ | $\lambda, \alpha;\ \lambda, \alpha > 0$ | $\dfrac{\alpha}{\lambda}$ | $\dfrac{\alpha}{\lambda^2}$ | Lengths of waiting time, time intervals between accidents |
| Beta $B(\alpha, \beta)$ | $\dfrac{x^{\alpha-1}(1-x)^{\beta-1}}{B(\alpha, \beta)} \quad 0 \leq x \leq 1$ | $\alpha, \beta;\ \alpha, \beta > 0$ | | | Life length of some components over finite time intervals |

If a density function $f$ exists for $F$,

$$E(X) = \int_{-\infty}^{\infty} xf(x)\,dx$$

If $X$ has mass function $p$ on the points $\{a_i : 1 \leq i \leq m\}$, then

$$E(X) = \sum_{i=1}^{m} a_i p(a_i)$$

As an example, suppose $X$ has an exponential distribution with parameter $\lambda$. Then

$$E(X) = \int_0^{\infty} xf(x)\,dx = \int_0^{\infty} \lambda x e^{-\lambda x}\,dx$$

Integrating by parts yields a value of $1/\lambda$.

For the binomial distribution we compute

$$E(X) = \sum_{k=0}^{n} k \binom{n}{k} p^k (1-p)^{n-k}$$

which gives

$$E(X) = \sum_{k=1}^{n} \frac{n!}{(k-1)!(n-1)!} p^k (1-p)^{n-k}$$

We can set $j = k - 1$ so that we have

$$E(X) = \sum_{k=1}^{n} \frac{n!}{j!(n-1-j)!} p^{j+1} (1-p)^{n-1-j}$$

Factoring out $np$ to obtain a binomial summation we obtain

$$E(X) = np \sum_{j=0}^{n-1} \frac{(n-1)!}{j!(n-1-j)!} p^j (1-p)^{n-1-j} = np \cdot 1 = np$$

This can be generalized to obtain the $r$th moment and variance of $X$. [$E(X^r)$ and VAR $(X)$ or $\sigma^2(X)$, respectively.] The discrete counterpart appears in parentheses.

$$E(X^r) = \int_{-\infty}^{+\infty} x^r\,dF(x) \quad (\sum_i a_i^r p(a_i))$$

$$\text{VAR}(X) = E(X - E(X))^2 = \int_{-\infty}^{+\infty} (x - E(X))^2\,dF(x)$$

$$(\sum_i (a_i - E(X))^2 p(a_i))$$

The variance of a distribution can be computed using the identity

$$E(X - E(X))^2 = E(X^2) - (E(X))^2$$

For the exponential distribution we first compute the second moment of $X$ using integration by parts to obtain

$$E(X^2) = \int_{-\infty}^{\infty} x^2 \lambda e^{-\lambda x} \, dx = \frac{2}{\lambda^2}$$

Subtracting $(E(X))^2$ from this, we obtain $1/\lambda^2$. The variance gives a measure of the spread of concentration of mass under a density function. For a general function $g$ of $X$ we have

$$E(g(X)) = \int_{-\infty}^{\infty} g(x) \, dF(x)$$

For a given $\Omega$ and $P$, a number of r.v.'s can be constructed that are built around the payoff, risk, or some other function of $X$. For example, define $X_1$ and $X_2$ for a die toss by

$$X_1(i) = 1 \text{ for } i = 1, 2, 3$$
$$X_1(i) = 5 \text{ for } i = 4, 6$$
$$X_1(5) = 10$$

and

$$X_2(i) = 0 \quad \text{for } i = 1, 4, 6$$
$$X_2(i) = 15 \quad \text{for } i = 2, 3$$
$$X_2(5) = 28$$

For a fair die the expected payoff for $X_1$ and $X_2$ is given by

$$E(X_1) = (1)(\tfrac{1}{6}) + (1)(\tfrac{1}{6}) + (1)(\tfrac{1}{6}) + (5)(\tfrac{1}{6}) + (10)(\tfrac{1}{6}) + (5)(\tfrac{1}{6})$$
$$= \frac{23}{6}$$

and

$$E(X_2) = (0 + 0 + 0 + 15 + 15 + 28)16 = \frac{29}{3}$$

For events and r.v.'s, several definitions can be derived that relate multiple events or r.v.'s. Two events, $A$ and $B$, are said to be *independent* if

$$P(A \cap B) = P(A)P(B)$$

If a die and a coin are tossed separately, then any two simple events, one involving only the die and the other involving only the coin, are independent.

This notion of independence can be generalized to r.v.'s. Suppose $X_1$ and $X_2$ are r.v.'s on $\Omega$ with probability $P$. Then $X_1$ and $X_2$ are said to be *independent* if

$$P[X_1 \leqslant x_1, X_2 \leqslant x_2] = P[X_1 \leqslant x_1]P[X_2 \leqslant x_2]$$

for any two real numbers $x_1$ and $x_2$. Independent r.v.'s are reflected in sampling procedures and experiments. Suppose a coin is tossed 10 times. Let $X_i$ be the outcome of the $i$th toss with $X_i = 1$ if a head appears and 0 if a tail appears. Then $X_1, X_2, ..., X_{10}$ are independent r.v.'s. Their outcomes do not depend on each other. This is because any toss is not assumed to be affected by earlier tosses and outcomes.

A random sample is characterized by an experiment performed repeatedly under the same conditions on similar specimens. These specimens are said to be drawn from a population at random. For a random sample of size $n$ ($n$ experiments), the random variables associated with the outcomes on the individual experiments, $X_1, ..., X_n$, are independent and have the same distribution function.

In statistics a random sample of some fixed size $n$ is often taken. A purpose of performing the sequence of experiments or trials is that some property or parameter must be estimated or shown to have small probability of occurrence. For example, in a reliability experiment the life length of a component may be estimated by operating $n$ components (assumed to be identical in distribution of life length) until failure. In a drug testing program it is necessary to show that the drug does not cause a worsening in the patient. This is considered by a series of tests on animals assumed to have been drawn at random whose behavior is assumed to be similar to human behavior with respect to the drug.

### 5.1.2 *Estimation*

Statistics involves procedures associated with sampling and testing. Two classes of statistical problems will be considered here: estimation and testing hypotheses. Suppose a sample has been collected. A parameter $\theta$ associated with the common r.v. of the sample is unknown. Estimation attempts to approximate the true value of $\theta$ by using a function $g(x_1, ..., x_n)$ of the sample outcomes, $x_1, ..., x_n$. The selection of the function $g$ is based on a specific criterion. For example, the criterion of unbiasedness is to select an unbiased estimate of $\theta$. An *unbiased estimate* $g$ is a function of $x_1, ..., x_n$ that satisfies

$$E(g(x_1, ..., x_n)) = \theta \tag{5.1}$$

Note that $x_1, ..., x_n$ are independent and have the same distribution as X. An added criterion is to select among all $g$ satisfying Eq. (5.1) the function with smallest variance. This is called the *minimum variance unbiased estimate*.

In Table 5-2 some estimates for parameters of common distributions are given. If $\theta$ is the mean of a r.v. X, then

$$\bar{x}_n = \sum_{i=1}^{n} \frac{x_i}{n}$$

is the usual estimator for $\theta$. $\bar{x}_n$ is called the *sample mean*.

In some applications the sample sizes are large so that large sample properties would be useful. One of the main results in this area is the central limit theorem. Suppose a random sample of size $n$ is drawn from a r.v. X with sample mean $\bar{x}_n$. Also, assume X has a finite mean and variance $\sigma^2$. Then the central limit theorem states that

$$\lim_{n \to \infty} P[\sqrt{n}\, \frac{(\bar{x}_n - \mu)}{\sigma} \leqslant x] = \int_{-\infty}^{x} e^{-y^2/2}\, dy\, /\sqrt{2\pi}$$

## Overview of Probability and Statistics / 139

**Table 5-2.** ESTIMATES OF PARAMETERS FOR SOME COMMON DISTRIBUTIONS

| Distribution | Parameters | Estimate |
|---|---|---|
| Binomial | $p$ | $\bar{x}_n$ |
| Geometric | $p$ | $\dfrac{1}{\bar{x}_n}$ |
| Poisson | $\lambda$ | $\dfrac{1}{\bar{x}_n}$ |
| Normal | $\mu, \theta^2$ | $\bar{x}_n, \quad \dfrac{1}{n-1} \Sigma (x_i - \bar{x}_n)^2$ |
| Exponential | $\lambda$ | $\dfrac{1}{\bar{x}_n}$ |

The result is of major use in cases where the sample size is large and either the distribution of $X$ is unknown except for $\mu$ and $\sigma^2$ or the distribution is unwieldly.

This section has so far centered on obtaining a point estimate of a parameter. Another form of estimate is based on a confidence interval. Formally, a $100(1 - \alpha)\%$ *confidence interval* $[a, b]$ for $\theta$ is an interval that satisfies the inequality $P[\theta \text{ lies in } [a, b]] \geq 1 - \alpha$.

### 5.1.3 Testing hypotheses

Suppose the accuracy of a monitoring device for a vital human function is being evaluated. If the error ($\epsilon$) exceeds 0.05, it is possible that erroneous actions will be taken on a patient. Before sampling devices of this type, a hypothesis and an alternative hypothesis can be formulated as

$$H: \epsilon \geq 0.05$$

versus

$$K: \epsilon < 0.05$$

The hypothesis $H$ is the *null hypothesis.* The alternative hypothesis $K$ consists of a set of alternative values of the parameter(s) involved. The adjective simple is added to any hypothesis if that hypothesis specifies exactly one value of a parameter.

If a tolerance level of 0.03 between the error and 0.05 was desirable, then the hypotheses could be formulated as

$$H{:}\epsilon > 0.05$$

versus

$$K{:}\epsilon \leqslant 0.05 - 0.03 = 0.02$$

For a given set of hypotheses, the next step is to analyze the sample data to make a decision of acceptance or rejection of the null hypothesis ($H$). In making this decision two types of errors are possible. In the present example the most serious error is to reject $H$ and accept $K$ when $H$ is really true. This can be serious since erroneous devices could possibly be approved for distribution and use. This type of error is called *type I error.* The *size* of the test is its probability and is given by

$$\text{size} = P\,[\text{reject } H \text{ when } H \text{ is true}]$$

The other type of error (type II) is that of accepting $H$ when $K$ is true. This leads to sending back good devices to the factory for improvement or check-out and/or treating healthy patients. The power of the test is the probability of the complement of type II error. That is,

$$\text{power} = 1 - P\,[\text{accept } H \text{ when } K \text{ is true}]$$

The goal is to minimize the probability of both types of error or equivalently to minimize the size and maximize the power. Because of the difficulty in working with two error types simultaneously, however, the size of the test is given an admissible upper bound, say, $\alpha$. The goal is then to select the testing procedure for $H$, which maximizes the power of the test.

To obtain the procedure consider a r.v. $X$ with density $f(x, \theta)$, size $\alpha$, and hypotheses

$$H: \theta = \theta_0$$

versus

$$K: \theta = \theta_1$$

where $\theta_1 > \theta_0$. The first step is to form the ratio (*Likelihood ratio*)

$$L = \frac{\prod_{i=1}^{n} f(x_i, \theta_1)}{\prod_{i=1}^{n} f(x_i, \theta_0)}$$

Here $x_1, \ldots, x_n$ is a random sample of size $n$. The decision is to reject $H$ if $L > C_\alpha$ where $C_\alpha$ is a function of $\alpha$ derived from the equation $P[L > C_\alpha] = \alpha$, given $H$ is true. This inequality is usually reduced to an equivalent form so that an estimator of $\theta$ can be used.

To illustrate this, consider a $N(\theta, 1)$ r.v. Then the inequality

$$L = \frac{\prod_{i=1}^{n} (1/\sqrt{2\pi}) e^{-(x_i - \theta_1)^2 / 2}}{\prod_{i=1}^{n} (1/\sqrt{2\pi}) e^{-(x_i - \theta_0)^2 / 2}} > C_\alpha$$

is equivalent to

$$\frac{-\sum_{i=1}^{n} (x_i - \theta_1)^2}{2} + \frac{\sum_{i=1}^{n} (x_i - \theta_0)^2}{2} > \ln(C_\alpha)$$

or

$$\bar{x}_n = \frac{\sum_{i=1}^{n} x_i}{n} > D_\alpha$$

$$= \frac{2 \ln(C_\alpha) - n\theta_0 + n\theta_1}{2n(\theta_1 - \theta_0)}$$

This last inequality is much easier to use. In fact, $D_\alpha$ can be found from the table of the $N(0, 1)$ distribution using

$$\alpha = P[\sqrt{n}(\bar{x}_n - \theta_0) > \sqrt{n}(D_\alpha - \theta_0) \text{ given } \theta = \theta_0]$$

142 / Statistics

The sample mean $x_n$ is called the *test statistic*. Similar procedures hold for other distributions. Composite (nonsimple) hypotheses are more difficult.

The problem lies in obtaining an expression for the power of the test. Let the general test statistic be $T(x_1, ..., x_n)$. Some sample rejection regions for various tests are given by

| Hypotheses | Reject when |
|---|---|
| $H: \theta = \theta_0$ versus $K: \theta \neq \theta_0$ | $T(X_1, ..., X_n) < B_\alpha$ or $> C_\alpha$ |
| $H: \theta = \theta_0$ versus $K: \theta \geq \theta_1 (> \theta_0)$ | $T(X_1, ..., X_n) > C_\alpha$ |
| $H: \theta \leq \theta_0$ versus $K: \theta \geq \theta_0$ | $T(X_1, ..., X_n) > C_\alpha$ |

The statistic $T(x_1, ..., x_n)$ can be formed from the distribution of the $x_i$'s using a single value of the composite hypothesis and alternative hypothesis with the procedure above. An example for the exponential distribution with mean $(1/\lambda)$ is the hypotheses

$$H: \lambda \leq 1$$
versus
$$K: \lambda \geq 2$$

Letting $\lambda_0$ be a point in $[0, 1]$ and $\lambda_1$ in $[2, \infty]$, we have as an inequality

$$L = \frac{\lambda_1^n \exp\left(-\lambda_1 \sum_{i=1}^{n} x_i\right)}{\lambda_0^n \exp\left(-\lambda_0 \sum_{i=1}^{n} x_i\right)} > C_\alpha$$

Rejection occurs if $L$ is greater than $C_\alpha$ because of the form of the hypothesis. This reduces to

$$\sum_{i=1}^{n} x_i < \frac{C_\alpha \lambda_0^n / \lambda_1^n}{\lambda_1 - \lambda_0} = D_\alpha$$

In Section 5.1 the emphasis has been on defining estimation and testing hypotheses using elements of probability theory as a base. In the next section specific areas of statistics are considered.

## 5.2 Statistical Methods

### 5.2.1 Regression Analysis

A major problem in both statistics and numerical analysis is the prediction of a quantity based on presently existing data on the quantity. In numerical analysis the data is usually assumed to be exact. Randomness, except in terms of errors, is suppressed. Prediction of a future value is called *extrapolation*. In statistics the data are from a random sample. The purpose in statistics is to predict the values of quantities such as the future sales of a firm, the rate of emissions from classes of vehicles with new control devices, and the future position of a maneuverable vehicle. In each case there is assumed to be a number of independent variables such as time and environmental conditions and a dependent variable.

In regression analysis a curve (usually of polynomial type) is fitted to the data over the range of observation. Extending this curve to points beyond the range provides an estimate at future values of the independent variable. The easiest case to consider is that of linear regression where the curve is merely a straight line. Denote an independent variable by $X$ and the dependent variable by $Y$. Suppose there are $n$ observations that can be viewed as pairs $(x_i, y_i)$, $i = 1, ..., n$. In a linear regression setting it is assumed that $Y = mX + b$. The sum of squares ($SS$) is constructed as in Eq. (5.2)

$$SS = \sum_{i=1}^{n} (y_i - mx_i - b)^2 \tag{5.2}$$

Now $m$ and $b$ in Eq. (5.2) are not known and must be estimated using the data and $SS$. Differentiating $SS$ with respect to $m$ and $b$ and setting these partial derivatives equal to 0 yields

$$\sum_{i=1}^{n} y_i - m \sum_{i=1}^{n} x_i - bn = 0$$

and

$$\sum_{i=1}^{n} x_i y_i - m \sum_{i=1}^{n} x_i^2 - b \sum_{i=1}^{n} x_i = 0$$

Solving these equations simultaneously yields as estimates of $m$ and $b$

$$\hat{m} = \frac{\sum_{i=1}^{n} y_i \sum_{i=1}^{n} x_i^2 - \sum_{i=1}^{n} x_i y_i \sum_{i=1}^{n} x_i}{n \sum_{i=1}^{n} x_i^2 - \left(\sum_{i=1}^{n} x_i\right)^2}$$

and

$$\hat{b} = \frac{\sum_{i=1}^{n} x_i y_i - \sum_{i=1}^{n} x_i \sum_{i=1}^{n} y_i/n}{\sum_{i=1}^{n} x_i^2 - \sum_{i=1}^{n} x_i{}^2/n}$$

Similar procedures would be followed for a general polynomial in place of $mX + b$ in Eq. (5.2). Complexity occurs in solving for a larger number of polynomial coefficients and equations. Weight functions can be introduced to weigh past observations. This occurs when predicting the future location of a maneuverable object. In the preceding, neither $x$ nor $y$ were assumed to be random variables. Now suppose both are random and that $X(Y)$ has a mean $\mu(X)$ $(v(Y))$ and variance $\sigma^2(x)$ $(\tau^2(y))$. Then in place of Eq. (5.2), we wish to take expectation of the variables inside the summation of $SS$. Doing this, we obtain

$$ESS = E(Y - mX - b)^2$$

This will be minimized by setting

$$\hat{b} = v(Y) - \mu(X)$$

and

$$\hat{m} = \frac{1}{\sigma^2(X)} E[(Y - v(Y))(X - \mu(X))]$$

to give a minimum value

$$ESS_{min} = \frac{\sigma^2(X) - E^2[(Y - v(Y))(X - \mu(X))]}{\sigma^2(x)}$$

The *least squares of Y on X* is then

$$Y = \hat{m}X + \hat{b}$$

Similarly, we could derive the least squares regression line of $X$ on $Y$. Two terms that are frequently used are the *covariance* of $X$ and $Y$ given by

$$\text{COV}(X, Y) = E[(X - \mu(X))(Y - v(Y))]$$

and the *correlation coefficient* of $X$ and $Y$, $\rho(X, Y)$, defined by

$$\rho(X, Y) = \frac{\text{COV}(X, Y)}{\sigma(X)\tau(Y)}$$

It can be shown that $\rho^2(X, Y) \leq 1$ and that if $\rho^2(X, Y)$ is unity, then $Y = AX + B$ for some $A$ and $B$ constants. The general polynomial case for estimating $Y$ from $X$ follows analogously.

### 5.2.2 Fitting procedures

A frequently encountered problem in statistics is to verify or disprove with some degree of certainty that a random variable such as life length of components or drug degradation has a certain probability distribution. Such a determination must be made on the basis of observations of the property.

One method for carrying out this fitting is known as $\chi^2$ goodness of fit. In the goodness-of-fit procedure, the ordered observations are grouped into a certain number of cells, say, $K$. An example is given in Fig. 5-2. Here the life lengths (in hours) of a sample of size 10 have been ranked increasingly.

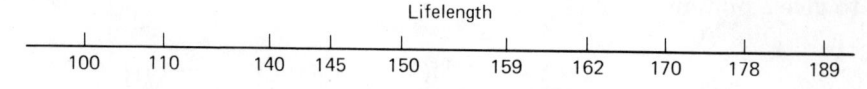

```
                              Lifelength
 ├─────┼─────┼──┼──┼─────┼─────┼─────┼─────┼─────┤
100   110   140 145 150  159   162   170   178   189
```

**Figure 5.2.** Ordered observations of life length.

Four cells have been selected and are the following intervals:

$$C_1 = [0, 125)$$
$$C_2 = [125, 155)$$
$$C_3 = [155, 174.5)$$
$$C_4 = [174.5, \infty)$$

The fitting problem can be interpreted in terms of hypothesis testing. Thus, a hypothesis and alternative would be

$$H: p(C_i) = p_i, \quad 1 \leq i \leq 4$$

versus

$$K: p(C_i) = p_i \text{ for some } i, \quad 1 \leq i \leq 4$$

Here $p(C_i) = P[X \text{ is in } C_i]$.

For a specific density function $f(x)$, the $(p_i)$ are found by intergrating over the cell intervals $C_i$. Thus,

$$p_i = \int_{C_i} f(x)\, dx$$

Caution must be exercised here, in that many distributions can satisfy the null hypothesis. Thus, if we test whether the variable has an exponential distribution with a specified parameter value and accept the null hypothesis, we can only say that we are relatively certain on the value of the $p_i$'s (not on the exact distribution).

Suppose $m_i$ observations out of $n$ total observations fall in cell $C_i$. The test procedure is to reject $H$ if the quantity

$$Q_1 = \sum_{i=1}^{K} \frac{(m_i - np_i)^2}{np_i} \tag{5.3}$$

exceeds some real number $C_\alpha$ depending on the size of the test ($\alpha$), $K$, and the $\chi^2$ distribution. For a large sample size $n$ and if $\{m_i\}$ are sizable, then $Q_1$ has approximately a $\chi^2$ distribution with $K - 1$ degrees of freedom.

In the example $K = 4$, $n = 10$, and if we hypothesize that $p_1 = 0.25, p_2 = 0.20, p_3 = 0.35,$ and $p_4 = 0.20,$ then $Q_1$ is $0.671$. With $\alpha = 0.05$ we find $C_{0.05}$ from the following equation using the $\chi^2$ table value (Table C-2 in the Appendix),

$$P[Q_1 > C_{0.05}] = 0.05$$

This gives $C_{0.05} = 7.815$. Since $Q_1 < C_{0.05}$, we do not reject $H$.

Another problem is to have a number of different random variables whose values are divided into cells. For these variables, we wish to test if they have the same distributions. This is referred to as a test of homogeneity. Suppose a collection of automobiles that are either new or year-old models is gathered. Each car is then evaluated to determine the level of carbon monoxide emission. This level is compared to a specified standard. The numerical results are summarized in Table 5-3 (called a *contingency table*).

**Table 5-3.** SAMPLE CONTINGENCY TABLE

|  | Below Standard | Above Standard | Total |
|---|---|---|---|
| New | 25 | 12 | 37 |
| Year Old | 15 | 13 | 28 |
| Total | 40 | 25 | 65 |

Let $m_{ij}$ be the $(i, j)$ entry in the table and let $m_i.$ $(m._j)$ be the total for the $i$th row ($j$th column). Then using the data, for $r$ rows and $c$ columns we compute the quantity

$$Q_2 = \sum_{i=1}^{r} \sum_{j=1}^{c} \frac{[m_{ij} - np_i p_j]^2}{np_i p_j} \quad (5.4)$$

In Eq. (5.4), $p_i(p_j)$ is estimated by $m_i./n$ $(m._j/n)$. Thus, $np_i p_j$ will be estimated by $m_i.m._j/n$. For the example, $Q_2 = 1.294$.

Now it can be shown for large $n$ that $Q_2$ has approximately a $\chi^2$ distribution with $(r-1)(c-1)$ degrees of freedom.

If we test the null hypothesis that the new and year-old cars have the same distribution with size $\alpha$, we shall seek a critical value $C_\alpha$ such that $P[Q_2 > C_\alpha] = \alpha$ from the tables of the $\chi^2$ distribution. For $\alpha = 0.30$ and $(r-1)(c-1) = 1$, $C_\alpha$ is equal to 1.074. Since $Q_2 > C_\alpha$, we reject the hypothesis that they have the same distribution.

In the preceding paragraphs, the variables were listed along the rows and the cell titles were column headings. It is also possible to test whether two random variables $X$ and $Y$ are independent using contingency tables. For this situation the row headings are cells or possible values of one variable $X$, and the column headings are possible values for the other variable $Y$. In the $(i, j)$th entry of the table is the frequency of occurrence for the $i$th value of $X$ and $j$th value of $Y$ simultaneously. For example, $X$ might be the usable total mileage for a tire and $Y$ the life length of a shock absorber. The data appears in Table 5-4.

Table 5-4. DATA FOR TEST OF INDEPENDENCE OF TWO RANDOM VARIABLES

| Tire Shock Absorber | 0–10,000 | 10,000–15,000 | 15,000–20,000 | Over 20,000 | Total |
|---|---|---|---|---|---|
| 0–5,000 | 5 | 1 | 5 | 9 | 20 |
| 5,000–10,000 | 6 | 2 | 5 | 17 | 30 |
| 10,000–15,000 | 6 | 20 | 10 | 4 | 40 |
| 15,000–20,000 | 3 | 12 | 15 | 5 | 35 |
| 20,000–25,000 | 5 | 5 | 15 | 7 | 32 |
| Over 25,000 | 5 | 15 | 20 | 3 | 43 |
| Total | 30 | 55 | 70 | 45 | 200 |

The quantity $Q_2$ is computed as in Eq. (5.4) with the same degrees of freedom, $(r-1)(c-1)$. With $\alpha = .10$, we determine $C_\alpha$ from the table (Table C-2 in the Appendix) of the $\chi^2$ distribution with 15 degrees of freedom and find $C_{0.10} = 22.307$. The calculated value exceeds 22.307 so that we reject the hypothesis that the variables are independent.

## 5.2.3 Analysis of variance

Suppose a series of experiments is performed on a number of different types of components that perform the same function. These could be different brands of soap, spark plugs, or computer programs. Each observation is a measurement of a characteristic of a sample of one type of component. The characteristic could be life length, speed, or durability. Analysis of variance (ANOVA) seeks to test hypotheses to detect differences in the distributions of the random variables being observed.

Unfortunately, to allow these random variables to possess any distribution leads to intractable expressions. Therefore, several assumptions are made on the variables. Each variable $X_i$ is assumed to be normally distributed with mean $\mu_i$ and variance $\sigma^2$. Thus, not only is normality assumed but also that there is a common variance.

Let the number of component types be $m$ and the number of observations of the $i$th type be $n_i$. The $j$th observation of the $i$th type is denoted by $x_{ij}$. Suppose we consider a problem in which we are evaluating five different computer programs written in the same language and capable of being run at the same computer facility. Each program is designed to integrate real-valued functions over a finite interval. We observe the total running time. The data is summarized in Table 5-5.

**Table 5-5.** DATA FOR TEST OF COMMON MEANS

| $i$ | $x_{ij}$ | $n_i$ |
|---|---|---|
| 1 | 10.2, 9.5, 5.7, 7.8, 26.1 | 5 |
| 2 | 11.7, 13.8, 9.0, 8.8 | 4 |
| 3 | 14.1, 12.1, 7.6, 7.2, 8.7 | 5 |
| 4 | 9.5, 17.7, 14.3, 9.3, 8.9, 8.6 | 6 |
| 5 | 4.5, 5.6, 4.9 | 3 |

The hypothesis is that all variables have a common mean. Then with the assumptions of normality and common variance, accepting the hypothesis will lead to believing the variables are identically distributed. Since we are testing on the means, it would appear that the sample means and sums of squares of differences between observations should be considered. The notation is as follows:

$$SS_1 = \sum_{i=1}^{m} \sum_{j=1}^{n_i} (x_{ij} - \overline{x}_i)^2 \quad \text{sum of squares within types}$$

$$SS_2 = \sum_{i=1}^{m} \sum_{j=1}^{n_i} (x_{ij} - \overline{x})^2 \quad \text{sum of squares}$$

$$SS_3 = \sum_{i=1}^{m} n_i (\overline{x}_i - \overline{x})^2 \quad \text{sum of squares between types}$$

$$\overline{x}_i = \sum_{j=1}^{n_i} \frac{x_{ij}}{n_i}$$

$$\overline{x} = \frac{\sum_{i=1}^{m} \sum_{j=1}^{n} x_{ij}}{\sum_{i=1}^{m} n_i}$$

Then the quantity to test the hypothesis of common means is

$$AN_1 = \frac{SS_2/(m-1)\sigma^2}{SS_1/(\sum_{i=1}^{m} n_i - m)\sigma^2} \tag{5.5}$$

or simplifying

$$AN_1 = \frac{\sum_{i=1}^{m} n_i - m}{m-1} \frac{SS_2}{SS_1} \tag{5.6}$$

Under the null hypothesis the numerator and denominator of Eq. (5.5) are both $\chi^2$ distributed and independent. From this it follows that $AN_1$ is Snedecor's $F$ or $F$ distributed with $m-1$ and $\sum_{i=1}^{m} n_i - m$ degrees of freedom.

The hypothesis of common mean is rejected if $AN_1$ is too large. This is in part due to this quantity having a higher expectation if the means are not the same.

In the example, $AN_1 = 7.05$ with 4 and 18 degrees of freedom. If $\alpha = 0.05$, then using Table C-4 in the appendix, we see that $F_{4,18,0.95}$ is less than 6 so that we reject $H$. This test is termed a *one-way analysis of variance*.

The experimental situation can be complicated by the presence of additional factors. Suppose each of the computer programs is tested on three different levels of compilers with a single problem. Then for program $i$ and compiler level $j$ the running time is $x_{ij}$. The presence of two factors makes this problem one of a two-way classification ANOVA. One assumption is that each $x_{ij}$ has an $N(\mu_{ij}, \sigma^2)$ distribution. In general, let $1 \leqslant i \leqslant m$ and $1 \leqslant j \leqslant n$. For convenience we shall define the following means.

$$\bar{\mu}_{i\cdot} = \frac{1}{n} \sum_{j=1}^{n} \mu_{ij} \qquad \bar{x}_{i\cdot} = \frac{1}{n} \sum_{j=1}^{n} x_{ij}$$

$$\bar{\mu}_{\cdot j} = \frac{1}{m} \sum_{i=1}^{m} \mu_{ij} \qquad \bar{x}_{\cdot j} = \frac{1}{m} \sum_{i=1}^{m} x_{ij}$$

$$\bar{\mu} = \frac{1}{mn} \sum_{i=1}^{m} \sum_{j=1}^{n} \mu_{ij} \qquad \bar{x} = \sum_{i=1}^{m} \sum_{j=1}^{n} x_{ij}/mn$$

It is also assumed that $\mu_{ij} = (\mu_{i\cdot} + \mu_{ij}) - \mu$ for all $i$ and $j$. Consider now two hypothesis:

$$H: \bar{\mu}_{\cdot j} = \bar{\mu}, \quad 1 \leqslant j \leqslant n$$
$$H': \bar{\mu}_{i\cdot} = \bar{\mu}, \quad 1 \leqslant i \leqslant m$$

These have interpretations in the experiment. Accepting the hypothesis $H$ will lead to believing that the different programs or types do not affect the characteristic of running time. Accepting $H'$ means that the compiler or treatment does not affect running time.

Define:

$$SS'_1 = \sum_{i=1}^{m} \sum_{j=1}^{n} (x_{ij} - \bar{x})^2 \qquad \text{sum of squares}$$

$$SS'_2 = n \sum_{i=1}^{m} (\bar{x}_{i\cdot} - \bar{x})^2 \qquad \text{sum of squares between types}$$

$$SS'_3 = m \sum_{j=1}^{n} (\bar{x}_{\cdot j} - \bar{x})^2 \qquad \text{sum of squares between treatments}$$

$$SS'_4 = \sum_{i=1}^{m} \sum_{j=1}^{n} (x_{ij} - \bar{x}_{i\cdot} - \bar{x}_{\cdot j} + \bar{x})^2 \qquad \text{residual sum of squares}$$

The quantities for testing $H$ and $H'$ are, respectively,

$$AN_2 = (n-1)\frac{SS'_2}{SS'_4}$$

and

$$AN'_2 = (m-1)\frac{SS'_3}{SS'_4}$$

where $AN_2$ and $AN'_2$ have $F$ distributions. $AN_2$ has $(m-1)$ and $(m-1)(n-1)$ degrees of freedom; $AN'_2$ has $(n-1)$ and $(m-1)(n-1)$ degrees of freedom. Rejection of $H$ or $H'$ occurs if the respective quantity is too large. Computationally, we would find $SS'_1$, $SS'_2$, and $SS'_3$ and then note that $SS'_4$ is the difference of $SS'_1$ and the sum of $SS'_2$ and $SS'_3$.

### 5.2.4 Nonparametric statistics

In the previous sections we have assumed that the underlying phenomena have a general known distribution. This is supportable if it is known from data that have been collected and goodness-of-fit procedures have been followed. In some cases, however, nothing can be assumed about the distribution as to shape or other properties. The area of statistics that treats this subject is called *nonparametric* or *distribution-free statistics*.

Suppose that a random variable $X$ has a continuous but unknown distribution function $F$ and that a sample of size $n$ has been taken. We wish to estimate $F$ using the sample points. Suppose the observations are ordered increasingly so that the ordered sample is $y_1 \leq y_2 \leq y_3 \leq y_4 \leq \cdots \leq y_n$. Define the function $F_n$ to take jumps of height $1/n$ at each sample point and be constant between sample points. Formally,

$$F_n(x) = \begin{cases} 0 & x < y_1 \\ \frac{k}{n} & y_k \leq x < y_{k+1} \\ 1 & x \geq y_n \end{cases}$$

A typical curve for $F_n$ is shown in Fig. 5-3.

The function $F_n$ is called the *empirical distribution function*. For large $n$, $F_n$ approximates $F$ at every point [see Loeve[7] for a proof that $F_n$ converges everywhere to $F$ as $n \to \infty$]. Under certain conditions a discrete jump function may not be a good approximation. Several alternatives have been proposed. Parzen[8] has offered a method based on kernel functions and Tartar and Kronmal[15] have obtained an estimate based on orthogonal polynomials.

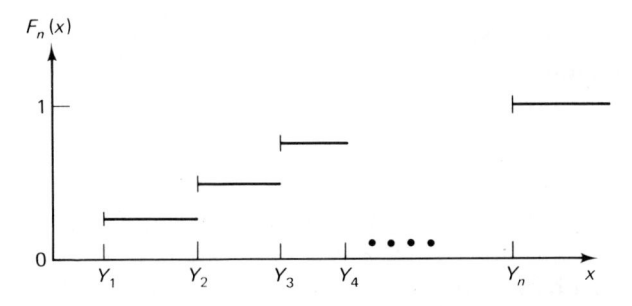

Figure 5-3. Graph of empirical distribution $F_n$.

For a given testing situation a decision can be based on a function of $F_n$ and $F$. An example is

$$\max_{\{x : a \leq F(x) \leq b\}} [F_n(x) - F(x)]$$

These functions have the important property that their distributions do not depend on $F$ (and so the name *distribution-free*).

Suppose we are testing a new helicopter rotor blade and we wish to estimate the life length of the blade. Since we wish to be conservative with our estimate $F_n(x)$, we need to have the following inequality hold.

$$P[\{\sup_x \{F(x) - F_n(x)\} < 0\}] \geq \gamma$$

for some $\gamma$ close to unity. Using the empirical distribution function, we can find an estimate $\tilde{F}_n(x) = F_n(x) - C_{n,\gamma}$ where $C_{n,\gamma}$ is found from $\gamma$ and tables of the variable $\sup_x \{F(x) - F_n(x)\}$.

Often the entire distribution function $F$ is not of interest, rather, some property such as the mean or variance is of interest. A related problem is comparing two distributions with respect to this property.

Suppose observations are taken from two populations. The aim is to determine if the difference in means for the two populations is sizable. Let these observations be given by

$$X \quad x_1, x_2, \ldots, x_m$$
$$Y \quad y_1, y_2, \ldots, y_n$$

Now these observations can be ranked and arranged by increasing order of magnitude to give

$$z_1, z_2, \ldots, z_{m+n}$$

Assigning rank $i$ to $z_i$, the sum of ranks for $X$ and $Y$ can be computed. Let these be denoted by $SR_X$ and $SR_Y$, respectively. It may happen that several observations are identical. In this case the sum of the ranks for the identical observations is divided by the number of identical observations to give the rank to each of the identical observations.

Suppose two aircraft engines are tested for use in the same craft and type. The times to first repair for these engines ($X$ and $Y$) are given by

$$X: 15, 18, 14, 24, 32, 32, 16$$
$$Y: 13, 17, 32, 21, 23$$

The ranks are given by

| Observations | 13 | 14 | 15 | 16 | 17 | 18 | 21 | 23 | 24 | 32 | 32 | 32 |
|---|---|---|---|---|---|---|---|---|---|---|---|---|
| Rank | 1 | 2 | 3 | 4 | 5 | 6 | 7 | 8 | 9 | 10 | 11 | 12 |
| Source Variable | Y | X | X | X | Y | X | Y | Y | X | X | X | Y |

The rank for 32 is found from

$$\frac{10 + 11 + 12}{3}$$

The sum of the ranks for $X$ and $Y$ are $SR_X = 46$ and $SR_Y = 32$. If there are $n$ observations, then

$$SR_X + SR_Y = \frac{n(n+1)}{2}$$

where $n(n+1)/2$ is the sum of the numbers $1, 2, \ldots, n$. The statistic used to test the hypothesis that the means of $X$ and $Y$ are the same is

$$W = \frac{2mn + m^2 + m - 2SR_X}{2}$$

By a form of the central limit theorem it can be shown that $W$ is approximately distributed as a normal variable with mean $mn/2$ and variance $mn(m+n+1)/12$. The approximation is acceptable if $m$ and $n$ are at least 10. Using the normal tables the hypothesis of identical means is rejected if

$$\left| \frac{W - E(W)}{\sqrt{\text{VAR}(W)}} \right| > C_\alpha$$

for an $\alpha$-size test.

In the engine example if we are willing to use a normal approximation with $\alpha = 0.10$, then

$$\frac{W - E(W)}{\sqrt{\text{VAR}/W}} = \frac{17 - 17.5}{\sqrt{105}} = \frac{-0.5}{10.25} = -0.00488$$

Since $C_{0.10} = 1.645$, we do not reject $H$.

This test is referred to as the *Mann-Whitney nonparametric test*. It is weak in the sense that it ignores the magnitude of the observations even though it does take into account the rank of observations. Unless there is a simple alternative hypothesis, the power of the test cannot be determined.

A weaker test is the *sign test*. This is often used in cases for paired observations, that is, each observation of a variable $X$ is paired with exactly one observation of the other variable $Y$. Suppose there is a sample of $n$ $X$'s and $n$ $Y$'s. If the distributions of $X$ and $Y$ were the same, then $E(X) = E(Y)$ or $E(X - Y) = 0$. A version of the sign test has the null hypothesis.

$$H:p = P[X - Y > 0] = \tfrac{1}{2}$$

versus

$$K:p \neq \tfrac{1}{2}$$

The quantity used for acceptance or rejection of $H$ is the number of times $X_i > Y_i$, $1 \leq i \leq n$. Let this be denoted by $N$. Under the null hypothesis, $N$ is distributed as a binomial variable with parameters $n$ and $\tfrac{1}{2}$. Because of the alternative $p \neq \tfrac{1}{2}$, we shall reject $H$ if $N$ is too small or too large.

Suppose 10 twin-jet aircraft are used to evaluate a pollution emission device. For each jet one engine is fitted with the device and the other engine is not. The aircraft are then flown for 1 hour and the pollution labels are checked every 10 minutes. The individual aircraft are flown at a variety of altitudes. It is suspected that the device's efficiency may actually increase pollution at some altitudes. For the given aircraft the engines (without the devices) are assumed to be identical.

The mean levels of emission are given in Table 5-6.

**Table 5-6.** SAMPLE DATA FOR SIGN TEST

| Aircraft | 1 | 2 | 3 | 4 | 5 | 6 | 7 | 8 | 9 | 10 |
|---|---|---|---|---|---|---|---|---|---|---|
| Without Device | 56.2 | 48.7 | 55.8 | 27.6 | 32.1 | 47.5 | 49.5 | 65.7 | 59.4 | 46.1 |
| With Device | 57.0 | 40.0 | 56.8 | 13.5 | 15.0 | 39.3 | 49.4 | 72.1 | 62.2 | 45.5 |

With this data, $N = 6$. Using Table C-1 of the appendix for $N = 10$ and $\alpha = 0.10$, we would reject $H$ if $N > 8$ or $N < 3$ (or $N > 7$ and $N < 2$). Thus, we do not reject $H$ using this test.

Suppose a product is being mass-produced on an assembly line basis. This could be, for example, soft drinks in bottles. It is noticed that some of the bottle caps have been put on in a defective manner by one or several of the installation machines. The problem then is to test to see if these errors are being made at random or are really being done according to a pattern. An example set of results would be

S S F S S S F S F F S S S F S

where S denotes a success (the cap is attached properly) and F denotes a failure (improperly attached cap). A run is a set of consecutive results on outcomes that have the same value. The runs in the sequence above are

$$SS, \ F, \ SS, \ F, \ S, \ FF, \ SSS, \ F, \ S$$

The number of runs, is then 9. The quantity to test randomness is the number of runs, denoted by $NR$. If $NR$ is too large or small, a pattern is indicated. To perform a test we need to obtain the distribution of $NR$ under the hypothesis of random errors.

Suppose that the sample size is $n$ and is partitioned into $n_S$ successes and $n_F$ failures (so that $n_F + n_S = n$). Under the hypothesis of randomness each arrangement of the sample is equally likely so that the probability of any arrangement is $n_F!n_S!/n!$. Using this we can obtain

$$P(NR = t) = \begin{cases} \dfrac{2\binom{n-1}{t/2-1}\binom{n-1}{t/2-1}}{\binom{n}{n_F}} & \text{if } t \text{ is even} \\[2em] \dfrac{\binom{n-1}{(t-1)/2}\binom{n-1}{(t-3)/2} + \binom{n-1}{(t-1)/2}\binom{n-1}{(t-3)/2}}{\binom{n}{n_F}} & \text{if } t \text{ is odd} \end{cases}$$

It is also possible to compare two random variables using the runs test. The sample of one variable is given the label of $S$ and the other $F$ after all the observations have been arranged in order of magnitude. The weakness of this lies in not considering the value of the actual observations and only using their comparative magnitude.

## 5.3 Applications

This section considers some applications of statistics that can be addressed by either an existing program or a modification of an existing program.

### 5.3.1 Traffic flow

In traffic flow, statistical analysis is concerned with estimating the behavior of vehicles of various types in traffic patterns under a variety of conditions. There are a number of properties of interest. These include traffic volume, maximal flow or capacity, and gaps between vehicles. A general description of these properties appears in Haight.[13] Here we shall consider the time gap between vehicles, also called the *time headway*. The other gap between vehicles is that of distance.

In analyzing time headways, the objective is to fit a distribution to the data obtained under a set of environmental conditions. The conditions include the rate of flow, the number of lanes, the type of roadway (freeway, two-lane road, etc.), and the mixture of traffic. There have been a number of proposed distributions [see Ashton,[11] Buckley,[12], Lientz[14]]. For a given distribution, estimates are obtained for each of the parameters of the distribution. For example, the proposed distribution might have density

$$f(x) = \begin{cases} \alpha f_1(x), & 0 \leqslant x \leqslant \mu \\ (1-\alpha)f_2(x), & \mu \leqslant x < \infty \end{cases}$$

where

$$f_1(x) = \frac{2}{\mu^2}x$$

and

$$f_2(x) = \frac{2}{\mu(1-\alpha)}e^{-2\alpha(x-\mu)/\mu(1-\alpha)}$$

The general shape of $f$ is given in Fig. 5-4.

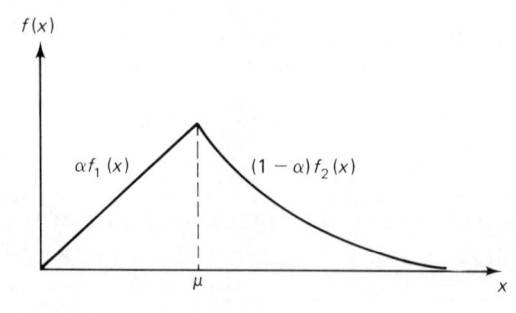

Figure 5-4. Sample graph of time headway density.

Estimates are needed for $\alpha$ and $\mu$. Suppose from previous data we set $\mu = 6$. Then $\alpha$ is the proportion of observations below $\mu$.

The procedure in Subsection 5.2.2 can be followed to test the goodness of fit for a given significance level. Goodness-of-fit problems occur in other traffic parameters such as distance gaps. Work continues in finding better fitting distributions for higher flow rates. The use of a fitted distribution has application in simulation and design analysis. Suppose a stretch of proposed arterial has been designed. Using the design a simulation program can generate time headways from the distribution. In this way with other parameters a design can be evaluated for capacity, bottlenecks, and concentration of vehicles.

### 5.3.2 Insecticide testing

A continuing research program is devoted to obtaining nonpersistent but effective chemical compounds that can control various species of pests. This can be viewed as an analysis of variance problem. Fields or sample tracts are divided into areas that are separated to minimize interaction effects. The test is designed to evaluate the efficiency of dosage levels of the chemical. Several levels are selected.

Data is gathered on pest concentration for the various areas. Analysis of variance would then be used to test whether the means were equal. If this were rejected, further testing could then be used to determine the difference in effect. In applying ANOVA, attention must be paid to the model assumptions on the underlying distributions and sample sizes necessary to substantive results.

### 5.3.3 Credit card and investment analysis

A problem encountered by banking and commercial firms is to classify the risks and borrowing ceiling for any applicant. Variables that can be used are income, job stability, marital status, outstanding debts, education level, and housing. Often regression and correlation analysis are used to determine the key "independent" variables. Independence here is an assumption since some of the variables may be by nature highly correlated. Oversimplification can lead to incorrect debt ceilings that may either deter customers from using the particular card or increase the size of bad debts and nonpayment. Additionally, the variables that can be accessed are restricted to data the applicant supplies and that available through credit bureaus.

## 5.4 Programs

There are many statistical programs available for both specialized and general usage. In this section the BMD series produced at the University of California[16],[17] and SPSS[18] will be considered in detail. These were chosen because of their wide availability and usage at various universities and companies. Both BMD and SPSS list the variable sizes that can be handled.

The BMD sequence of programs is one of the most general and inclusive in existence. BMD has over 40 programs written in FORTRAN IV for handling multivariate analysis (including factor analysis, discriminant analysis), regression analysis, Guttman scaling, time series, analysis of variance, and general linear hypotheses. BMD arose from the need for statistical procedures in medical and biological research. Estimates of running time as a function of the number of variables, classifications, and cells are given. The order and layout of the card deck and sample problem printouts are presented as well as options for each program. Included are transformation of basic input of variables to be used by the program. Standard FORTRAN formats for variables are allowed. BMD has the advantage of having been through several editions. Later editions have increased parameter size and additional options as well as increased reliability.

SPSS is a collection of programs written in FORTRAN for the social sciences for both IBM and CDC computers. SPSS can compute the correlation between one dependent and one independent variable while holding other variables at various values (partial correlation). In regression analysis, SPSS contains a program to handle linear multiple regression. That is, from a collection of independent variables it selects the linear combination of a subcollection to estimate a given dependent variable. SPSS can also perform factor analysis and Guttman scaling. SPSS allows for manipulation of files to add and modify data. Although intended for social science applications, the programs are of a general statistical nature.

The file structure of SPSS allows both a fixed format, where data must be entered in specific columns on a card, and a flexible card format, where the restrictions are that each data sequence length is fixed and values of quantities must be offset by a comma or spaces. Subsets and subsequences of data can be handled by subfiles. SPSS files are limited to 500 variables with each file containing no more than 100 subfiles.

SPSS prints out error messages according to a numerical code. Error messages are mainly to indicate incorrect list structures and excessive or dependent data.

A property of both BMD and SPSS is that output is in a standard statistical format so that the task of interpretation is eased.

Emerging recently have been interactive statistical programs. These include general collections such as Dartmouth's IMPRESS and the University of Alberta's STATPAK.

A number of individual programs for specific applications have been written for classification and related statistical problems, however, on-line, interactive statistical routines are appropriate only in some commercial and government situations where rapid turnaround is necessary. Examples are credit card risk analysis and ballistic missile defense.

Other packages and programs are available from the user groups mentioned in previous chapters. Some of these are general packages that have imbedded the BMD programs. Most are specialized for a specific type of regression, correlation, or analysis of variance situations.

Several textbooks are listed in References that range from the elementary level [Brownlee,[1] Freund,[6]] to the advanced Loeve,[7] and Cochran and Cox.[4] Chakravarti, et al.[3] and Walsh[10] are reference books that present summaries of methods for a variety of situations. Parzen[8] and Brunk[2] are good intermediate level texts in probability and statistics, respectively. Sources in experimental design and analysis of variance are Finney[5] and Scheffé[9].

## REFERENCES

*Textbooks*

1. BROWNLEE, K. A., *Statistical Theory and Methodology in Science and Engineering*. New York: John Wiley & Sons, Inc., 1960.
2. BRUNK, H. D., *An Introduction to Mathematical Statistics*, 2nd ed. Waltham, Mass.: Blaisdell Pub. Co., 1965.
3. CHAKRAVARTI, I. M., R. LAHA AND J. ROY, *Handbook of Methods of Applied Statistics*, Vol. 1. New York: John Wiley & Sons, Inc., 1967.
4. COCHRAN, W. G. AND G. M. COX, *Experimental Designs*. New York: John Wiley & Sons, Inc., 1957.

5. FINNEY, D. J., *Experimental Design and Its Statistical Basis.* Chicago, Ill.: University of Chicago Press, 1955.
6. FREUND, J. E., *Modern Elementary Statistics.* Englewood Cliffs, N. J.: Prentice-Hall, Inc., 1967.
7. LOEVE, M., *Probability Theory.* Princeton, N. J.: Van Nostrand Co., Inc., 1963.
8. PARZEN, E., *Modern Probability Theory and Its Applications.* New York: John Wiley & Sons, Inc., 1960.
9. SCHEFFE, H., *The Analysis of Variance.* New York: John Wiley & Sons, Inc., 1959.
10. WALSH, J. E., *Handbook of Nonparametric Statistics.* Princeton, N. J.: Van Nostrand Co., Inc., 1962.

*Other References*

11. ASHTON, W. D., "Distributions for Gaps in Road Traffic," *J. Inst. Math. and Applications*, VIII (1971), 37–46.
12. BUCKLEY, D. J., "Road Traffic Headway Distributions," *Proceedings of the First Conference of Australian Road Research Board*, 1962.
13. HAIGHT, F. A., *Mathematical Theories of Traffic Flow.* New York: Academic Press, 1963.
14. LIENTZ, B. P., "Estimation of Mass Concentrations for Problems in Traffic Flow," *Transportation Research*, V (1971), 75–81.
15. TARTAR, M. AND R. KRONMAL, "The Estimation of Probability Densities and Cumulatives by Fourier Series Methods," *J. Amer. Statistical Assn.*, 63 (Sept., 1968), 925–952.

*Program Manuals*

16. DIXON, W. J. (ED.), *BMD Biomedical Computer Programs.* Berkeley, Calif.: University of California Press, 1968.
17. ———, *BMD Biomedical Computer Programs, X-Series Supplement.* Berkeley, Calif.: University of California Press, 1970.
18. NIE, N., D. BENT, AND C. H. HULL, *SPSS: Statistical Package for the Social Sciences.* New York: McGraw-Hill Book Co., 1970.

## PROBLEMS

Give the set of events and express the probability function for the situations described in Problems 1 to 3.

1. Balls are drawn from an urn containing five white balls, seven black balls, and three red balls. Each time a ball is drawn at random, its color is re-

corded and the ball returned to the urn (drawing with replacement). There are a total of five balls drawn.

2. A deck of 52 playing cards is shuffled and 6 cards are drawn at random in succession. Each time a card is drawn, its suit is noted and the card is set aside (drawing without replacement).

3. A number of tires is being tested for mileage before blowout or puncture. There are 10 tires. The experiment stops when all tires are tested or a failure occurs. Failure occurs if the mileage on the worn-out tire is below 10,000. From previous experiments it is estimated that the probability that a tire will fail before 10,000 miles is 0.11.

In Problems 4 to 6, corresponding to Problems 1 to 3, respectively, derive the density function and distribution function. Write a program to perform these calculations.

4. (a) Number of red balls drawn;
   (b) Number of nonwhite balls drawn.
5. (a) Number of hearts in the first three draws;
   (b) Number of spades in the last three draws.
6. Number of tests required to get failure.
7. Suppose $X$ is exponential with mean 2 and range $(1, \infty)$. Derive the distribution of the following functions of $X$.
   (a) $\ln(X)$
   (b) $X^{1/2}$
   (c) $X^2$
   (d) $2 - X$
8. A random variable $X$ is Poisson with parameter $\lambda = 0.5$. Determine the distributions of the following functions of $X$.
   (a) $X^k$, $k$ is an even, positive integer.
   (b) $1/(X + 2)$
9. A light bulb has an expected life length of 200 hours, given that it is turned on at time zero. Find the variance of the life length. Find the probability that a bulb will last more than 500 hours.
10. Pollution measurements are made on a paint factory to measure to a certain type of pollutant. The level of pollution $X$ is thought to be normal with mean $\mu$ and variance 2. A sample of size 8 is taken, giving

    $$500 \quad 510 \quad 600 \quad 470 \quad 620 \quad 550 \quad 710 \quad 540$$

    (a) Test the hypothesis that $\mu$ is 600 versus $\mu \neq 600$ with $\alpha = 0.05$. Find the rejection region.
    (b) Using the same data, test the hypothesis $\mu$ is 570 versus the alternative $\mu$ is 750 with $\alpha = 0.10$. Find the power of the test.

11. The distribution of heights of students in a certain age level is thought to be normally distributed with mean 38 inches and variance 3 inches. The observations in cells are

| Interval | Number |
| --- | --- |
| [0, 32) | 3 |
| [32, 33) | 5 |
| [33, 34) | 5 |
| [35, 36) | 7 |
| [36, 37) | 8 |
| [37, 38) | 15 |
| [38, 39) | 10 |
| [39, 40) | 10 |
| [40, 41) | 9 |
| [41, 42) | 6 |
| [42, ∞) | 6 |

Test the hypothesis that the cell probabilities are those of an $N(38, 3)$ distribution.

12. A set of components is tested in a laboratory. The life length of the components is suspected to be gamma distributed with density

$$f(x) = \begin{cases} \dfrac{x^2 e^{-x/2}}{8\Gamma(2)} & x \geq 0 \\ 0 & x < 0 \end{cases}$$

The times of failure of 20 components are as follows:

3.2, 7.8, 1.8, 1.5, 1.7, 2.1, 6.2, 11.1, 1.8, 1.6,
1.7, 0.8, 1.3, 1.4, 9.6, 10.3, 20.1, 12.4, 0.5, 1.8

Test the goodness of fit to the gamma distribution at the $\alpha = 0.05$ and $\alpha = 0.10$ significance levels.

13. It is thought that the relationship between the fertilizer concentration per acre and yield per acre for corn are linearly related. Use regression analysis and the following data to find the linear avenue.

Concentration: 0.1, 0.2, 0.25, 0.4, 0.42
Yield: 2.8, 5.1, 5.5, 8.1, 8.3

14. Suppose that the relationship between drug dosage and potency is being tested to see if there ia a linear relationship. The initial seven observations are given by

| x | 0.001 | 0.002 | 0.005 | 0.007 | 0.0081 | 0.009 | 0.0092 |
|---|---|---|---|---|---|---|---|
| y | 0.05 | 0.091 | 0.241 | 0.333 | 0.341 | 0.411 | 0.487 |

Now 10 other observations on potency are made. The mean of these observations is 0.153. Using linear regression, obtain a point estimate for the corresponding mean dosage level.

15. Suppose an emission device is being tested on several types of engines. The level of carbon monoxide emission is measured for several engines of each type tested. The percentage reduction in levels with the device are given as

| Type | | Observations |
|---|---|---|
| Diesel | 1 | 15.2, 17.4, 20.1, 10.8 |
| 4 Cylinder | 2 | 22.3, 21.7, 21.1, 24.7, 26.3 |
| 6 Cylinder | 3 | 20.7, 21.2, 20.1 |
| 8 Cylinder | 4 | 19.3, 20.8, 21.3, 21.4 |

Test the hypothesis that the mean reductions are the same using analysis of variance.

16. A producer of gears has achieved a high standard of uniformity by maintaining the same machine configuration in manufacturing the gears. The producer must now evaluate the impact of increased production on the uniformity. The production increase will be derived by a new collection of machines. Explain how the producer could set up a test to determine whether there is a significant mean difference in uniformity. Uniformity is measured by calculating the square of the difference between errors for the individual gear and the uniform standard. Apply analysis of variance and nonparametric methods.

17. A maker of toasters has two models ($M_1$ and $M_2$) for testing to determine durability before repair. From the guarantee registration card they know the date of purchase. The times (in months) until breakdown for samples of both models were recorded as follows:

$M_1$: 1.5, 2.7, 6.1, 7.2, 7.5, 8.9, 9.0, 9.0, 9.2, 9.3

$M_2$: 1.0, 7.1, 8.1, 8.2, 8.7, 9.1, 9.4, 9.7, 9.8, 11.0

Using the normal approximation for $\alpha = 0.05$, test the hypothesis that each model has the same mean.

18. Use the same data as in Problem 9, and assume that because of geography pairing can be done between corresponding observations. Test the probability that the time to repair of $M_1$ exceeds that of $M_2$ by $\frac{1}{2}$.

19. Write a program to compute
    (a) The first four moments of an exponential distribution with parameter $\lambda = 2$.
    (b) The points at which a Poisson distribution function with parameter 3 attains the value 0.1, 0.25, 0.5, 0.75, 0.9, 0.99.
    (c) The values of the parameter $p$ in a geometric distribution of $X$ that give $P[X \geq 5] \geq 1/2 \geq P[X \geq 6]$

20. A drug firm wishes to install a management information system in order to perform extensive statistical testing of drug information. In order to be timely and of use in experimentation planning, the programs and data base must be rapidly accessible by the various laboratory testing groups. Discuss the structure and content of a data base, development of programs, and implementation with hardware.

21. A component for an earth resource satellite is being designed. As part of the design phase, the testing layout must be examined and specified. The cost of a component is small if at least 100 copies are made; 10 will be needed with 2 being installed in each of five satellites. Then 40 additional copies are needed as spares. There are four types of tests that must be performed independently. Each component is tested until failure under a set of conditions. Describe how the testing could be carried out and discuss how inference can be made on the distribution of life length under each set of conditions.

# 6

# SIMULATION AND QUEUING THEORY

## 6.1 Introduction

In the preceding chapters we have examined problems in scheduling and planning. Although these situations appeared complex, they are relatively simple compared to more ill-defined problems in the same areas of operations research. Suppose, as an example, that we wish to assign and route empty railroad cars from storage yards to demand points. There could be several objective functions based on such goals as the maximization of the number of cars assigned; the minimization of total travel time; and the minimization of engine, switching, and crew times. These would be conflicting because the optimal solution and feasible region would depend on the objective function employed and which of the other factors become constraints.

Another problem involves investment selection. Here a model must be constructed to reflect market averages, corporate profits and sales, industry behavior, and other factors along with historical information in performance. The problem becomes so complex with these factors that the model would normally be employed to test strategies under a variety of assumptions. This is one example of sensitivity analysis and provides a user of the model with some idea of relationships between many ill-defined, fuzzy quantities.

The examples above provide insight into the use of modeling in complex situations where there is no known complete analytical approach. Simulation is the process of defining, constructing, and using such a model of an operations system. Simulation can assist in the determination of underlying relationships between variables, analysis of tradeoffs between strategies, and solution of complex scheduling and allocation problems.

Because simulation is oriented toward complex situations, there is less emphasis on obtaining an "optimal" solution. As in some integer programming and network problems, simulation can assist in deriving operationally optimal solutions. Thus, our discussion of simulation must be viewed from a nonalgorithmic standpoint. There are no simplex- or branch and bound-type algorithms in simulation, although simulation can involve operations research methods such as these.

Having defined the reason for and benefits from simulation as well as properties it fails to possess, some of its applications can be considered. Simulation has been employed in large-scale scheduling, production, and planning. Simulation languages have been specially developed for general applications. These languages are gradually becoming as important as FORTRAN IV is to scientific applications. Some of the common simulation languages are explored in this chapter along with applications of simulation. The use of simulation has grown to the extent that there are annual simulation conferences where papers are presented on theory, standards, and applications. These conferences attract people from universities, government, and businesses and are held in addition to sessions in simulation at operations research and statistical society meetings.

Construction of a simulation model is of critical importance because of the need to fit the operations system environment being modeled. The next section is concerned with specific steps in this process.

Having constructed a model, we wish to know if it reflects the behavior of the operations system accurately. Secondly, it must be sufficiently flexible and usable so that the model can be employed in tradeoffs between alternatives or general system analysis tasks.

Validation here assumes the program embodying the model is working so that validation of the model is the concern. Validation of a model depends on the system being considered. A vague, ill-defined system such as the economic activities of a nation is difficult to evaluate since the model, to be reasonable, would have many underlying assumptions and simplifications. In that case several historical cases would have to be considered by the model. The results would then be compared to events and to consistency with the economic theories relating to the assumptions. The assumptions must be at least related to the operations system. This analysis not only must be for assumptions taken singly but also must be taken in combinations to reveal inconsistencies. The model runs may also reveal other assumptions that evolved without being explicity stated.

For a more specific system such as a production line, inventory system, or scheduling problem, past data is available along with timings on average completion time, production levels, usage of raw materials, and service and arrival times. This data can be processed using the model. Goodness-of-fit procedures could be employed to compare the distribution of goods produced and times. Attention must be paid to the selection of data for validation. It must in the "normal operating range" of the system so that it accurately reflects the physical behavior of the facility. Validation is discussed in more detail in References on p. 207.

Suppose now that a model has been developed and validated. Another step is to make sure that the model is easily usable under varying circumstances. This includes easy input and output for the user, user manuals that can be rapidly understood, and report formats that are sufficiently comprehensive. The input format can be in a logically arranged card format that can be entered by cards or through a CRT (cathode-ray tube) or other terminal for remote use. Through a minicomputer a user can input information on the CRT screen, which is then stored on a cassette tape. After entry of all items, teleprocessing can begin to transmit the data for processing.

In using the model the user must be aware of the results needed in terms of quantity. In statistical terms and for statistical analysis a sufficient sample size is necessary. Another use of statistics is regression analysis to determine the effects of values of specific parameters or a probability distribution of input data to the simulation.

Not only must output reports present summary information on the activities of the model but also they should have the option to produce detailed listings of tables and parameters for diagnostic checking of the program itself as well as the model logic. The reports should provide summaries and in addition should give statistical and economic analysis of the results. This would allow the user to test hypotheses by setting up additional runs and considering trends in output.

The user documentation is important because of the complexity of the model and the range of various applications. In previous chapters we have considered a variety of operations research methods and programs. Simulation models sometimes compare in complexity to management information systems. Although not as general purpose as data management systems, simulation models may be required to serve a number of users including engineers, financial advisors, and marketing personnel. Documentation must encompass the detailed inputs and outputs along with program capabilities to do error checking. Descriptions and analyses of intermediate data must be detailed so that if the hardware configuration changes, the program can be modified without undue effort. Programs are available that give a flow chart of the program. This flow chart can then be annotated and incorporated into the documentation. Documentation should extend to the source code with comment statements that describe the variables, arrays, tables, and algorithms of the program.

Having discussed how we check out, use, and document a simulation model, we are now prepared to consider how it is constructed and what its constituent parts are. Subsection 6.2.1 discusses nonprobabilistic simulation; Subsections 6.2.2 and 6.2.3 provide a basis for generating pseudo-random numbers for various distributions and queuing theory. The results of Subsections 6.2.1 to 6.2.3 are then combined and discussed in Subsection 6.2.4 with probabilistic simulation. Applications appear in Section 6.3. Existing simulation languages and references are examined in Section 6.4.

## 6.2 Simulation and Queuing Analysis

### 6.2.1 *Nonstochastic simulation*

*6.2.1.1. Initial Analysis of a Problem.* Suppose we are attempting to simulate the operation of a production line that makes some type of product. We first visit the production line if it exists and examine the individual steps involved at each stage to completion. The purpose of such a simulation could be first to model the existing system and then to study the effects of adding or deleting machinery, manpower, or other resources or of reassigning priorities if different stages require the same production step. The steps in the production line might include milling, grinding, drilling, cleaning, shaping, stamping, dipping, painting, or performing other processes. For each of these steps there is the unfinished product or part of the product as input. Typically, it would be positioned and then some operation performed. This operation could involve additional parts or subassemblies such as bolts, paint, or a printed circuit. After the operation is completed, the product is removed and shipped to the next stage. This processing continues until the finished product is produced. This product does not have to be a complete, standing usable item such as an automobile but could be a subassembly or component such as a battery, tire, or transmission.

In some factories, inventories are sufficient so that raw materials can be made available at will. In these situations, arrival of raw materials and subassemblies are nonrandom. If processing times at each stage are also fixed, then the time to "service" a product at a given stage is fixed. These assumptions will be removed in later discussions after this subsection.

Major decisions are needed prior to the construction of the model as to the degree of flexibility desired and the detail necessary in the model. More detail will require more data collection, perhaps longer program execution times, and sometimes less accuracy. The reduced accuracy can result from statistical error, incorrect measurement, or the omission of a process step. This is not to say that detail is not needed; rather, attention must be paid to the detail necessary. The proper level of detail can be characterized as the minimum amount necessary to satisfy the purposes of the simulation and yet still provide the necessary realism.

Having selected the level of detail, the next step is to collect information on processing times, delays, and the flow of parts in the production line. The processing and delay times can be measured by statistical sampling procedures. Using results of Chapter 5, the mean times of such samples could be used as the processing and other times. Later, the simulation model could be run repeatedly with varying processing times to find bounds on the time needed to process a certain number of items.

*6.2.1.2. Construction of a Simulation Model.* Having collected the basic information and constructed a system flow of parts, the next

**172 / Simulation and Queuing Theory**

step is to begin the construction of the simulation model. One method of constructing such a model is to use one of the simulation languages in Section 6.4 or References. The model would be constructed using the user manual and language documentation. Because we wish to consider an actual simulation program, we shall assume that a decision has been made to construct the model in a nonsimulation language such as FORTRAN IV.

Suppose the product system flow is given as shown in Fig. 6-1.

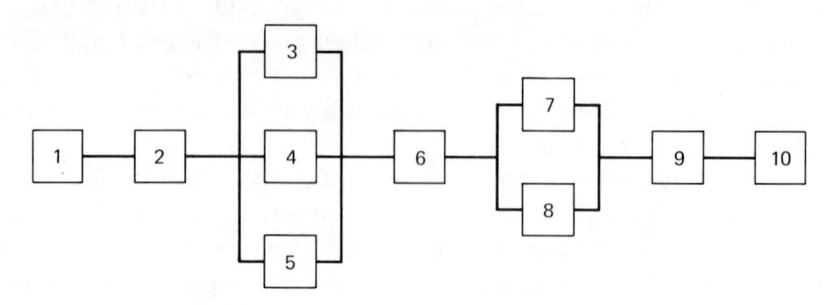

**Figure 6-1.** Sample system flow.

There the flow of parts is from left to right so that we begin at node 1 and end at node 10. Node 1 is the first processing step. Nodes 2, 6, and 9 are conveyers to move materials between successive stages. For example, node 2 moves the output of node 1 to one of nodes 3, 4, or 5. Nodes 3, 4, and 5 are in parallel to each other as are nodes 7 and 8. In an operations sense this means that nodes 3, 4, and 5 (7 and 8) accomplish the same task. These nodes could be drill presses, paint machines, etc. We should keep in mind that the nodes in parallel need not have the same mean time to complete a processing.

Now for each node and each type of part we have a mean processing time and a priority level for processing. Node 1 may, in addition, have a mean arrival rate to get the production line started. Before considering how we simulate the production line, we should briefly examine the input structure. We shall assume the program will be constructed on a terminal using a time-sharing system. For a batch-processing system, data cards are put in and then accessed by I/O statements after dimensioning the various arrays needed in the simulation.

A sample input format is shown in Fig. 6-2.

This input is arranged so that the program asks the user for input and types a question mark. The user then responds with an input response.

ENTER THE NUMBER OF NODES FOR THIS RUN.

? 10

ENTER THE NUMBER OF JOB TYPES.

? 1

FOR EACH OF THE 10 NODES AND FOR EACH JOB TYPE

　　　ENTER THE ARRIVAL RATE, PROCESSING TYPE, AND

PRIORITY NUMBER

NODE

1 - ? 1., 1., 2

2 - ? .9, 3

3 - ? 1.5, 1

4 - ? 1.6, 1

5 - ? 1.9, 1

6 - ? .1, 4

7 - ? 1, 2

8 - ? 1, 2

9 - ? .5, 6

10 - ? 2, 1

ENTER THE PATH FOR EACH JOB TYPE

JOB TYPE 1? 1 * 2 +3 4 5 * 6 * 7 8 * 9 * 10

ENTER THE NUMBER OF CONVEYER MODULES

? 1

FOR EACH CONVEYER MODULE, GIVE THE NODES

WHICH COMPRISE THE MODULE

MODULE NUMBER 1? 2, 6, 9

ENTER THE TIME DESIRED FOR SIMULATION

? 10

DO YOU WISH TO HAVE INTERMEDIATE

OUTPUT FOR ERROR CHECKING (ENTER YES OR NO)?

? NO

Figure 6-2. Sample input format.

If the user is satisfied with his input, he depresses carriage return and the input is acted on by the program. Most such programs would have the capability to perform error checking. For example, if a letter was entered when a number was required, the program would respond by asking for the input again. The actual means of entry will depend on the type of terminal device and system.

In the input in Fig. 6-2, we first entered the number of nodes. This then initialized the program to request information on nodes for the proper numbers of nodes. The number of job types is requested to initialize arrays for input format. The basic input is then requested for each node. For each node we need to put in the arrival rate of outside inputs (in this case only at node 1) and for each job type the processing time and priority are needed. Although the processing time has been discussed before, some discussion of priorities is necessary. In our priority system the higher the number, the higher the priority. Now for the nodes that are not conveyer modules, priorities in this example do not matter (why?). If a number of jobs or parts are waiting for processing at a given node and they possess the same priority, then the job that arrived first will be processed first. To summarize, each node processes the highest priority job with ties being resolved by first arrival. This priority system is merely an example and should not be taken as the only one possible.

For each job type, we enter the network path that the job type follows. In this example, we enter 1 and then a space and asterisk to indicate that node 1 and the remainder of the path are in series. Entries continue until we encounter a part of the system in parallel. Nodes 3, 4, and 5 are in parallel and so no asterisk is placed between 3, 4, or 5. Similar remarks hold for nodes 7 and 8. Therefore, asterisks are used to offset series modules of nodes in the system.

The next inputs relate to conveyor nodes. The program requests the number of such nodes for initialization and then the user must input the nodes that serve for each conveyer node. In this example, nodes 2, 6, and 9 are separate conveyers. If these nodes were the same conveyer, then the priority arrangement for these nodes is of importance because of this. If the highest priority was assigned to node 2 or 6, it is conceivable and in fact highly likely that no units would be produced since the conveyer would never be able to move jobs from nodes 7 and 8 to node 10. This is the motivation for giving the highest priority to node 9 and the lowest to node 2. In that way, jobs will enter the system and be assured of ultimate completion.

Simulation and Queuing Analysis / 175

The final input is the desired length of time for the simulation run. In this example, 10 units of time were entered.

The program is storing these inputs in arrays as they become available. For example, each node can have an associated matrix where rows are job types and columns are arrival times, processing times, and priorities. Paths for each job type can be stored as vectors. A conveyer module comprising several nodes can have an associated vector whose entries are the node numbers.

*6.2.1.3. Master Event List and Example.* In execution the program must advance time and update tables and events to reflect the processing in the operations system. An easy way to perform this is to work from a table or list. Because this is the major means of checking events, we shall call this list the *master event list*. It will keep track of everything that is going on in the system. A row entry in the master event list would correspond to an event of single job or product of a given job type. The column information for event I contains the following information:

M1 (I) — node where event is going next
M2 (I) — time for happening of event I
M3 (I) — node at which event I is located
M4 (I) — job type of event I
M5 (I) — number of event that is predecessor to I

At the beginning of program execution, the master event list is empty and all six of the variables above are initialized at zero.

We begin the simulation by looking for the first event for the master event list. Since no activity is going on at any nodes, the first event will be the arrival of a job at node 1. For this event we have

| Job | Event | M1 | M2 | M3 | M4 | M5 |
|-----|-------|----|------|----|----|----|
| 1 | 1 | 1 | 1.001 | 0 | 1 | 0 |

This indicates that a job is arriving at node 1 (M1(1) = 1). The job will arrive at time 1 + current time. For convenience we begin with current time (CURR) set equal to a small positive number (0.001). The job type is 1 (M4(1) = 1). Since it is not at M3 yet (CURR

= 0.001), M3(1) = 0 and M5(1) = 0. Now having constructed the first entry in the master event list, we look for what can happen next. We know that the first job will be completed at node 1 at time 1.001 + 1 = 2.001. A job will arrive at node 1 at the same time. No other events can occur between 1.001 and 2.001 so that the current time should be advanced to 2.001 and two entries put into the master event list.

| Job | Event | M1 | M2 | M3 | M4 | M5 |
|-----|-------|----|----|----|----|----|
| 1 | 1 | 1 | 1.001 | 0 | 1 | 0 |
| 1 | 2 | 2 | 2.001 | 1 | 1 | 1 |
| 2 | 3 | 1 | 2.001 | 0 | 1 | 0 |

We now look at our master event list and see what event can occur next. We see that node 2 is a conveyer module that is unoccupied (why?). This module can transfer the first job from node 1 to one of nodes 3, 4, or 5. Since these are all idle, processing would be fastest at node 3. The time for transfer plus CURR is 2.001 + 0.9 = 2.901. Now a new job will arrive at node 1 at time 2.001 + 1 = 3.001 and the second job will finish at node 1 at time 3.001. Therefore, we enter the conveyer module action in the master event list to get the following list.

| Job | Event | M1 | M2 | M3 | M4 | M5 |
|-----|-------|----|----|----|----|----|
| 1 | 1 | 1 | 1.001 | 0 | 1 | 0 |
| 1 | 2 | 2 | 2.001 | 1 | 1 | 1 |
| 2 | 3 | 1 | 2.001 | 0 | 1 | 0 |
| 1 | 4 | 3 | 2.901 | 2 | 1 | 2 |

The next step is to move CURR to 3.001 when the next events can occur. Doing this we obtain the following master event list.

| Job | Event | M1 | M2 | M3 | M4 | M5 |
|-----|-------|----|----|----|----|----|
| 1 | 1 | 1 | 1.001 | 0 | 1 | 0 |
| 1 | 2 | 2 | 2.001 | 1 | 1 | 1 |
| 2 | 3 | 1 | 2.001 | 0 | 1 | 0 |
| 1 | 4 | 3 | 2.901 | 2 | 1 | 2 |
| 2 | 5 | 2 | 3.001 | 1 | 1 | 3 |
| 3 | 6 | 1 | 3.001 | 0 | 1 | 0 |

Now we look at those events still active in the master event list (4 to 6) and find the next time that an event will occur. Job 1, which is event 4, will finish at $2.901 + 1.5 = 4.401$. The third job will finish at node 1 at 4.001 at the same time a new job arrives. The second job finishes at 2 at time 3.901. We advance time to 3.901 and construct the sublist.

| Job | Event | M1 | M2 | M3 | M4 | M5 |
|---|---|---|---|---|---|---|
| 1 | 4 | 3 | 2.901 | 2 | 1 | 2 |
| 2 | 5 | 2 | 3.001 | 1 | 1 | 3 |
| 3 | 6 | 1 | 3.001 | 0 | 1 | 0 |
| 2 | 7 | 4 | 3.901 | 2 | 1 | 5 |

Next we advance to 4.001 to obtain

| Job | Event | M1 | M2 | M3 | M4 | M5 |
|---|---|---|---|---|---|---|
| 1 | 4 | 3 | 2.901 | 2 | 1 | 2 |
| 2 | 5 | 2 | 3.001 | 1 | 1 | 3 |
| 3 | 6 | 1 | 3.001 | 0 | 1 | 0 |
| 2 | 7 | 4 | 3.901 | 2 | 1 | 5 |
| 4 | 8 | 1 | 4.001 | 0 | 1 | 0 |
| 3 | 9 | 2 | 4.001 | 1 | 1 | 6 |

As can easily be seen, the situation is becoming more complex. There are four jobs in the system. Job 2 was assigned to node 4 because it would complete the job earliest since node 3 is busy until time $2.901 + 1.5 = 4.401$. Job 1 will be conveyed to node 7 at time 4.501. Job 3 will be conveyed at time $4.001 + 0.9 = 4.901$. Job 4 will move to node 2 at time $4.001 + 1 = 5.001$, which is the same time that job 5 will enter the system. Advancing time to 5.001, the master event list appears as follows.

| Job | Event | M1 | M2 | M3 | M4 | M5 |
|---|---|---|---|---|---|---|
| 2 | 7 | 4 | 3.901 | 2 | 1 | 5 |
| 4 | 8 | 1 | 4.001 | 0 | 1 | 0 |
| 3 | 9 | 2 | 4.001 | 1 | 1 | 6 |
| 1 | 10 | 6 | 4.401 | 3 | 1 | 4 |
| 1 | 11 | 7 | 4.501 | 6 | 1 | 10 |
| 3 | 12 | 3 | 4.901 | 2 | 1 | 6 |
| 4 | 13 | 2 | 5.001 | 1 | 1 | 8 |
| 5 | 14 | 1 | 5.001 | 0 | 1 | 0 |

Notice that job 3 goes to node 3 since job 1 has previously been completed and node 3 has the fastest completion time. Proceeding in this same vein, we can continue to advance CURR to the next event and update the master event list. For 10 units of simulation time we obtain the master event list for M2 from 4.501 to 10 as shown in Table 6-1.

In programming this model we must be careful to check that all possible events are considered. Updating must be precise so that times are correct and no jobs are lost. Also, with each event, M1 must be constructed from the path array for the given job type. The output of the program should provide details on the activities at each of the nodes, including the number of jobs produced, the number of jobs waiting, and idle time for each node. This would be done for each job type. This output for the example above is an exercise that the reader should definitely perform.

Specific questions concerning the example appear in Problems at the close of the chapter. Some general remarks can be made on these events. First, node 5 is not used at all. If we ran the simulation time for a much longer period and this continued to hold, then we could remove this piece of equipment.

A second remark is that node 10 is a bottleneck. By simulation time 10, node 10 has processed the first job and is still working on the second. Meanwhile, jobs 3 and 4 are waiting in line or are queued up for service. This bottleneck at node 10 can be resolved by inserting other machines parallel to node 10 or by replacing node 10 by a machine with a faster processing time.

*6.2.1.4. Comments on Simulation.* These remarks reveal some of the applications of simulation. Bottlenecks and idle machinery can be detected. Variation in process times and priorities can be evaluated along with modifications in network structure.

The routing logic of selection of alternative nodes is based on observing where a job can be processed first. In a complex situation we need a network algorithm to find the optimal choice based on data on the status of each node. A modified shortest path method could be used to select the next node for a job.

There are other implementation considerations beyond routing. First, a great deal of effort is required to perform updates of the various tables. The search for the next event is much less time consuming. The lists and arrays consume substantial blocks of core, which in FORTRAN must be dimensioned in advance. Thus, if the operations

Table 6-1. SAMPLE MASTER EVENT LIST

| Job | Event | M1 | M2 | M3 | M4 | M5 |
|---|---|---|---|---|---|---|
| 2 | 7 | 4 | 3.901 | 2 | 1 | 5 |
| 1 | 11 | 7 | 4.501 | 6 | 1 | 10 |
| 3 | 12 | 3 | 4.901 | 2 | 1 | 6 |
| 4 | 13 | 2 | 5.001 | 1 | 1 | 8 |
| 5 | 14 | 1 | 5.001 | 0 | 1 | 0 |
| 1 | 15 | 9 | 5.501 | 7 | 1 | 10 |
| 2 | 16 | 6 | 5.501 | 4 | 1 | 7 |
| 2 | 17 | 7 | 5.601 | 6 | 1 | 16 |
| 4 | 18 | 3 | 5.901 | 2 | 1 | 8 |
| 1 | 19 | 10 | 6.001 | 9 | 1 | 15 |
| 5 | 20 | 2 | 6.001 | 1 | 1 | 14 |
| 6 | 21 | 1 | 6.001 | 0 | 1 | 0 |
| 3 | 22 | 6 | 6.401 | 3 | 1 | 12 |
| 3 | 23 | 8 | 6.501 | 6 | 1 | 22 |
| 2 | 24 | 9 | 6.601 | 7 | 1 | 17 |
| 5 | 25 | 4 | 6.901 | 2 | 1 | 20 |
| 7 | 26 | 0 | 7.001 | 0 | 1 | 0 |
| 6 | 27 | 2 | 7.001 | 1 | 1 | 21 |
| 2 | 28 | 10 | 7.101 | 9 | 1 | 24 |
| 4 | 29 | 6 | 7.401 | 3 | 1 | 18 |
| 4 | 30 | 7 | 7.501 | 6 | 1 | 29 |
| 3 | 31 | 9 | 7.501 | 8 | 1 | 23 |
| 6 | 32 | 3 | 7.901 | 2 | 1 | 27 |
| 1 | 33 | — | 8.001 | 10 | 1 | 19 |
| 3 | 34 | 10 | 8.001 | 9 | 1 | 31 |
| 7 | 35 | 2 | 8.001 | 1 | 1 | 26 |
| 8 | 36 | 1 | 8.001 | 0 | 1 | 0 |
| 4 | 37 | 9 | 8.501 | 7 | 1 | 30 |
| 5 | 38 | 6 | 8.501 | 4 | 1 | 25 |
| 5 | 39 | 7 | 8.601 | 6 | 1 | 38 |
| 7 | 40 | 4 | 8.901 | 2 | 1 | 35 |
| 4 | 41 | 10 | 9.001 | 9 | 1 | 37 |
| 8 | 42 | 2 | 9.001 | 1 | 1 | 36 |
| 9 | 43 | 1 | 9.001 | 0 | 1 | 0 |
| 6 | 44 | 6 | 9.401 | 3 | 1 | 32 |
| 6 | 45 | 7 | 9.501 | 6 | 1 | 44 |
| 5 | 46 | 9 | 9.601 | 7 | 1 | 39 |
| 8 | 47 | 3 | 9.901 | 2 | 1 | 42 |

system is expanded in scope or detail, a substantial amount of reprogramming may be necessary. Buffer areas in core and temporary storage on disk may be necessary.

The simulation model above marched in time from event to event. This is one of the two time-event methods of advancing in time. The other method is to advance time by some increment and then enter all events that occurred during the intervening time interval.

The example above was incomplete in that the model was not run for a sufficient time to be in a steady state condition. To be realistic, we would run the model of any operations system until the initial, starting conditions had diminished or dampened in effect. Tradeoff analysis and alternative evaluation should be done only for the steady state case unless the transient case is of major interest.

### 6.2.2 *Pseudo-random and random number generation*

*6.2.2.1. Random Number Generation.* In some production and scheduling problems customer arrivals and/or servicing is random in the sense that arrivals of customers have such extensive variation that the model described in Subsection 6.2.1 is not realistic. Suppose as an example that customers can arrive at 10-minute intervals and that the number of customers arriving at any one time can be 0, 1, 2, 3, 4, or 5. Also, it is believed that each of these is equally likely. In the context of probability we have an experiment with six possible outcomes, each of which has a probability of $\frac{1}{6}$ of occurring.

How can we handle this situation of random arrivals? Manually, we could take a fair die and say that if a 1, 2, 3, 4, or 5 appear on a toss, then that number of customers arrives. If a 6 appears, no customers arrive. This is fine for manual work with only a few experiments. Obviously this method is unsuitable for most realistic operations systems. We need to develop a method to handle the generation of random numbers inside a computer. A random number here is a number generated by a statistical experiment. In statistical terms we need to construct an array or sequence of independent observations of a random variable with a known distribution. In the literature this is called *Monte Carlo sampling*.

In a realistic sense we know that truly random generation is difficult and theoretically impossible to achieve. This is because no device or experiment is perfectly random. This should not be cause for despair since we can develop generators that statistically appear to be random. An example of a statistical test for randomness was the runs test of the previous chapter. The RAND Corporation produced a large volume of random digits.[25] This can be used for manual work.

Simulation and Queuing Analysis / 181

Since we cannot generate truly random numbers, we shall attempt to generate pseudo-random numbers that pass the statistical tests for randomness. We shall review one of these methods here. Generally, pseudo-random number generators are available through simulation languages for various distributions. If a FORTRAN or other non-simulation language based program is being used, number generators are available through utility programs in the computer program library accessible by the operating system.

Generation methods depend for their appearance of randomness on their initial starting values input prior to generation. These often are based on the computer machinery properties such as word size.

*6.2.2.2. Lehmer Congruential Method.* The Lehmer congruential method is based upon number theory concepts. Let $a$, $b$, and $c$ be three integers. If $c$ divides the quantity $a - b$ without a remainder, then this is denoted by

$$a \equiv b \pmod{c}$$

This means that $a$ is congruent to $b$ modulo (mod $c$). We say that integers $f$ and $g$ are relatively prime if the only positive integer that divides both $f$ and $g$ without remainder is 1. Symbolically, this is expressed by

$$(f, g) = 1$$

One of the properties of congruences involves composition. For $x$ and $c$, suppose integers $\{a_i\}$ are a sequence of integers defined by

$$a_1 \equiv xa_0 \pmod{c} \tag{6.1}$$

and

$$a_{n+1} \equiv xa_n \pmod{c} \quad \text{for } n \geq 1 \tag{6.2}$$

This means, for example, that $c$ divides $a_1 - xa_0$ and $c$ divides $a_2 - xa_1$. From this it follows that $c$ divides $xa_1 - x^2a_0$ and $a_2 - xa_1$ and hence divides $a_2 - xa_1 + xa_1 - x^2a_0 = a_2 - x^2a_0$ (why?). Therefore,

$$a_2 \equiv x^2 a_0 \pmod{c}$$

182 / Simulation and Queuing Theory

In general, we can prove by induction on the subscript of $a_i$ that $a_{n+1} \equiv x^n a_0$ (mod $c$).

The Lehmer congruential method is based on Eq. (6.1) and (6.2). The pseudo-random sequence is $\{a_i\}$. Remaining is the task of selecting $a_0$, $c$ and $x$ so that the sequence appears statistically to be random. This implies that the sequence $\{a_i\}$ should not repeat itself since repetition would indicate nonrandomness (explain this). To avoid repetition it is desirable that $(x, c) = 1$ and $(a_0, c) = 1$. Usually the word length of the computer is chosen for $c$. Thus, for a 32-bit word machine, $c$ is 32. A summary for various word lengths appears in Table 6-2. The value of $x$ is either $8I \pm 3$ where $I$ is an

**Table 6-2.** INITIAL VALUES FOR PSEUDO-RANDOM GENERATION USING THE LEHMER CONGRUENTIAL METHOD

| Word Length of Machine | $c$ | $x$ | $a_0$ |
|---|---|---|---|
| $2^k$ | $2^k$ | $8I \pm 3$ | Any odd integer |
| $10^m$ | $10^m$ | $x = +(3, 11, 13, 19)$ (mod 200) | Any odd integer and $1 = (a_0, 5)$ |

integer or an integer congruent to $\pm 3$, 11, 13, or 19 modulo 200. There are other values besides these and these appear in Mize and Cox[9] along with a more detailed development. Integer $a_0$ is odd for both types of word size. In addition, for word sizes of the value $10^m$ $a_0$ is relatively prime to 5.

As an example, suppose $c$ is 32, $x$ is 5 ($8 \cdot 1 - 3$), and $a_0$ is 3. Then we obtain

$$a_1 = 15 \text{ (mod 32)}$$

Now $a_1$ must be any integer such that $a_1 - 15$ can be divided by 32. Some candidates are $-17$, 47, and $-49$. Suppose we let $a_1 = 47$. Next we have

$$a_2 = 5(47) \text{ (mod 32)}$$

and set $a_2 = 11$ since 32 divides $11 - 235$. We continue and obtain a sequence

3, 47, 11, 23, 19, 31, 57, 93, 81, 53, 73

### 6.2.2.3. Statistical Tests of Randomness.

The example above represents a pseudo-random generation that purports to be selected from a uniform distribution on the integers 1, 2, ..., 100. We say *purports* since we must now consider how to test statistically for randomness. The statistical tests for randomness can be drawn from the preceding chapter. For a sequence of integers generated by some pseudo-random generator we can use the $\chi^2$ goodness of fit to test whether these appear statistically to be close to numbers generated from a uniform distribution. If we perform such a test at a selected $\alpha$ significance level and it is not rejected, then we do not reject the hypothesis of randomness.

As an example, suppose $\alpha = 0.05$ and we wish to test for randomness with the data of the Lehmer method example. For subintervals we shall select [0, 20), [20, 40), [40, 60), [60, 80), [80, 100]. The probability of drawing a number that is in one subinterval is $\frac{1}{5}$ for a uniform distribution. Now the sequence has 11 numbers so that the expected number of observations in each subinterval is $\frac{11}{5}$ (11 · $\frac{1}{5}$). Using the $\chi^2$ test, we compute

$$Q_1 = \sum_{i=1}^{5} \frac{(m_i - \frac{11}{5})^2}{\frac{11}{5}} = 1.168$$

Here $m_i$ is the actual number of terms in the sequence that fell into the *i*th subinterval. From the $\chi^2$ table for 4 degrees of freedom and $\alpha = 0.05$, we find that we should reject the hypothesis if $Q_1 > 9.488$. Since $9.488 > 1.168$, we do not reject $H$.

The significance level, subintervals, and number of terms are interdependent and dependent on the actual situation. Note that we must take into account conditions such as sample size for a valid statistical test as well as for simulation.

### 6.2.2.4. General Distributions.

To generalize, we know that a distribution function for a random variable $X$ is defined by

$$F(y) = P[X \leq y]$$

Suppose we set $z$ equal to $F(y)$. Now since $F$ is a nondecreasing function from 0 to 1, we can define $F^{-1}$ by

$$F^{-1}(z) = \min \{q : F(q) = z\}$$

That is, $F^{-1}(z)$ is the smallest quantity whose functional value is $z$. Now set $Z = F(X)$ so that $Z$ is a random variable. Its distribution is given by

$$P[Z < z] = P[F(X) \leq z]$$

and

$$P[F(X) \leq z] = P[X < F^{-1}(z)] = F(F^{-1}(z)) = z$$

for $0 \leq z \leq 1$. Therefore, $Z$ is a uniform random variable on $[0, 1]$. Now we can generate uniform pseudo-random numbers and by dividing by 100 or some other scale factor the range can be $[0, 1]$. Using the transformation above we can use these pseudo-random numbers and obtain a sequence for any other distribution.

For our earlier example we first scale the sequence to obtain 0.03, 0.47, 0.11, 0.23, 0.19, 0.31, 0.57, 0.93, 0.81, 0.53, 0.73. If we wish a pseudo-random sequence from an exponential distribution on $[0, \infty)$ with mean 1, we solve.

$$P[X < b_1] = \int_0^{b_1} e^{-x}\, dx = 0.03$$

to obtain $b_1 = \ln(0.97)$.

In general, we solve for $b_i$ from

$$P[X < b_i] = \int_0^{b_i} e^{-x}\, dx = a_i$$

An analogous procedure would be followed for other distributions.

Frequently in simulation it is necessary to deal with several random variables simultaneously. For example, if there are several service people at a counter and the number of arrivals to all servers exceeds some number, a new server might be called to reduce waiting times. Other examples would involve more complex interactions between variables.

For sums of random variables we can employ separate starting values with a generator and then use the method outlined above to get observations on the variables desired. For example, if one random variable was normal with mean 1 and variance 1 and another had a mean of 1.5 and variance of 2, then we could use the generated sequences for a uniform distribution and the above procedure to find a sequence for each of these. The combining of variables assuming independence could be quite easy since the sum of two independent normal random variables is normal with mean $1 + 1.5 = 2.5$ and variance $2 + 1 = 3$. Similar properties hold for other known distributions and are discussed in References in Chapter 5. Combinations of random variables in queuing theory will be taken up in Subsection 6.2.3.

### 6.2.3 Queuing theory

In Subsection 6.2.1 we examined a production line system where the service times and times between arrivals were fixed. Often this is not the case. Arrivals and service times are random variables. If we could derive expressions for factors involving the random variables, then a sequence could be generated using the results of Subsection 6.2.2. This subsection will deal with queuing theory and analysis. Several detailed texts on queuing analysis appear in References on p. 207. These texts present results in more theoretical detail than we shall use here.

Analysis of queues means the study of waiting lines. People or commodities (customers) arrive at certain places to be serviced in some way. After servicing one unit, the server handles the next customer. The process continues in this way. Since waiting lines and servicing play such a prominent role in our lives, there has been much research into queueing problems.

A queuing system can be viewed as a system in which a single input of customers arrives at the system from outside sources. The customers then enter a queue where they await service. The customers are served by some apparatus. The output of the system is the served customers. To describe the system we need to detail the number and rate at which customers arrive for service, the capacity of the queue, the logic for selecting customers for service, the number of servers, and the length of time it takes for service.

Let $N_t$ be the number of arrivals at the system between the start time 0 and $t$. Thus, if a customer enters the system at time $t'$ and the previous customer entered at time $t(< t')$, we would have

$$N_{t'} = N_t + 1$$

A sample graph of $t$ versus $N_t$ appears in Figure 6-3. $N_t$ is a counting function and has the property that

$$N_0 = 0$$

$N_t$ is a random variable dependent on time and the rate of arrivals to the system.

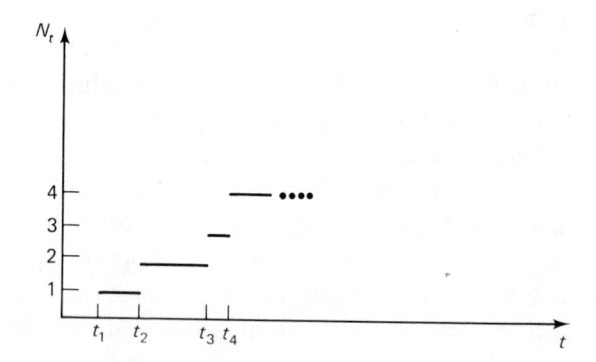

Figure 6-3. Graph of a sample counting function.

A common assumption in queuing analysis is that customers arrive independently for service. Another common assumption is that the probability of an arrival in an interval $[t, t + \Delta t]$ is the same regardless of the value. If a sequence of random variables $\{N_t\}$ has this property, then $\{N_t\}$ is said to have *stationary increments*. Another assumption is that if $[t, t + \Delta t]$ is a very short interval ($\Delta t$ is very small), then the probability of a single arrival is approximately proportional to the length of the interval. This is expressed by

$$P[N_{t+\Delta t} - N_t = 1] = \lambda \Delta t + o(\Delta t) \qquad (6.3)$$

and

$$P[N_{t+\Delta t} - N_t > 1] = o(\Delta t) \qquad (6.4)$$

where $\lambda$ is a constant and $o(\Delta t)$ is a function of $\Delta t$ with the property

$$\frac{o(\Delta t)}{\Delta t} \to 0 \quad \text{as} \quad \Delta t \to 0$$

These assumptions and conditions lead to $\{N_t\}$ being called a *Poisson counting process*. From Eq. (6.3) and (6.4) and the property of $o(\Delta t)$, it follows that the probability of no arrival is

$$P[N_{t+\Delta t} - N_t = 0] = 1 - \lambda t + o(\Delta t)$$

We now have enough information to derive the distribution of $\{N_t\}$. Let $p_k(t)$ denote the probability that $N_t$ is $K$ and let $p_{ij}(t, t+\Delta t)$ be defined by

$$p_{ij}(t, t + \Delta t) = P[N_{t+\Delta t} = j \mid N_t = i] \tag{6.5}$$

Then because of the stationarity we have

$$p_{ij}(t, t + \Delta t) = P[N_{t+\Delta t} = j \mid N_t = i] = P[N_{t+\Delta t} - N_t = j - i]$$

and

$$p_{ij}(t, t + \Delta t) = P[N_t - N_0 = j - i] = P[N_{\Delta t} = j - i]$$
$$= p_{j-i}(\Delta t) \tag{6.6}$$

For the probability of no arrivals in $[0, t + \Delta t]$, we have

$$p_0(t + \Delta t) = P[N_{t+\Delta t} = 0] = p_0(t) p_{0,0}(\Delta t)$$

and using Eq. (6.5) and (6.6) we obtain

$$p_{0,0}(\Delta t) = 1 - \lambda t + o(\Delta t)$$

Combining the above, we can begin to obtain the derivative of $p_0$ at $t$. First, we can show

$$\frac{p_0(t + \Delta t) - p_0(t)}{\Delta t} = \frac{p_0(t)[1 - \lambda \Delta t + o(\Delta t) - 1]}{\Delta t}$$

188 / Simulation and Queuing Theory

or

$$\lim_{\Delta t \to 0} \frac{[p_0(t + t) - p_0(t)]}{\Delta t} = \lim_{\Delta t \to 0} \frac{-\lambda p_0(t) \Delta t + p_0(t) o(\Delta t)}{\Delta t}$$

Simplifying, we find

$$\frac{dp_0(t)}{dt} = -\lambda p_0(t) \qquad (6.7)$$

The solution to this differential equation is

$$p_0(t) = e^{-\lambda t}$$

so that

$$P[N_t = 0] = e^{-\lambda t} \qquad (6.8)$$

Using the identity

$$p_k(t + \Delta t) = \sum_{j=0}^{k} p_j(t) p_{jk}(\Delta t)$$

we can show that

$$P[N_t = k] = \frac{e^{-\lambda t}(\lambda t)^k}{k!} \qquad (6.9)$$

Thus, $N_t$ has a Poisson distribution ($\{N_t\}$ is then a Poisson process).

Now since $N_t$ is Poisson, we can compute the expectation of $N_t$ to obtain

$$E(N_t) = \lambda t$$

or

$$\lambda = \frac{E(N_t)}{t}$$

Having examined the number of arrivals $\{N_t\}$, we should consider the arrival times themselves. Let $T_k$ be the time of the $k$th arrival and let $F_k(t)$ be the distribution function of $T_k$. Then

$$F_k(t) = P[T_k < t]$$

is the probability that the $k$th arrival occurs at or before time $t$. This is equivalent to the number of arrivals in $[0, t]$ being at least $k$. This gives

$$F_k(t) = P[T_k \leq t] = P[N_t \geq k]$$

or

$$F_k(t) = 1 - P[N_t \leq k - 1]$$
$$= 1 - \frac{\sum_{j=0}^{k-1} e^{-\lambda t}(\lambda t)^j}{j!}$$

Let the interval between the arrival of the $(k-1)$st and $k$th customer be denoted by $D_k$ so that $D_k = T_k - T_{k-1}$. Let $G_k$ denote the distribution function of $D_k$. Now

$$G_k(t) = P[D_k \leq t] = P[T_k - T_{k-1} \leq t]$$
$$= 1 - P[T_k - T_{k-1} > t]$$

The event that $T_k - T_{k-1}$ exceeds $t$ means that no arrival occurred in the interval $[0, t]$. By stationarity it follows that

$$G_k(t) = 1 - P[N_t = 0] = 1 - e^{-\lambda t} \qquad (6.10)$$

From Eq. (6.10) it follows that the $\{D_k\}$ have the same exponential distribution with parameter $\lambda$.

From the discussion above we can characterize a Poisson process as having exponential interarrival rates and the number of arrivals as Poisson distributed. The Poisson process and the expressions obtained above can be used to obtain values for the expected number of arrivals, variance, and other properties. We should remark that this only applies to the arrivals of customers and does not reflect on the servicing of the customers. We should now consider the queuing situation as a system.

Early research of queues was based in part on studies of epidemics and population. Customers arriving for service can be viewed as births and customers who have completed service are deaths. If customers are arriving faster than the rate of service, then births exceed deaths. Preventing arrivals results in a pure death process. Conversely, providing no service is a pure birth process. We shall follow a development similar, to Hillier and Lieberman[21] and Lee.[23] More detailed descriptions appear in these sources.

To consider queues, we shall define $\lambda_n$ and $\mu_n$ positive numbers by

$\lambda_n$ expected arrival rate of customers when $n$ customers are in the system.

and

$\mu_n$ — expected service rate of customers when $n$ customers are in the system.

For most simulation applications we are interested in the state of operations systems when the model has stabilized or reached steady state. For this reason and for mathematical tractability most of our attention will be in the steady state case.

We can now use $\lambda_n$ and $\mu_n$ for considering births and deaths. Generalizing upon the linearity assumption of the Poisson process, we shall assume that the probability of exactly one arrival (or both) in the interval $[t, t + \Delta t]$ is $\lambda_n \Delta t - o(\Delta t)$ when there are $n$ customers in the system. Similarly, the probability that exactly one customer is serviced (dies) in $[t, t + \Delta t]$ with $n$ customers in the system is $\mu_n \Delta t + o(\Delta t)$. Analogously to the Poisson process, we shall assume that the probability of more than one birth or death in $[t, t + \Delta t]$ is $o(\Delta t)$. The function $o(\Delta t)$ has the same property as previously given. Let $P_n(t)$ be the probability that $n$ customers in the system at time $t$.

The probability of one arrival in $[t, t + \Delta t]$ when $n$ are in the system is $P_n(t)[\lambda_n \Delta t + o(\Delta t)]$. Similarly, the probability of one customer ending servicing when $n + 2$ are in the system is $P_{n+2}(t)$

$[\mu_{n+2} \Delta t + o(\Delta t)]$. The probability of more than one arrival or servicing is $o(\Delta t)$. The probability that no arrivals or servicings occur is

$$P_{n+1}(t)[1 - \lambda_{n+1} \Delta t - \mu_{n+1} \Delta t + o(\Delta t)]$$

(The reader should verify these probabilities). The probability that $n + 1$ customers are in the system at time $t + \Delta t$ is the sum of the probabilities above. Adding these and combining $o(\Delta t)$ terms, we obtain

$$P_{n+1}(t + \Delta t) = P_n(t)\lambda_n \Delta t + P_{n+2}(t)\mu_{n+2} \Delta t + P_{n+1}(t)$$
$$- \lambda_{n+1} P_{n+1}(t) \Delta t - \mu_{n+1} P_{n+1}(t) \Delta t + o(\Delta t) \quad (6.11)$$

We now use this to compute the derivative of $P_{n+1}$ at $t$. Doing this we obtain

$$\frac{dP_{n+1}(t)}{dt} = \lim_{\Delta t \to 0} \frac{(P_{n+1}(t + \Delta t) - P_{n+1}(t))}{\Delta t}$$
$$= \lambda_n P_n(t) + \mu_{n+2} P_{n+2}(t) - (\lambda_{n+1} + \mu_{n+1}) P_{n+1}(t)$$
$$(6.12)$$

For $n = -1$, set $\lambda_{-1} = \mu_0 = 0$ to obtain

$$\frac{dP_0(t)}{dt} = \mu_1 P_1(t) - \lambda_0 P_0(t) \quad (6.13)$$

$P_n(t)$ would be obtained for a particular case by solving these differential equations. Solution of the cases with no arrivals or no servicing are addressed in Problems on p. 209.

As we stated earlier, we are most interested in a steady state solution. Then $P_n(t)$ converges to a constant, say, $P_n$, as $t$ tends to infinity. The derivative $dP_n(t)/dt$ converges to 0. Applying this to Eq. (6.12) and (6.13) gives

$$P_1 = \frac{\lambda_0 P_0}{\mu_1}$$

and

$$P_{n+2} = \frac{\lambda_{n+1}P_{n+1} + \mu_{n+1}P_{n+1} - \lambda_n P_n}{\mu_{n+2}}$$

We can show by induction that the general term $P_n$ is given by

$$P_n = \frac{\prod_{i=0}^{n-1} \lambda_i P_0}{\prod_{i=1}^{n} \mu_i}$$

Since the sequence $\{P_n\}$ sums to unity, $P_0$ can be derived as

$$P_0 = \left( \frac{1 + \sum_{n \geqslant 1} \prod_{i=0}^{n-1} \lambda_i}{\prod_{i=1}^{n} \mu_i^{-1}} \right)^{-1}$$

We could use modified expressions and follow a similar technique to determine $\{P_n\}$ under various conditions. Some of these are sumarized in Table 6-3. Also given in this table are the expected number of customers, the expected time in the system for both queuing and service, and the expected waiting time while in a queue. Blanks in the table mean there is no simple closed expression.

The expected number of customers waiting, but not being served, can be computed as the difference of the expected number in the system and the probability that at least one customer is in the system.

The first three cases are for one server. The third case is for a fixed number of customers permitted to wait in the queue. Then $\lambda_n$ is equal to a constant $\lambda$ until there are $L$ customers in the system above which it becomes zero. This case also assumes the $\{\mu_n\}$ are all equal to a constant $\mu$.

The fourth case involves $s$ servers. Then the service rate $\mu_n$ is $n\mu$ if the number in the system does not exceed the number of servers and $s\mu$ if it does.

More complicated models can be obtained by taking account of priority traffic or having a dependence between $\lambda_n$ and $\mu_n$ and $n$ itself. These are explored in References on p. 207.

Table 6-3. QUEUING EQUATIONS

| Distribution of Number of Arrivals | Distribution of Service | $P_0$ | $P_n$ | Expected Number Customers in System | Expected Time in System | Expected Time in Queue | Other Conditions |
|---|---|---|---|---|---|---|---|
| Poisson | Exponential | $1 - \dfrac{\lambda}{\mu}$ | $\dfrac{\lambda^n}{\mu^n} P_0$ | $\dfrac{\lambda}{\mu - \lambda}$ | $\dfrac{1}{\mu - \lambda}$ | $\dfrac{\lambda}{\mu(\mu - \mu)}$ | — |
| Poisson | Any; mean $1/\mu$ and variance $\tau^2$ | $1 - \dfrac{\lambda}{\mu}$ | — | $\dfrac{1}{\mu} + \dfrac{\lambda}{\mu}$ | $\dfrac{1}{\lambda} + \dfrac{1}{\mu}$ | $\dfrac{1}{\lambda}$ | $\lambda < \mu$ |
| Poisson | Exponential | $\dfrac{(1 - \lambda/\mu)}{(1 - \lambda/\mu)^{L+1}}$ | $\left(\dfrac{\lambda}{\mu}\right)^n P_0$ | $\dfrac{\lambda}{\mu - \lambda} - \dfrac{(L+1)^{m+1}}{\mu^{m+1} - \lambda^{m+1}}$ | — | — | Only $L$ allowed in queue |
| Poisson | Exponential | $\left( \displaystyle\sum_{j=0}^{s-1} \dfrac{(\lambda/\mu)^j}{j!} + \dfrac{(\lambda/\mu)s}{s!(1 - \lambda/s\mu)} \right)^{-1}$ | $\dfrac{(\lambda/\mu)^n P_0}{n!} \quad n \leq s$ $\dfrac{(\lambda/\mu)^n P_0}{s! s^{n-s}} \quad n > s$ | $\dfrac{Q+1}{\mu}$ | $\dfrac{Q+1}{\mu}$ | $Q = \dfrac{P_0(\lambda/\mu)^{s+1}}{\lambda s (s!)(s - \lambda/\mu)^2}$ | $\lambda < s\mu$ $s$ servers |

The service philosophy we have assumed was first in/first out (FIFO). There are other more elaborate priority systems. For evaluation many require simulation since the mathematical expressions become difficult to solve. Another common queuing logic is last in/first out (LIFO). This occurs in inventory systems of nonperishable goods. A person stacking plates or storing glasses usually uses a LIFO queuing method.

Queuing in applications permits the modeling analytically of some waiting line systems without resorting to a full-scale simulation. In Subsection 6.2.4 we explore how queuing can be combined in the discrete simulation method of Subsection 6.2.1.

Application of queuing models involves the same steps as most other methods. We first must examine the operations system to see what assumptions on a model can be used. This step includes the distributions of the arrivals and service times as well as the logic as to the order in which customers are selected for service. A queuing model could be treated as a simulation model wherein the queuing equations govern the events of the model. Some questions that could be addressed by such a simulation include the number of servers and the priority arrangement for service.

### 6.2.4 *Simulation modeling*

Having discussed time–event simulation, random number generation, and queuing analysis, we are now prepared to develop models more general than that described in Subsection 6.2.1. The time–event relationship and master event list concepts will remain. Instead of having a fixed arrival, however, we shall generate arrival times using a pseudo-random number generator. In place of having fixed process times as before, we shall call upon generators to give times according to a specific distribution. Thus, the net difference between the models here and those of Subsection 6.2.1 are in the detail of allowing nondeterministic quantities.

In considering an operations system, we follow the same procedures as in Subsection 6.2.1. We identify processing steps or nodes, system inputs arriving from the outside environment, outputs of each step, and outputs of the system. The information flow and other system parameters must be understood. Understanding must be gained as to which factors can be controlled and uncontrolled in the simulation models and which variables are independent and dependent on each other. This dependence must be specified in the model definition phase as clearly as possible. This formulation stage must be carried out carefully since the entire simulation process is dependent on a clear conceptual understanding of the operations system. Classifying system components and relationships is explored in more detail in texts listed in References on p. 207-9.

In addition to specifying the system, we need to state the assumptions to be used by the simulation model. These assumptions relate to distributions of variables such as arrival rates and service times as well as conditions on relationships between variables.

As an example of a simulation model, consider the network of Subsection 6.2.1, which is repeated in Fig. 6-4. A single product type is assumed.

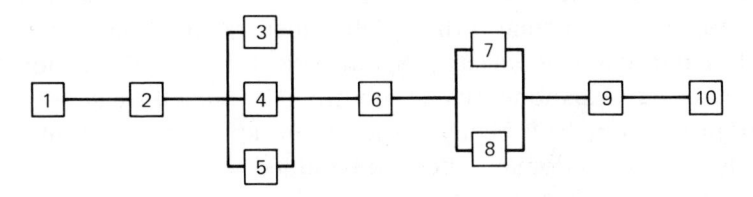

Figure 6-4. Networks of single product.

As before, nodes 2, 6, and 9 constitute conveyer modules. Nodes 3, 4, and 5 (7 and 8) are parallel servers for the jobs created by the processing at node 1. Nodes 1 and 10 are single servers. Materials, we shall assume, arrive at random at node 1 with an exponential interarrival distribution with mean $\lambda_1$. The service times for nodes 1, 3, 4, 5, 7, 8 and 10 are exponential random variables. Nodes, 2, 6, and 9 have a common exponential service time random variable. These would have to be justified based on actual data of the operations system.

The next step is to apply the results of Subsection 6.2.3 to the implementation of the simulation model. One method that could be employed for such a small network is to employ pseudo-random number generators with appropriate parameters and generate sequences for each node up to some preassigned number. Each sequence could be stored as a vector for access by the program. Then for a service or arrival time the program would not consider a deterministic fixed number but would instead access the appropriate vector for a value. The time-event part of the program would remain as in Subsection 6.2.1. For a complex network we would generate parts of the sequence as required. For parallel nodes such as 3, 4, and 5 we would look at the earliest expected time of completion rather than the fixed service time. The algorithm for finding the shortest path of a part in the network for a complex case would be based upon the expected values of the various times, and probabilistic confidence intervals could be developed to estimate earliest and latest completion times for the complete product.

For multiple products the queuing situation becomes more complex. There is no simple first in/first out queuing system but instead priorities that can cause rearrangement of queues. Rather than employ complex queuing results, the algorithm for assignment to parallel nodes can have the priority structure designed so that the model itself progresses over time with available queuing equations.

For our example we can generate arrivals by pseudo-random generators using an exponential distribution. At time 0 we generate one random number. This becomes the arrival time of the first unit. The second pseudo-random number can be added to the first to obtain the time of arrival of the second unit. We next use another pseudo-random number generator (perhaps the same method with different starting values) to generate service times for node 1. This then produces input units for node 2. Pseudo-random number generators can supply service times for each of the successive nodes. The simulation model really provides the framework and glue to control the entire model. Each node is governed by an appropriate queuing model that utilizes the pseudo-random number generators as a tool. Nodes, 3, 4, and 5 are parallel servers and hence are governed by a single queuing model if a FIFO logic is assumed and a common mean service time is appropriate. The flow is portrayed in Fig. 6-5.

Numerically we proceed as in Subsection 6.2.1. The same master event list structure can be used. Now, however, the program logic accesses different subprograms that handle the queuing for the modules comprising nodes 1; 2, 6, and 9; 3, 4, and 5; 7 and 8; and 10.

Using the queuing equations, we can compute the mean waiting time for each module of nodes. Interarrival times for arrivals at the modules other than that comprising node 1 can be obtained from statistics by running the simulation model or by using mean service rates of previous modules.

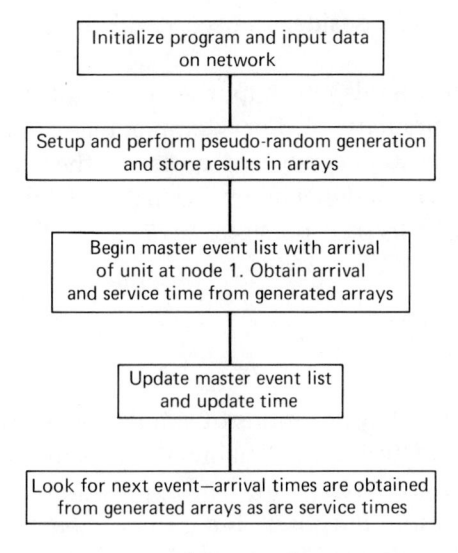

```
┌─────────────────────────────────┐
│ Initialize program and input data│
│          on network              │
└─────────────────────────────────┘
                │
┌─────────────────────────────────────┐
│ Setup and perform pseudo-random generation│
│      and store results in arrays    │
└─────────────────────────────────────┘
                │
┌─────────────────────────────────────┐
│   Begin master event list with arrival│
│   of unit at node 1. Obtain arrival │
│ and service time from generated arrays│
└─────────────────────────────────────┘
                │
┌─────────────────────────────┐
│   Update master event list  │
│      and update time        │
└─────────────────────────────┘
                │
┌──────────────────────────────────────────┐
│Look for next event—arrival times are obtained│
│ from generated arrays as are service times│
└──────────────────────────────────────────┘
```

Figure 6-5. Example program flow.

In this section the program flow is outlined in Fig. 6-5. We have considered deterministic discrete simulation random number generation, queuing, and probabilistic simulation. The same considerations hold for all simulations in that we must give attention to assumptions, distributions, uses of the model, model structure, and model validation.

An example of stochastic simulation is an inventory system where the demand of units in storage is a random variable dependent on the time between orders to replenish inventory. Suppose $T$ is the time between orders and $D(T)$ is the demand for the part in time interval of length $T$. Without examining inventory theory we shall remark that, for a particular $T$ and a demand $D(T)$, the firm incurs a cost (which may be negative) $C(T, D(T))$, which is also a function of holding costs of a unit, cost of ordering, and cost of failing to meet the demand.

To address this problem we select a given value of $T$ and generate a value of $D(T)$ using a pseudo-random number generator. The steps in Fig. 6-5 can now be followed. As time passes, the cost $C(T, D(T))$ can be computed. The master event list maintains information on demand and supply with respect to the inventory.

After processing the simulation model for various values of $T$ and $D(T)$, we can then analyze the results to find the value of $T$ that gives the lowest expected cost over the period of time desired. Analysis can also be done to consider the sensitivity of cost to the distribution of demand.

This example reveals the importance of statistical methods and their relation to simulation. For example, regression analysis can be used to detect the dependence of costs on the values of time and demand. This analysis depends on having available sufficient results so that statistical analysis is possible.

## 6.3 Applications

That the range of applications of simulation is broad is evidenced by the spectrum of topics in the annual proceedings of the Winter & Summer Simulation Conferences. The applications discussed here are not for computation purposes, but rather their goal is to provide insight into the benefits and consideration in construction simulation models.

One area of application is health care and services. This example is due to Kennedy.[31] In this case a projected 18-story medical care facility was being considered in the light of an estimated patient load double current capacity. A department of importance, due to resources consumed, is that of physical therapy. Physical therapy attempts to restore physical capability through exercises and coordination. This requires a great deal of labor by licensed medical staff members. The purpose of the simulation model is to become more cost-beneficial by adjusting parameters associated with labor. Staffing levels and work assignments and flows are among these parameters.

Kennedy[31] constructed a FORTRAN IV based simulation model using software routines available for the hardware. The simulation time for a model run was approximately 5 minutes. As indicated in the previous section the model is composed of the basic simulation module surrounded by an output report generator and an input psuedo-random generation step for feeding in patients. Parameters are modified in the simulation module. In the terminology of some simulation languages, there are temporary and permanent entities. Temporary entities include the patients and their tasks, while doctors, aides, and facilities are permanent entities.

Each entity possesses certain attributes. These characterize the entity. Some of these for various entities are given here.

| Entity | Attributes |
|---|---|
| Therapist | Scheduled times for treatments, number of treatments, wages, sex, and capabilities. |
| Doctor | Diagnosis, classes of patients, and therapists assigned. |
| Equipment | Space requirements, costs, and capacity. |
| Patients | Arrival time, admission date, and tasks in therapy with associated times. |

The model first enters a patient, evaluates his case medically, and assigns appropriate staff members. Given a schedule, the day begins and treatments occur unless lateness, absence, or some other condition delays treatment. This is how randomness enters the model. Therapists activities are modeled by taking into account training and conferences, as well as treatments of patients.

Input to the model is a collection of therapy task prescriptions for various disabilities along with the size and composition of the patients to be generated in the first stage. The generator then provides a file of patients, disability groups, and treatment times. The model then can assign and reassign therapists within the constraints of the number of working hours, patients, and other conditions. With a schedule the model generates arrival times of patients for therapy. Allowance is made for cancellation of therapy sessions as well as discharge.

The output reports provide statistical information on utilization of the department's resources, distribution of patient loads, and demands for service from various disability groups. Specific reports include diagnosis versus tasks rendered; staff assignment versus diagnosis class; number of patients, inpatients, and outpatients for various times of day.

Using this model, tradeoffs were made between centralized and decentralized care. Reductions in staff were shown to be possible in various areas. Productivity increased with better scheduling and improved task assignment.

This is but one example of simulation in health care. Other health care simulation models have been constructed for clinics, emergency wards, ambulance service, and general health requirements analysis.

Another area of application involves public safety. This includes fire and police protection. Larson[32] developed a simulation model for manpower planning in a police department. The model has been employed to evaluate the design of patrol zones, car locator systems, and effect of alterations in patrol resources and scheduling. Instead of patients being generated, crime incidents are generated pseudo-randomly according to a preassigned distribution over the entire city. An incident is classified by severity and patrol units are attempted to be assigned. Incidents not taken care of await action in a queue. The model can be employed to study the method of manpower deployment and dispatching. The city is subdivided into cells so that the probability density over the cell is uniform. Cells are assigned to patrol zones. Incidents are generated by means of a Poisson process. Location of an incident and its priority are based on historical data. Dispatching is then performed under geographic and operational constraints. Units that have taken care of or serviced an incident either are reassigned to another incident or are returned to preventive patrol.

An on-line, interactive version of the model was developed. The user at a terminal is led through a decision or logic tree to select among various alternatives. The user must specify the method of car location, geographical data, dispatching logic, and length of the model run. Output can be obtained at various levels of detail.

The model has been used to redesign patrol zones and evaluate the addition of more cars and various dispatching methods. Models similar to the preceding can be used to study integration of adjacent police forces in emergency as well as concentrated patrolling.

A much more general situation was considered by Fourcans and Hindelang.[27] The operations system considered is a capital budgeting problem for a multinational firm. In addition to presenting a simulation model, Reference 27 contains a good review of existing capital budgeting simulation models along with presenting a model in two stages. At the first stage the subsidiary simulation model selects among a set of alternative investments with the subsidiaries' goals in mind. The next stage is the simulation model of the parent corporation, which considers the acceptable alternatives presented by the subsidiary model.

In the subsidiary model the user inputs parameters of the various alternatives. This includes the number of simulation runs, depreciation rate, selling price, cost of capital, and other similar factors.

The output of the model includes net income after taxes and annual cash flow over the period of the investment. Cash inflows are composed of sales revenue and salvage value. Outflows include initial capital requirements, cost of financing, taxes, and costs resulting from operations.

The simulation for the subsidiary then takes the inputs and generates values for the following variables: market growth rate, market share or percentage captured, investment cost at initiation, life of investment, market size at time of initial investment, operating costs (fixed and variable), interest costs, tax rate for nation location, probability of war and percentage of loss if war occurs, inflation rate, and probability of expropriation and percentage of loss due to expropriation. Having completed the generation of independent variables, the model computes totals for sales, costs, profit, net income, book value, net cash inflow, net present value, discounted rate of return, terminal inflow if war or expropriation occurs, and book value.

The subsidiary model could be run repeatedly for each of a variety of subsidiaries. Output of these runs produces alternatives for the parent corporate model to consider. For convenience we shall call this the *corporate model*. The corporate model generates values for more global variables than the subsidiary model. These include the foreign exchange rate, royalties, and payments to the parent corporation; principal and interest payments received by the parent corporation; transportation costs associated with importation; costs paid by the parent corporation for production by the subsidiary; direct savings generated by the project; and the parent corporation tax rate. Using this information, the model computes the same economic information including total revenue and cost, net cash inflow, and net income for the parent corporation. This model handles the effects of inflation and war.

Tradeoffs between investments can be accomplished using these models by measuring such economic quantities as the internal rate of return versus the cost of capital. Statistical analysis is available to rank projects by desirability. Payback analysis is available to determine when the original investment will be repaid. This is important if the subsidiary is located in a politically or economically volatile country. Sensitivity to devaluation can be examined by modifying the basis for generating the foreign exchange rates. Not treated by the models are relationships between proposed and on-going projects.

As a last example we shall consider a simulation model developed by Menke[33] to determine strategies for pest management. The goal of the model is to analyze interactions between an insect population and its food and other factors affecting growth and control. The growth of the population is viewed as a queuing process. Arrivals are discrete. There are an infinite number of servers and continuous service time distributions. This model is of interest because the system is not of major interest at steady state. The model instead is employed to find critical initial values that minimize damage to crops. Also, the model could be employed to determine the time in the pests life at which pesticide application is most effective.

A specific crop and pest were chosen for the simulation. The crop was soybeans and the pest was a species of caterpillar. The moth invades the soybean crop and two generations of pests develop prior to natural death in the Fall. Growth to adulthood is through six stages with the time in each stage being a normal random variable with distinct parameter values for each stage.

The model is characterized by discrete arrival times that represent the incursion of the moth. The starting population (eggs) is discrete. The servers that represent the life cycle for each insect are infinite. The service times are on the distributions at each life phase and so are multistage. Crops developed are assumed to be a function of time. At weekly intervals the damage and pest population are counted. These are averaged over acre areas.

The model discretely simulates the growth of each egg until death or transformation to a moth. If the egg is female, the time of spawning for the next generation is computed. The model handles eggs a generation per cycle. Pseudo-random generations are used to obtain values for times at each stage, survival, and sex of the egg. The program performs a simualtion over a specified number of generations. For weekly intervals after this, the model gives the population for various life stages, the damage, area available, and percent eaten by the pests.

The model runs indicated that two pest generations were possible prior to the time of susceptability of the crop to economic damage. Using the results obtained by the model, the early pest population for each generation and the pest population in later stages of growth experienced substantial variance between model runs.

Validation of the model was done using field population counts. The graphs of average pest population versus time were done for both the model and direct observations.

Analysis was done for finding the worst case. Experimental design and analysis of variance were employed with the model to test the effect of pesticides on population growth. A one-time application was found to be as statistically effective in either the first or second generation. Application once in each generation was found to be superior to a one-time application in either generation. The conclusion combined with economic considerations is that pesticides should be applied early in the first generation and if the pests are undetected, then the pesticides should be applied early in the second generation.

The examples above only consider some of the possible applications that have been explored. Sources for other applications include the proceedings of simulation conferences as well as the journals that contain simulation articles.

## 6.4 Languages

From time to time, survey articles appear on the state-of-the-art in simulation and simulation languages. Several of these are Krasnow and Merikallio,[4] Teichroew and Lubin,[5] and Tocher.[6] A bibliography on simulation is given in Reference 1. Early simulation languages arose from generalized simulation programs written in a higher-order language such as FORTRAN or ALGOL. The reason for this was due to similarities between various operations systems and applications being considered. From this beginning, simulation languages written in higher level languages were developed. These languages have not as yet reached the level of sophistication of, say, FORTRAN IV or PL/1. New languages designed for various applications are still being constructed. There is also the unfortunate circumstance that not all simulation languages function on all types of computing machinery. Compilers are not available for all machines. This is one reason why scientists still write simulation programs in transferable languages such as FORTRAN IV.

The basic goal of a simulation language is to assist the programmer and analyst in performing a simulation in a way that is preferential to using a general-purpose higher level language. This advantage can be measured by the speed in constructing and testing a simulation program; the lesser programmer sophistication in using the simulation language; the easier use of the program in terms of input, output, and intermediate storage; and the flexibility for future alteration and change for later analyses.

There is no formula for making the language decision. Each situation is an individual entity and the decision must be based on such factors as the sophistication and experience of the programmers; the types of hardware on which the program will be constructed, tested and employed; the amount of time available to construct the program; and the nature and use of the program. In theory this last factor should be considered first. In practice it is last since each of the previous facts act to exclude certain possibilities so that the feasible alternatives will be quite limited.

From a general approach to simualtion languages, we now turn to a consideration of features and elements of the languages. We shall not be concerned here with the exact construction of a language but instead shall take a user's point of view. As indicated earlier in this chapter, simulation models can involve continuous or discrete time. For continuous time we have differential or analytic equations that describe a phenomenon over time. Analog simulation is one major means of implementing a continuous time model. Using a digital computer, approximations and finite differences can replace the analytic formulas. A continuous time simulation language is DYNAMO.[19] It employs difference equations and can work on IBM equipment. Other continuous time languages are explored in Teichroew and Lubin.[5] Hybrid simulation is another approach to continuous time simulation and combines both digital and analog elements. The digital part of such a model is employed so that the user can modify and adjust parameters more easily than through hardware changes. Reviews of hybrid simulation appear in Brennan and Linebarger[2] and Clancy and Fineberg.[3]

The major simulation area that is of concern in operations research is that of discrete simulation. As pointed out earlier, a discrete model marches across time by finite time steps or from successive event to event. Some of the major simulation routines and languages are GASP, GPSS, SIMSCRIPT, and SIMULA. Each of these is based on a higher-order language. For the four simulation languages, the base languages are given by

| Simulation Language | Base Language |
| --- | --- |
| GASP | FORTRAN |
| GPSS | FAP, FORTRAN |
| SIMSCRIPT | FORTRAN |
| SIMULA | ALGOL |

It should be noted that compiler efficiency for simulation languages remains a major restriction. In some cases modifying input data requires a recompile.

These and other languages are reviewed in References, 4, 5, and 6. Here we summarize some of the major features of these languages.

GASP has been widely used in job shop simulations (Hurst and Pritsker.[30]) GASP permits the user to define events, time settings, and parameters and to call forth random number generators with ease. A standard reference for GASP-II is Pritsker and Kiviat.[18] GASP was written and designed to be used in FORTRAN. This permits GASP to be employed on almost any machine with a FORTRAN compiler. Another advantage is that GASP rather than being a homogeneous language consists of a series of subroutines. GASP has modules that permit a programmer to select, prevent, and schedule events. Standard statistics of output are available with random number generators from most common distributions. Some error detection is permitted. GASP is most often used in medium-sized computers. SIMSCRIPT and GPSS require larger core and can take advantage of operating system features found on larger machines.

GPSS (*G*eneral *P*urpose *S*ystem *S*imulator) was one of the first languages specially built for simulation modeling for a wide variety of applications. GPSS is based in FORTRAN and FAP and has been successfully employed in small-to-medium applications. GPSS and SIMSCRIPT are the two most widely employed discrete simulation languages. GPSS is user oriented rather than execution oriented as compared to SIMSCRIPT. While it is relatively easy to run GPSS, it requires a greater amount of time and effort to learn SIMSCRIPT. GPSS is useful where the simulation model will undergo many changes over a period of time. GPSS is also good for problems that are queuing oriented. In contrast, SIMSCRIPT is used when the model modifications required are infrequent; rapid execution time is desired; and the scale of the problem is large. There are a number of differences in language structure. Some of these are described in Naylor, et al.,[10] and the user manuals.[16],[17] In GPSS the operations system being simulated is input in the logic of a block diagram. Activities or jobs that move through the model are viewed as transactions. GPSS allows equipment for processing, storage, and switching. Arrays are created for maintaining statistics on the processing at various nodes. For nodes in parallel, random or preselected choice is allowed. Additional information is given in References 12 and 15.

SIMSCRIPT, like GPSS, is FORTRAN based. SIMSCRIPT allows the user to define the basic components of the operations system. GPSS is not capable of this level of generalization. An example is arrays for data. SIMSCRIPT permits two-dimensional arrays. GPSS operates from a set of fixed one-dimensional arrays. For SIMSCRIPT, the user defines events and activities. Timing for both SIMSCRIPT and GPSS is based on considering the next successive event in relation to the last event. Table updates occur in SIMSCRIPT after each event and in GPSS after a change of state occurs.

SIMULA is based in ALGOL. In SIMULA the user defines the nodes and processing at the nodes. These are called *objects*. After this the activities are then begun by specifying the activation of a new job at a specific time. SIMULA can be viewed as an extension of ALGOL and its subroutines can be accessed using a code for simulation. SIMULA is not as easy to work with as GPSS. Details on the use of SIMULA are available in Dahl and Nygaard[14] and Dahl, Myhrhang, and Nygaard.[13]

It should be noted that these languages are not the only ones in existence. There are several others that have been used quite successfully. Information and references can be found in the review articles on p. 207. In addition, some language manuals are also listed there.

The number of textbooks in simulation theory and applications has grown considerably over the years. Some of these, such as Mize and Cox[9] and Gorden,[8] present not only the methods of simulation but also the formulation, validation, and use of simulation models. Tocher[11] is one of the first basic texts in simulation. Naylor, et al.,[10] present queuing results, random number generation, and building simulation models with application to economic systems. There is also a chapter on several simulation languages that, although the book has been in print several years, are still relevant. A recent text oriented toward computerization is Enshoff and Sisson.[7] Several specialized texts in simulation application areas are economics (Naylor[34]), industrial systems (Schmidt and Taylor[35]), Schrieber[36]), psychology (Tomkins and Messick[37]), Dutton and Starbuck[26]), social science (Guetzkow[28]), and international relations (Guetzkow et al.[29]).

# REFERENCES

*Survey Articles*

1. "Bibliography on Simulation," IBM Corp. Document Rep. 320-0924-0 (1966).
2. BRENNAN, R. D. AND R. LINEBARGER, "An Evaluation of Digital Analogue Simulator Languages," *Proc. IFIP Congress*, 2.
3. CLANCY, J. J. AND M. S. FINEBERG, "Digital Simulation Languages: A Critique and a Guide," *Proc. AFIPS Fall Joint Comp. Conf.*, 27 (1965), 23-36.
4. KRASNOW, H. S. AND R. MERIKALLIO, "The Past, Present, and Future of General Simulation Languages," *Mgmt. Science*, 11 (1963), 236-267.
5. TEICHROEW, D. AND J. F. LUBIN, "Computer Simulation—Discussion of the Technique and Comparison of Languages," *Comm. of ACM*, 9 (1966), 723-741.
6. TOCHER, K. D., "Review of Simulation Languages," *Oper. Res. Quart.*, 15 (1965) 189-218.

*Textbooks on Simulation*

7. ENSHOFF, J. R. AND R. L. SISSON, *The Design and Use of Computer Simulation Models*. New York: The Macmillan Co., 1970.
8. GORDEN, G. *System Simulation*. Englewood Cliffs, N. J.: Prentice-Hall Inc., 1969.
9. MIZE, J. H. AND J. G. COX, *Essentials of Simulation*. Englewood Cliffs, N. J.: Prentice-Hall, Inc., 1968.
10. NAYLOR, T. H., J. L. BALINTFY, D. S. BURDECK, AND K. CHU, *Computer Simulation Techniques*. New York: John Wiley & Sons, Inc., 1966.
11. TOCHER, K. D., *The Art of Simulation*. Princeton, N. J.: Van Nostrand Co., Inc., 1963.

*Simulation Language Textbooks and Manuals*

12. *General Purpose Simulation System V-User's Manual*. IBM Publications SH-20-0851, 1970.
13. DAHL, O. J., B. MYHRHANG, AND K. NYGAARD, "Some Features of the SIMULA 67 Language, *Proc. Second Conf. on Simulation*. 1968.
14. DAHL, O. J. AND K. NYGAARD, "SIMULA—An ALGOL Based Simulation Language," *Comm. of ACM*, 9 (1966), 671.
15. GREENBERG, S., *GPSS Primer*. New York: Wiley-Interscience, 1972.
16. KIVIAT, P., H. MARKOWITZ, AND R. VILLANEUVA, *The SIMSCRIPT II Programming Language*. Englewood Cliffs, N. J.: Prentice-Hall, Inc., 1968.

17. MARKOWITZ, H., B. HOUSNER, AND H. KARR, *SIMSCRIPT: A Simulation Programming Language*. Englewood Cliffs, N. J.: Prentice-Hall, Inc., 1963.
18. PRITSKER, A. A. B. AND P. J. KIVIAT, *Simulation with GASP-II*. Englewood Cliffs, N. J.: Prentice-Hall, Inc., 1969.
19. PUGH, A. L., *DYNAMO User's Manual*. Cambridge, Mass.: MIT Press, 1961.

*Textbooks on Queuing Theory*

20. COX, D. R. AND W. L. SMITH, *Queues*. London: Methuen & Co., 1961.
21. HILLIER, F. S. AND G. J. LIEBERMAN, *Introduction to Operations Research*. San Francisco, Calif.: Holden-Day, Inc., 1967.
22. KARLIN, S., *First Course in Stochastic Processes*. New York: Academic Press, 1966.
23. LEE, A. M., *Applied Queuing Theory*. London: MacMillan & Co., 1966.
24. PARZEN, E., *Stochastic Processes*. San Francisco, Calif.: Holden-Day, Inc., 1962.

*Other References*

25. *A Million Random Digits with 100000 Normal Deviates*. RAND Corp., New York: Free Press of Glencoe, 1955.
26. DUTTON, S. M. AND W. H. STARBUCK, *Computer Simulation of Human Behavior*. New York: John Wiley & Sons, Inc., 1971.
27. FOURCANS, A. AND T. J. HINDELANG, "Multinational Capital Budgeting: A Simulation Model," *Proc. Sixth Winter Simulation Conference*, 1973, 512-533.
28. GUETZKOW, H., *Simulation in Social Science*. Englewood Cliffs, N. J.: Prentice-Hall, Inc., 1963.
29. GUETZKOW, H., ET AL., *Simulation in International Relations: Developments for Research and Teaching*. Englewood Cliffs, N. J.: Prentice-Hall, Inc., 1963.
30. HURST, N. R. AND A. A. B. PRITSKER, "GASP IV: A Combined Continuous/Discrete FORTRAN Based Simulation Language," *Proc. 1973 Winter Simulation Conf.*, 1973, 795-803.
31. KENNEDY, O. G., "The Use of Computer Simulation in Health Care Planning," *Proc. Sixth Winter Simulation Conf.*, 1973, 172-198.
32. LARSON, R. C., "On-line Simulation of Urban Police Patrol and Dispatching," *Proc. Sixth Winter Simulation Conf.*, 1973, 371-385.
33. MENKE, W. W., "Identification of Viable Biological Strategies for Pest Management by Simulation Studies," *Proc. Sixth Winter Simulation Conf.*, 1973, 32-50.
34. NAYLOR, T. H., *Computer Simulation Experiments with Models of Economic Systems*. New York: John Wiley & Sons, Inc., 1971.

35. SCHMIDT, J. W. AND R. E. TAYLOR, *Simulation and Analysis of Industrial Systems*. Homewood, Ill.: R. D. Irwin, Inc., 1970.
36. SCHRIEBER, A. N. (ED.), *Corporate Simulation Models*. Seattle, Wash.: University of Washington Press, 1970.
37. TOMKINS, S. S. AND S. MESSICK, *Computer Simulation of Personality*. New York: John Wiley & Sons, Inc., 1963.

## PROBLEMS

In Problems 1-4, formulate each problem as a simulation problem. Discuss which are dependent and independent variables and which are inputs and outputs; describe the relationships between variables and between the operations system and the external environment. Explain how you would perform sampling and gather data for a simulation model.

1. A paint company makes three colors of paint in a certain factory. The factory receives raw materials in the form of white paint in 50-gallon drums. These drums must first be opened. Colors are added using three distinct pigment addition steps. The first has two parallel facilities for pigment addition. After this stage the 50-gallon drums are divided into 1-gallon cans and mixed. One of the colors, green, has a special preservative added. The 1-gallon cans are then sealed and packed, 4 cans to a box. A single conveyer is available to move the open 50-gallon drums to the pigment addition step and the finished 50-gallon drum to the 1-gallon separator phase.

2. A logistics problem exists in preparing troops for field duty. For each man, a weapon, food kit, shelter kit, and medical kit must be assigned, collected, and distributed. In addition, heavy weapons and supplies for the men must be distributed. Priorities of assignment exist so that artillary, infantry, and support armor receive priority in that order.

3. An owner of a launching ramp for outboard motorboats wishes to perform a simulation of his operation to see where bottlenecks are and where improvements will reduce delays. The flow in the system can be described as follows. A customer enters at a gatehouse that has three entry lanes and one exit lane. After a customer pays, he drives his car and trailer to the concrete ramp where he backs the trailer into the water and launches the boat. He then drives the car and trailer to a parking lot. After he is finished boating, he returns to the lot and drives his car and trailer to the ramp, loads the boat, and drives to a washrack where the boat is cleaned. After cleaning, he leaves through one exit gate where he shows his receipt. The owner's alternatives are to add to the number of stalls available for ramps or washrack. This, however, would reduce parking and could increase bottlenecks by increasing the amount of traffic in the ramp and washrack areas.

210 / Simulation and Queuing Theory

4. An underdeveloped nation has contracted with an operations research firm to conduct modeling to find ways of improving the nation's transportation system. Alternatives include the construction of more rail lines, highways, or a new deep-water port. The model must be sensitive to projections of future population and mineral extractions as well as world prices for the country's export products.

5. In Subsection 6.2.2 the Lehmer congruential method of pseudo-random number generation was explored. Construct a flow chart of a method of generation based on an initial value $a$ with an even number of digits $d$. The value $a$ is squared and the middle $d$ digits extracted for the next pseudo-random number in the sequence. In the event that $a^2$ has an odd number of digits, then we randomly select the $p$th digit from one end. The process is repeated. Why is this method eventually repeating or cyclic?

6. Using the method of Problem 5, generate a sequence of 10 pseudo-random numbers with the starting values

   (a) 34
   (b) 1222
   (c) 81
   (d) 20

7. Use the Lehmer congruential method for the following cases to generate 15 pseudo-random numbers in each case.

   (a) $c = 8, x = 5, a_0 = 1$
   (b) $c = 8, x = 5, a_0 = 3$
   (c) $c = 10, x = 181, a_0 = 3$
   (d) $c = 16, x = 5, a_0 = 1$

8. Use the network in the example of Subsection 6.2.1 to simulate the operation with the following inputs for 10 units of time.

| Job Type | Arrival Rate | 1 | 2 | 3 | 4 | 5 |
|---|---|---|---|---|---|---|
| 1 | 0.5 | (1, 1) | (1.1, 2) | (1, 4) | (0.7, 7) | (0.9, 5) |
| 2 | 0.6 | (1, 1) | (1.2, 3) | (1, 4) | (0.9, 5) | (0.7, 7) |

|  | 6 | 7 | 8 | 9 | 10 |
|---|---|---|---|---|---|
| 1 | (1, 4) | (0.5, 7) | (0.4, 6) | (1, 6) | (0.9, 5) |
| 2 | (1, 4) | (0.6, 8) | (0.7, 9) | (1, 5) | (2, 7) |

Here $(a, b)$ means the process time is $a$ and priority is $b$.

9. Discuss how an optimizing method can be used to determine the optimal priority levels for the data in Problem 8.

In Problems 10 to 13, use a pseudo-random number generator to obtain a pseudo-random sequence of the distribution given.

10. $N(1, 1)$

11. Exponential with mean $\frac{1}{2}$ and range $[1, \infty)$:

$$f(x) = \begin{cases} 2e^{-2(x-1)} & x \geq 1 \\ 0 & x < 1 \end{cases}$$

12. Binomial with $n = 10$ and $p = \frac{1}{4}$.

13. Poisson with mean 2.

14. The following sequence is proposed as being from an $N(0, 1)$ distribution. Test this hypothesis at the $\alpha = 0.10$ significance level.

    $-9.2$, $-6.5$, $-2.2$, $-2.1$, $-1.8$, $-0.7$, $0.1$, $0.3$, $0.5$, $0.9$, $1$, $1.1$, $6.3$, $17.2$

    Justify your choice of subintervals.

In each of Problems 15 and 16, perform a simulation based on the data given.

15. Using Problem 1, the data is the following. The arrival rate of 50-gallon drums is 1 per 30 seconds. The time for drum opening is 1 minute. The processing times for pigmentation by color is

    Pigmentation Step

    |       | 1          | 2           | 3      |
    |-------|------------|-------------|--------|
    | Green | 1 min      | 1 min 15 sec | 1 min  |
    | Black | 2 min      | 1 min       | 1 min  |
    | Red   | 1 min 30 sec | 2 min     | 30 sec |

    Service is first come, first served. Mixing time is 4 minutes. Preparing 1-gallon cans is 8 minutes per 50-gallon drum. The green preservative step takes 45 seconds. Conveyance at any stage averages 5 minutes. Packing of 1-gallon-can boxes takes 5 minutes.

16. In Problem 3, assume that there are launching areas for 4 cars. The washer can accommodate 5 cars. The parking lot can handle 250 cars with trailers. Interarrival rates are believed to be exponential with mean 10 minutes. The service times for payment are exponentially distributed with mean 5 minutes. Service times at the ramp and washracks are fixed at 15 and 25 minutes per vehicle, respectively. The time to go from the gatehouse to the ramp is 5 minutes. The time to go from the ramp to the parking lot is 3 minutes and

the time to go from the launching ramp to the washrack is 5 minutes. The time to go from the washrack to the gatehouse is 2 minutes.

In Problems 17 to 20, set up the problem in a queuing context. Compute $P_o$, $P_n$, the expected number of customers in the system, and the expected waiting time in the queue and in the system.

17. An automobile parts store has a service counter with one man dispensing parts. The interarrival times are believed to be exponential with mean $\frac{1}{2}$. Service time is also exponential with mean $\frac{1}{3}$.

18. A barbershop has three chairs. The mean arrival rate is 40 minutes, while the mean service rate is 30 minutes. Both distributions are exponential.

19. A service station has one car-wash facility. It is estimated that the mean time to wash a car is 15 minutes. The variance, due to how dirty a car is, is 5 minutes. Cars arrived according to a Poisson process with mean 20 minutes.

20. Same as Problem 18 except no more than four customers can wait in line.

21. A birth process where no customers are served is characterized by $\lambda_n = \lambda$ for all $n$ and $\mu_n = 0$. Derive the differential equation for $P_n(t)$ and find its general solution.

22. Perform the same steps as in Problem 21 for a system with no arrivals. Then $\lambda_n = 0, \mu_n = \mu$, for all $n$ and at $t = 0$ there are 50 customers in the system.

23. A meat market stays open until 5 p.m. Until 5 p.m. there are four servers available. At 5 p.m. the number goes to one. No new customers are admitted after 5 p.m. Construct a model for this system during the entire day.

For the operations systems in Problems 24 and 25, construct a simulation methodology and model.

24. Assume a system as shown in Fig. P6-24.

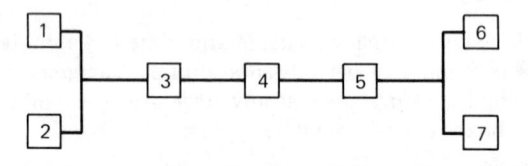

Figure P6-24

Units arrive at nodes 1 and 2 according to a Poisson process with mean interarrival rates of 1 and 1.1, respectively. Service times for all nodes are exponential with mean service times given by

| Node | Mean Service Time |
|------|-------------------|
| 1 | 0.9 |
| 2 | 0.8 |
| 3 | 1.1 |
| 4 | 0.6 |
| 5 | 1.1 |
| 6 | 0.5 |
| 7 | 0.5 |

Nodes 3 and 5 are a single-conveyer module. No other arrivals from outside occur except at nodes 1 and 2. Service is FIFO at all nodes.

25. Let an operation system be represented by Fig. P6-25.

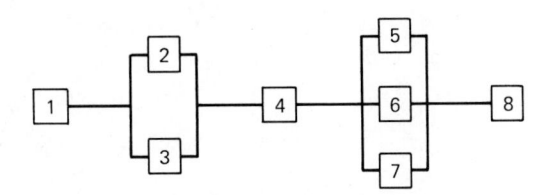

Figure P6-25

Service times are exponential. Let the mean service times be as follows:

| Node | Mean Service Time |
|------|-------------------|
| 1 | 0.9 |
| 2 | 0.7 |
| 3 | 0.7 |
| 4 | 0.5 |
| 5 | 0.4 |
| 6 | 0.3 |
| 7 | 0.2 |
| 8 | 0.5 |

The interarrival rate at node 1 has a mean of 1.1. Service logic at nodes 2 and 3 is FIFO. Service logic at nodes 5, 6, and 7 is according to where the earliest expected completion time would be.

# 7

# NUMERICAL ANALYSIS

## 7.1 Introduction

One of the first areas of applied mathematics to become computer oriented was numerical analysis. The need for computational speed and ease of use were two main reasons for this. Previously much work in numerical analysis was devoted to finding closed expressions and, more generally, formulas amenable to hand calculations on a desk calculator. The computer revolutionized the field in the sense that goals oriented toward ease of manual computation become much less important. One recent goal has been to develop computer based methods that are either very accurate or fast (or hopefully both). With the development of computing machinery the need for computer based numerical methods was felt in satellite and aircraft tracking, antisubmarine warfare, traffic flow analysis, and stock market and investment study.

Some major topics in numerical analysis are

Interpolation—given a set of points and corresponding values of an unknown function at those points, the value of the function is sought at an intermediate point.

Extrapolation—given a set of points and functional values at those points, the functional value at a point beyond the set of points is sought.

Quadrature and integration—the definite integral of a known or unknown function is obtained over a specified interval for given points and functional values.

Differentiation—the value of the derivative of an unknown function at a point is sought for a given set of points and corresponding values of the function.

Solution of differential equations at specific points for a set of initial conditions.

Determination of Eigenvalues and Eigenvectors.

For several of those topics, properties of an unknown function $f$ are sought. We shall assume that for a given point $x$ we can observe the true value of $f$ at $x$, $f(x)$.

If a set of points and their corresponding functional values are given, this set of points is referred to as the set of *tabular points*. As an example, consider the graph in Fig. 7-1. The dotted line is the graph of the unknown function. At the points 1, 2, 3, and 4 the functional values are known and can be summarized in a table as follows:

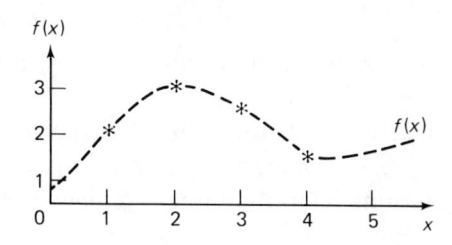

Figure 7-1. Sample function and tabular points.

| $x$    | 1 | 2 | 3   | 4   |
|--------|---|---|-----|-----|
| $f(x)$ | 2 | 3 | 2.5 | 1.8 |

Using this data, for example, we would use extrapolation if we seek $f(5)$, interpolation if we want $f(2.5)$, differentiation for $f'(1.3)$, and quadrature for $\int_1^4 f(x)\,dx$.

In performing numerical analysis, attention must be paid to errors and their sources. Errors are often classified into either truncation or roundoff categories. *Truncation error* is when an infinite summation or a definite integral is approximated by finite summations and summations of areas of parallelograms or other geometric figures, respectively. *Roundoff error* occurs when only a fixed number of digits can be retained in carrying out mathematical operations. Errors accumulate as rounding and truncation operations are successively performed. Superiority of one method over another is often based on the rate at which error is propagated using the method.

With data as given in the example above, a decision must be made as to the method of manipulating the data to obtain an approximation of the function over an interval or at particular points. A function $f$ is said to be *linearly approximated* by a class of functions $G$ if a finite sequence of functions $g_0, g_1, \ldots, g_n$ is selected from $G$ along with real constants $a_0, \ldots, a_n$ to form the sum

$$a_0 g_0(x) + a_1 g_1(x) + \cdots + a_n g_n(x)$$

This function is the approximation of $f(x)$

A *rational approximation* of $f(x)$ is of the form

$$\frac{a_0 g_0(x) + \cdots + a_n g_n(x)}{b_0 h_0(x) + \cdots + b_m h_m(x)}$$

where $\{g_i\}$, $\{h_i\}$ are members of $G$ and $\{a_i\}$, $\{b_i\}$ are collections of real numbers.

The most popular class of functions $G$ is the set of polynomials $G = \{1, x, x^2, x^3, \ldots\}$. One reason for this is that certain transformations or functions of polynomials remain polynomials. For example, if

$$p_n(x) = a_0 + a_1 x + \cdots + a_n x^n$$

is a polynomial of degree $n$, then $p_n(x + a)$ and $p_n(cx)$ are also polynomials of degree $n$. A more basic reason is given in the Stone-Weierstrass theorem, which states that if $f$ is a continuous function on an interval $[a, b]$, then for any $\epsilon > 0$ there exists an integer $n$ and a polynomial $p_n(x)$ of degree $G$ with

$$\max |f(x) - p_n(x)| < \epsilon \qquad a \leqslant x \leqslant b \qquad (7.1)$$

This states that if $f$ is sufficiently smooth, then we can find a polynomial that can uniformly approximate $f$ over the entire interval. The reason for continuity is revealed by considering the function in Fig. 7-2.

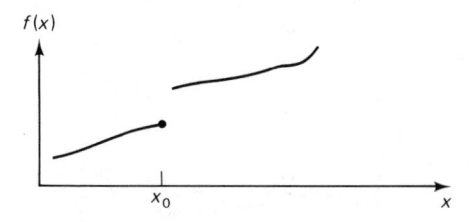

Figure 7-2. Discontinuous function.

If $\epsilon$ is set very small, problems are encountered in trying to approximate the function in the neighborhood around $x_0$.

Other classes of functions such as trigonometric and exponentiation functions can be used. The results are similar.

In the next section we shall examine some of the areas of numerical analysis and give some examples of applications. In Section 7.3 some of the existing programs are reviewed. References are examined on p. 238 in Section 7.4. Problems appear in Section 7.5 on p. 238-242.

## 7.2 Methods in Numerical Analysis

### 7.2.1. Interpolation

There are several possible methods of obtaining approximations to a function at a given point. For a given set of tabular points we might construct an approximating function $\tilde{p}(x)$ that goes through the known points $\{(x_i, f(x_i))\}_{i=0}^{n}$ (see Fig. 7-3). Substantial error may occur between and beyond the tabular points.

Another method is to select the polynomial that is obtained by minimizing the sum of squared errors. A polynomial $p(x)$, of specific degree, is found that minimizes

$$\sum_{i=0}^{n} (f(x_i) - \hat{p}(x_i))^2 \qquad (7.2)$$

218 / Numerical Analysis

The expression in Eq.(7.2) is the sum of squared errors function. A third method is the minimax rule, which is to select $\overline{p}(x)$ so as to minimize the worst absolute fit given by

$$\max_i |f(x_i) - \overline{p}(x_i)| \qquad (7.3)$$

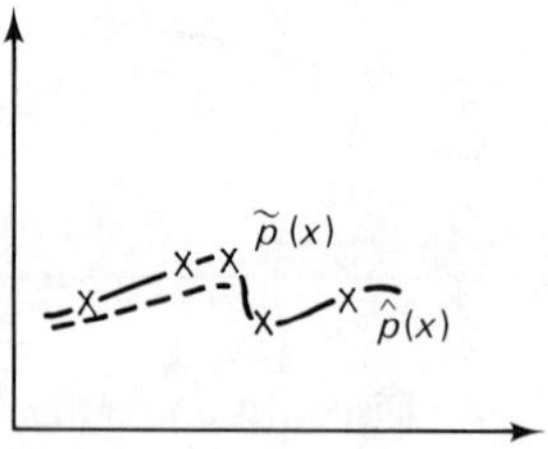

Figure 7-3. Exact and least squares polynomials.

The first method of exact fit is the most widely used. The process of fitting the points $\{(x_i, f(x_i))\}_{i=0}^n$ exactly is called *Lagrangian interpolation*. It is based on the existence of a unique polynomial $\tilde{p}(x)$ of lowest degree (at most $n$) that fits the points. It is given by

$$\tilde{p}(x) = \sum_{j=0}^{n} f(x_j) p_j(x) \qquad (7.4)$$

where

$$p_j(x) = \frac{\prod_{\substack{i=0 \\ i \neq j}}^{n} (x - x_i)}{\prod_{\substack{i=0 \\ i \neq j}}^{n} (x_j - x_i)} \qquad j = 0, 1, \ldots, n \qquad (7.5)$$

It can be shown that this polynomial takes the value $f(x_i)$ at $x_i$ ($0 \leq i \leq n$) (show this) and that it is the only polynomial of smallest degree with this property. Note that $\tilde{p}$ may have degree less than $n$. For instance, if all points were on a straight line, than $\tilde{p}$ would have at most degree 1.

When interpolation is done and $\tilde{p}$ is constructed, the errors in the estimate should be considered. Using Rolle's theorem from calculus, the error is given by

$$f(x) - \tilde{p}(x) = [\prod_{i=0}^{n} (x - x_i)] f^{(n)}(\tau)/n! \qquad (7.6)$$

where $f^{(n)}$ is the $n$th derivative of $f$ and $\tau$ is a specific point in the interval containing $x$, $x_0$, ...; $x_n$. The difficulty in using Eq. (7.6) lies in not knowing $f$ much less $f^{(n)}$ and in obtaining $\tau$. Bounds for errors can be obtained if there is some knowledge of $f$ beyond the tabular point values.

As an example of Lagrangian interpolation, consider the following tabular points for the function $f(x) = 5e^x$.

| $x$ | 0 | 0.5 | 1 |
|---|---|---|---|
| $f(x)$ | 5 | 8.25 | 13.60 |

The polynomials $\{p_j(x)\}$ are given by

$$p_0(x) = \frac{(x - 0.5)(x - 1)}{0.5} = (2x - 1)(x - 1)$$

$$p_1(x) = -4x^2 + 4x$$

$$p_2(x) = 2x^2 - x$$

Interpolating at $x = \frac{1}{4}$ gives

$$\hat{p}\left(\frac{1}{4}\right) = \left(\frac{3}{8}\right)(5) + \left(\frac{3}{4}\right)(8.25) - \left(\frac{1}{8}\right)(13.60)$$

or

$$\hat{p}\left(\frac{1}{4}\right) = 6.36$$

The true value is 6.42, while the error term is $(\frac{3}{128})(5e^\tau)$. In $[0, 1]$ this error is bounded by 0.319.

The Lagrangian interpolation method applies to any set of tabular points. Simplifications are possible if all points are equally spaced. An entire family of formulas has been constructed for equally spaced points. This development was in part due to ease of calculation by hand. These methods are based on finite differences. Forward finite differences, denoted by $\Delta$, are defined inductively by

$$\Delta^0 f(x) = f(x)$$

$$\Delta^1 f(x) = f(x + h) - f(x)$$

and

$$\Delta^k f(x) = \Delta^{k-1} f(x + h) - \Delta^{k-1} f(x) \qquad k \geqslant 2$$

The expression $\Delta^k f(x)$ is called the $k$th *forward difference* calculated at $x$. There are also *backward* ($\nabla$) and *central* ($\delta$) *differences*, which are defined respectively as follows:

$$\nabla^0 f(x) = f(x)$$
$$\nabla^k f(x) = \nabla^{k-1} f(x) - \nabla^{k-1} f(x - h) \qquad k \geqslant 2$$

and

$$\delta f(x) = f\left(\frac{x + h}{2}\right) f\left(\frac{x - h}{2}\right)$$
$$\delta^k f(x) = \delta^{k-1} f\left(\frac{x + h}{2}\right) - \delta^{k-1} f\left(\frac{x - h}{2}\right) \qquad k \geqslant 2$$

Finite difference interpolation formulas can be constructed by following a path through a table. For a set of tabular points ..., $x_{-2}'$, $x_{-1}'$, $x_0'$, $x_1'$, $x_2'$, ... and corresponding functional values ... $f_{-2}'$, $f_{-1}'$, $f_0'$, $f_1'$, $f_2'$, ... part of the table appears as in Table 7-1. The table is called the *Fraser diagram*. The quantity $\Delta^i f_j$ is the $i$th forward difference at $x_j$ written between $\Delta^{i-1} f_j$ and $\Delta^{i-1} f_{j+1}$. The quantity above $\Delta^i f_j$ is

$$(m - j:i) = \frac{(m - j)(m - j - 1) \cdots (m - j - i + 1)}{i!}$$

A formula is obtained by tracing a path from the left-hand column of $f_i$ values and proceeding to the right. The method of formula construction is described in the following steps.

1. We first write the starting functional value.
2. If we proceed up and to the right (northeast), we add the product of the ending difference and the coefficient below this difference.
3. If we proceed down and to the right (southeast), we add the product of the ending difference and the coefficient above this difference.

This process is continued and repeated until all available tabular points are used.

Table 7-1. FRASER DIAGRAM FOR FORWARD DIFFERENCE INTERPOLATION FORMULAS

$$
\begin{array}{cccccc}
\vdots \\
x_{-2} & f_{-2} & (m+2:1) & \Delta^2 f_{-3} & & \\
 & & \Delta f_{-2} & & (m+2:2) & \Delta^3 f_{-3} \\
x_{-1} & f_{-1} & (m+1:1) & \Delta^2 f_{-2} & & (m+2:3) \\
 & & \Delta f_{-1} & & (m+1:2) & \Delta^3 f_{-2} \\
x_0 & f_0 & (m:1) & \Delta^2 f_{-1} & & (m+1:3) \\
 & & \Delta f_0 & & (m:2) & \Delta^3 f_{-1} \\
x_1 & f_1 & (m-1:1) & \Delta^2 f_0 & & (m:3) \\
 & & \Delta f_1 & & (m-1:2) & \Delta^3 f_0 \\
x_2 & f_2 & (m-2:1) & \Delta^2 f_{+1} & & (m-1:3) \\
\vdots
\end{array}
$$

Suppose we start at $f_0$ and then go to $\Delta f_{-1}$. The formula starts as $f_0$ and then becomes $f_0 + (m:1) \Delta f_{-1}$. If we continue in a zigzag fashion, we would next go to $\Delta^2 f_{-1}$ to give

$$f_0 + (m:1) \Delta f_{-1} + (m+1:2) \Delta^2 f_{-1}$$

We would continue to add terms from the zigzag path. This formula is known as *Gauss's backward formula*. Other formulas are considered in Problems on p. 239.

Suppose we wanted to find $f(x)$ and knew the values $f(x_{-n})$ ... $f(x_0)$, ..., $f(x_n)$. Then $m$ is found from $x = x_0 + hm$ where $h = x_i - x_{i+1}$. An estimate of $f(x)$ can be found from constructing one of the forward difference formulas.

To compare several interpolation formulas the differences can be precomputed and stored in the main storage unit or on tape or disk. Programs for each formula can access the information to obtain estimates. Motivation for such a comparison lies in part in case of computation for specific problems.

One reason for comparing several formulas is that there is no general preference of one formula over another until the error bounds for each method are compared. Computation is eased since these methods all draw upon the same general table of finite differences.

Error terms for these formulas are as given in Eq. (7.6). The point $x_0$ is taken to be the central tabular point to minimize error.

A problem in interpolation is to estimate the point at which a function assumes a certain value. The most common example that we use here is to find a *zero* of a function [i.e., a point $x$ with $f(x) = 0$]. Suppose the tabular points and functional values are $(x_1, f(x_1))$, ..., $(x_n, f(x_n))$. Now if $f$ has many zeros in a small interval, our estimate may stray across the interval unless we have a great number of tabular points in this interval. Suppose we assume that $f$ is a one-to-one function in the interval so that for every point $x$ in the interval there is exactly one point where $f$ takes on the value $f(x)$. Then $z = f(x)$ has an inverse given by $x = f^{-1}(z)$. Reversing the roles of $x$ and $f(x)$ in the tabular values we have

| $z$ | $f(x_1)$ | ... | $f(x_n)$ |
|---|---|---|---|
| $f^{-1}(z)$ | $x_1$ | ... | $x_n$ |

We seek $f^{-1}(0)$ and can use Lagrangian interpolation to estimate this point with the usual procedure.

As an example, suppose we seek the zero between 2 and 3 using the data

| $x$ | 0 | 1 | 2 | 3 | 4 |
|---|---|---|---|---|---|
| $f(x)$ | 7 | 5 | 2 | −1 | −3 |

Transposing rows we have

| $z$ | 7 | 5 | 2 | −1 | −3 |
|---|---|---|---|---|---|
| $g(z) = f^{-1}(z)$ | 0 | 1 | 2 | 3 | 4 |

Using Lagrangian interpolation we have an approximation of 2.625.

More complex interpolation formulas involve knowing values of derivatives at tabular points. This will generally provide smaller errors than Lagrangian methods provided we know these derivative values. Interpolation formulas can be used for extrapolation purposes. The problem is that errors are larger because the point is beyond the interval containing the tabular points.

### 7.2.2 Differentiation and quadrature

Suppose we have an interpolation formula for $f(x)$ given by

$$f(x) = \sum_{j=0}^{n} f(x_j)g_j(x) + e(x) \tag{7.7}$$

where $e(x)$ is the error.

By differentiating and integrating Eq. (7.7), we obtain, respectively,

$$f^{(k)}(x) = \sum_{j=0}^{n} f(x_j)g_j^{(k)}(x) + e^k(x) \tag{7.8}$$

and

$$\int_a^b f^{(k)}(x) = \sum_{j=0}^{n} f(x_j) \int_a^b g_j(x)\,dx + \int_a^b e(x)\,dx \tag{7.9}$$

Here $f^{(k)}(e^k)$ is the $k$th derivative of $f(e)$. Provided $g_j$ and $e$ can be differentiated and integrated, respectively, we would expect to obtain a close approximation especially if the approximation in Eq. (7.7) is close. This is, in fact, how many derivative formulas are obtained.

For differentiation we would like to obtain the simplest expression for the error term. If the estimate is of the type in Subsection 7.2.1, then it can be shown that

$$\frac{d}{dx} \sum_{j=0}^{n}(x - x_j)f^{(n)}(\gamma)/n! = \sum_{j=0}^{n} \prod_{\substack{i=0 \\ i \neq j}}^{n}(x - x_i)f^{(n)}(\gamma)/n!$$

$$+ \prod_{j=0}^{n}(x - x_j)f^{(n+1)}(\gamma)/(n+1)!$$

where $\gamma$ is some point in the interval containing $(x_i)$ and $x$. Note that the derivative of $f^{(n)}(\gamma)$ is of the form $f^{(n+1)}(\gamma)$, for some point $\gamma$ in the interval containing $x, x_0, \ldots, x_n$.

Turning to quadrature or integration, consider Eq. (7.9). Let $E(f)$ represent the error integral so that

$$\int_a^b f(x)\, dx = \sum_{j=0}^n f(x_j) \int_a^b g_j(x)\, dx + E(f)$$

The term $\int_a^b g_j(x)\, dx$ is referred to as a *weight* for $f(x_j)$. Using a Lagrangian-type formula and transforming the interval $(a, b)$ to $(-1, 1)$ leads to the points $\{x_j\}$ being roots of a particular polynomial called the *Legendre polynomial*. These methods, where the tabular points are chosen to be roots of certain polynomials, are examples of *Gaussian-type quadrature*. This allows flexibility to minimize error since the tabular points can be selected without regard to equal spacing and other conditions.

Some weights and points $\{x_j\}$ are given in Table 7-2 for various values of $n$.

**Table 7-2.** WEIGHTS AND VALUES OF $x_j$ FOR LEGENDRE POLYNOMIAL

| $n$ | $\{x_j\}$ | Weight |
|---|---|---|
| 2 | $-0.5774, +0.5774$ | $1, 1$ |
| 3 | $-0.7746, 0, +0.7746$ | $\frac{5}{9}, \frac{8}{9}, \frac{5}{9}$ |
| 4 | $-0.8611, -0.3400, +0.3400, +0.8611$ | $0.3479, 0.6521, 0.6521, 0.3479$ |
| 5 | $-0.9062, -0.5385, 0, 0.5385, 0.9062$ | $0.2369, 0.4786, 0.5689, 0.4786, 0.2369$ |

The weights correspond to the location of the $x_j$ value. Suppose now we wish to estimate

$$\int_0^2 x^2 e^x\, dx$$

for $n = 3$. We first transform the integral so that the interval of integration is $[-1, 1]$. If $a \leqslant x \leqslant b$, then $2a \leqslant 2x \leqslant 2b$ or $a - b \leqslant 2x - b - a \leqslant b - a$. Dividing by $b - a$ we have

$-1 \leqslant (2x - b - a)/(b - a) \leqslant 1$. In our example then we set $z = (2x - 3)/3$ so that

$$\int_0^3 x^2 e^x \, dx = \frac{3}{2} \int_{-1}^1 \left(\frac{3z + 3}{2}\right)^2 e^{(3z+3)/2} \, dz$$

$$= \frac{27}{8} \int_{-1}^1 (z + 1)^2 e^{3(z+1)/2} \, dz$$

Applying the formula and using Table 7-2 for $n = 5$, we obtain the approximation

$\frac{27}{8}[(1 - 0.9062)^2 e^{3(1-0.9062)/2}(0.2369)$

$+ (1 - 0.5385)^2 e^{3(1-0.5385)/2}(0.4786) + e^{3/2}(0.5689)$

$+ (1.5385)^2 e^{3(1.5385)/2}(0.4786) + (1.9062)^2 e^{3(1.9062/2}(0.2369)]$

Upon evaluation, this is 98.543. The value obtained by direct integration is 98.43.

A major factor in using quadrature formulas is ease of computation. For hand calculations, finding roots of polynomials may be prohibitive. The same is true of limited storage and slow digital computers. Methods where tabular points are equally spaced are called *Newton-Cotes quadrature formulas.* These will be discussed in the remainder of this section. A Newton-Cotes method is called *closed* if the interval end points are tabular points and *open* if the end points are not and tabular points are symmetric within the interval. Closed formulas are of the form

$$\int_a^b f(x) \, dx = \sum_{j=0}^n \int_a^b g_j(x) \, dx \, f(a + sj) + E(f) \qquad (7.10)$$

where $s$ is the length of a subinternal $[(b - a)/n]$.

For two points $a$ and $b$, suppose $f$ is given as in Fig. 7-4. With only two points, a straight line would be used from Lagrangian methods. The approximation for the area under $f(x)$ between $a$ and $b$ is

226 / Numerical Analysis

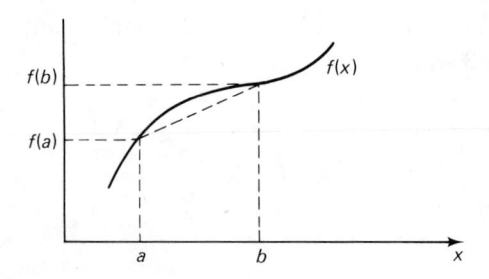

*Figure 7-4. Trapezoid approximation.*

then the area of the trapezoid $(\frac{1}{2})[f(a) + f(b)](b - a)$. The *general trapezoid rule* is

$$\int_a^b f(x)\, dx = \sum_{i=0}^{n} \frac{s[f(x_i) + f(x_{i+1})]}{2} + E(f) \quad (7.11)$$

The error term is $-(b-a)sf(\gamma)/12$ where $\gamma$ is a point between $a$ and $b$. The trapezoid rule is based on two points for $n = 1$. Taking higher values of $n$ to find more points in the approximation, we can reduce error. The next level of approximation is *Simpson's rule*, given by

$$\int_a^b f(x)\, dx = \frac{s[f(a) + 4f(a+s) + f(b)]}{3} + E(f)$$

where $E(f)$ is of the form $-s^5 f^{(4)}(\gamma)/90$ and $\gamma$ is in $(a, b)$. Simpson's rule can be pictured as fitting a second-degree polynomial through the points $(a, f(a))$, $(a + s, f(a + s))$, $(b, f(b))$ as in Fig. 7-5.

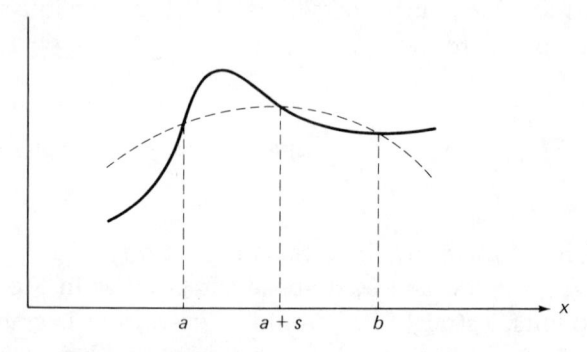

*Figure 7-5. Simpson's rule for a given function.*

The dashed line in the figure is a graph of the approximation. Higher-degree approximations can be constructed from Lagrangian interpolation formulas for four or more points.

The open Newton–Cotes methods are for symmetric tabular points about the end points but which exclude the end points. With one point between $a$ and $b$ the formula is

$$\int_a^b f(x)\, dx = 2sf(x_0) + E(f)$$

where $E(f)$ is $h^3 f^{(2)}(\gamma)/3$ and $x_0$ is the tabular point. For two and three points, respectively, the formulas with error terms are

$$\int_a^b f(x)\, dx = \frac{3s(f(x_0) + f(x_0 + s))}{2} + \frac{3s^3 f^{(2)}(\gamma)}{4}$$

and

$$\int_a^b f(x)\, dx = \frac{4s(2f(x_0) - f(x_1) + 2f(x_2))}{3} + \frac{14s^5 f^{(4)}(\gamma)}{45}$$

It is possible to apply a small degree of polynomial approximation to subintervals and then to sum these to obtain an approximation to the value of the integral over the entire interval. These methods are called *composite formulas* and Eq. (7.11) is an example. How error is affected depends on the error expression for each subinterval.

### 7.2.3 Linear systems of equations

Many problems in operations analysis involve solving systems of linear equations. This occurs, for example, in linear optimization methods and electrical circuits. Let a system of equations be given by

$$a_{11}x_1 + a_{12}x_2 + \cdots + a_{1n}x_n = c_1$$
$$\vdots$$
$$a_{m1}x_1 + a_{m2}x_2 + \cdots + a_{mn}x_n = c_m \qquad (7.12)$$

or in vector form as

$$A\mathbf{x} = \mathbf{c} \qquad (7.13)$$

The vector **x** contains the variables and the entries of $A$ as coefficients of $\{x_i\}$.

A result from linear algebra is that solutions exist to the system if and only if the rank of $A$ and that of $B = (A:\mathbf{c})$ are the same.* The matrix $B$ is formed by adjoining as a row the vector **c** to the matrix $A$. If the ranks of $A$ and $B$ are each equal to the number of variables, then there is exactly one solution. If $A$ and $B$ have the same rank (less than $n$), there is more than one solution.

The type of problem influences the structure of the matrix. In a large scheduling problem the matrix $A$ would be composed of 1's and 0's with a high percentage of zero entries. This is called a *sparse matrix*. The opposite problem is encountered in statistical problems wherein the size of $A$ is smaller but with few zero terms. Error is due to roundoff by computers and because of halting an iterative procedure for obtaining solutions. Methods that do not involve iterative procedures are called *direct methods*.

A popular direct method is that of *Gaussian elimination*, which we shall now consider. It should be noted that his procedure is equivalent to the technique of equation solving discussed in linear programming in Chapter 3. The purpose of Gaussian elimination is to successively reduce the problem by eliminating variables from subsets of equations. For convenience we shall assume $A$ is square ($n \times n$). We first eliminate $x_1$ from the 2nd–$m$th equations in Eq. (7.12) by defining

---

*See Appendix A for a discussion of rank, matrices, and related linear algebra topics.

$$d_{ij}(1) = a_{ij} - \frac{a_{i1}a_{1j}}{a_{11}}$$

$$d_{in+1}(1) = c_i - \frac{a_{i1}c_1}{a_{11}} \quad 2 \leq i \leq n, \, 2 \leq j \leq n$$

assuming $a_{11} \neq 0$. This yields the system

$$a_{11}x_1 + a_{12}x_2 + \cdots + a_{1n}x_n = c_1$$
$$d_{22}(1)x_2 + \cdots + d_{2n}(1)x_n = d_{2n+1}(1)$$
$$\vdots$$
$$d_{n2}(1)x_2 + \cdots + d_{nn}(1)x_n = d_{nn+1}(1)$$

If $a_{11}$ were zero, rows could be shifted and relabeled. We repeat the procedure by setting

$$d_{ij}(2) = d_{ij}(1) - \frac{d_{2j}(1)d_{i2}(1)}{d_{22}(1)} \quad 3 \leq i \leq n, \, 3 \leq j \leq n+1$$

The general transformation is

$$d_{ij}(s) = d_{ij}(s-1) - \frac{d_{is}(s-1)d_{sj}(s-1)}{d_{ss}} \quad \begin{array}{l} 1 \leq s \leq n-1, \\ s+1 \leq j \leq n+1, \\ s+1 \leq i \leq n \end{array}$$

At the end of the procedure we obtain

$$x_n = \frac{d_{nn+1}(n-1)}{d_{nn}(n-1)}$$

We then back up and solve for $x_{n-1}$ and continue to retrace until we obtain $x_1$. The recursive formula is expressed as

$$x_j = d_{jn+1}(j-1) - d_{jj+1}(j-1)x_{j+1} - \cdots - \frac{a_{jn}(n-1)x_n}{d_{jj}(j-1)}$$

$$1 \leq j \leq n \tag{7.16}$$

As an example of the Gaussian elimination method, consider the following system of equations:

$$2x_1 + 3x_2 + 8x_3 = 9$$
$$6x_1 + 12x_2 + 4x_3 = 4$$
$$4x_1 + 6x_2 + 4x_3 = 6$$

Gaussian elimination yields

$$2x_1 + 3x_2 + 8x_3 = 9$$
$$3x_2 - 20x_3 = -21$$
$$-12x_3 = -14$$

which gives $x_3 = 1.166$, $x_2 = 0.777$, and $x_1 = -1.330$. Although variants of the Gaussian elimination procedure exist that use slightly different transformations, Gaussian elimination is often preferred because it involves fewer operations.

Two iterative procedures will now be examined. The first is due to Jacobi. The rows and columns are first reordered so that $|a_{ii}| > |a_{ij}|$ and $|a_{ii}| > |a_{ji}|$ for all $j \neq i$. The system in Eq. (7.12) with $m = n$ can then be stated as

$$x_1 = \frac{c_1 - a_{12}x_2 - \cdots - a_{1n}x_n}{a_{11}}$$

$$\vdots$$

$$x_n = \frac{c_n - a_{n1}x_1 - \cdots - a_{nn-1}x_{n-1}}{a_{nn}} \tag{7.17}$$

An estimate of the solution $(x_1, \ldots, x_n)$ is inserted into the right-hand side of the equations in Eq. (7.17). Computing the right-hand sides gives new estimates of $x_1, \ldots, x_n$. This is repeated. The system in Eq. (7.17) can be represented as

$$\mathbf{x} = B\mathbf{x} + \tilde{\mathbf{c}}$$

where $B$ is the matrix of coefficients of $x_1, \ldots, x_n$ and $\tilde{\mathbf{c}} = (c_i/a_{ii})$. If $\mathbf{u}_0$ is a starting estimate and $\mathbf{u}_k$ is the $k$th stage estimate, then

$$\mathbf{u}_k = B\mathbf{u}_{k-1} + \tilde{\mathbf{c}} \tag{7.18}$$

or

$$\mathbf{u}_k = B^k \mathbf{u}_0 + (I + B + \cdots + B^{k-1})\tilde{\mathbf{c}} \tag{7.19}$$

From Eq. (7.19) it follows that convergence will occur if $B^k$ converges to 0 as $k \to \infty$. This occurs if

$$\sum_{\substack{j=1 \\ j \neq i}}^{n} |a_{ij}| < |a_{ii}|, \quad 1 \leq i \leq n$$

The Jacobi method can be written decomposing $A$ into diagonal ($A_1$), upper triangular ($A_2$), and lower triangular ($A_3$) parts. The result is

$$A = A_1 + A_2 + A_3 \tag{7.20}$$

where

$$A_1 = \begin{pmatrix} a_{11} & & 0 \\ & \cdot & \\ & \cdot & \\ & \cdot & \\ 0 & & a_{nn} \end{pmatrix}, A_2 = \begin{pmatrix} 0 & a_{12} & \cdots & 0 & a_{1n} \\ & \cdot & & & \\ & \cdot & & & \\ & \cdot & & & \\ 0 & 0 & \cdots & 0 & a_{n-1\,n} \\ 0 & 0 & \cdots & 0 & 0 \end{pmatrix} \tag{7.21}$$

$$A_3 = \begin{pmatrix} 0 & \cdots & 0 & 0 \\ a_{21} & \cdots & 0 & 0 \\ \cdot & & & \\ \cdot & & & \\ \cdot & & & \\ a_{n1} & \cdots & a_{nn-1} & 0 \end{pmatrix}$$

Then Eq. (7.18) becomes

$$\mathbf{u}_k = -A_1^{-1}(A_2 + A_3)\mathbf{u}_{k-1} + A_1^{-1}\tilde{\mathbf{c}} \qquad (7.22)$$

Another technique is called the *Gauss–Seidel method*, which uses each component of the $k$th estimate vector ($\mathbf{u}_k$) to obtain successive terms. Using the notation of Eqs. (7.20) and (7.21), the $k$th estimate is

$$\mathbf{u}_k = -(A_1 + A_3)^{-1}[A_2\mathbf{u}_{k-1} - \mathbf{c}]$$

Convergence follows if $A$ is positive definite.

As an example, consider the system

$$2x_1 + 3x_2 + 8x_3 = 9$$
$$6x_1 + 12x_2 + 4x_3 = 4$$
$$4x_1 + 6x_2 + 4x_3 = 6$$

Then

$$A = \begin{pmatrix} 2 & 0 & 0 \\ 0 & 12 & 0 \\ 0 & 0 & 4 \end{pmatrix}^{-1} \left[ \begin{pmatrix} 0 & 3 & 8 \\ 0 & 0 & 4 \\ 0 & 0 & 0 \end{pmatrix} \mathbf{u}_{k-1} - \begin{pmatrix} 9 \\ 6 \\ 4 \end{pmatrix} \right]$$

The inverse can then be computed, a starting value put in, and the iteration begun.

Computation using a computer is usually based upon efficient storage and manipulation of matrices. A matrix of 0's and 1's that is sparse can be stored as a one-dimensional array with an indicator indicating the end of a row. A record could be a row. Record entries would be column numbers where a 1 entry appears. Given a 5% density of nonzero entries, storage would be slightly more than 5% of the amount necessary to store the data as a matrix. For large matrices, rows (columns) could be aggregated so that part of the matrix would be maintained on disk. Two buffer areas in core would be required to permit data transfer in and out of core.

### 7.2.4 Solution of ordinary differential equations

In this section, we shall restrict our attention to ordinary differential equations of the first order. The general problem is to solve for

$y = y(x)$ at some point $x$ with the condition that $y' = g(x, y)$ subject to an initial condition $y(x_0) = y_0$. The relationship $y' = y(x, y)$ is known along with the initial condition, however, the function $y(x)$ is not known explicity in terms of $x$. We shall assume $g$ is well behaved in terms of being continuous and obeying the Lipschitz condition* so that a solution exists.

One method is to express $y$ at the point $x = x_0 + h$ as a Taylor series expansion so that

$$y(x_0 + h) = y(x_0) + hf(x_0, y_0) + \frac{h^2 f'(x_0, y_0)}{2!}$$

$$+ \frac{h^3 f^{(2)}(x_0, y_0)}{3!} + \cdots \tag{7.23}$$

Calculation of derivatives of $f$ follows from

$$f' = f_x + f_y y'$$

where $f_x$ and $f_y$ are partial derivatives with respect to $x$ and $y$, respectively. Usually computation limits Eq. (7.23) to the approximation

$$y(x_0 + h) = y(x_0) + hf(x_0, y_0) + E(h^2) \tag{7.24}$$

where $E(h^2)$ is the truncation error term. We could go from $x_0$ to $x_0 + h$ as in Eq. (7.14) and then continue to work our way using a general form of Eq. (7.24) given by

$$y(x_0 + h) = y(x_0) + hf(x_0, y_0) \tag{7.25}$$

and

$$y_i = y(x_0 + hi) = y_{i-1} + hf(x_i, y_i)$$

where $y_i$ is the estimate of $y(x_i)$, $i \geqslant 1$. The method in Eq. (7.25) is called *Euler's method*. It is restricted in use because of the limited accuracy due to the use of only two terms in the expansion.

---

*The function $f$ obeys the Lipschitz condition if there is a number $L$ with $|f(x, y) - f(x', y)| < L |x - x'|$ for any points $x, x', y$.

234 / Numerical Analysis

As an example, consider

$$y' = y$$

subject to

$$y(x_0) = y_0$$

The Taylor expansion is

$$y(x_0 + h) = y(x_0) + hy(x_0) + \frac{h^2(y(x_0))}{3!} + \cdots$$

$$= y(x_0)[1 + h + \frac{h^2}{3!} + \frac{h^3}{4!} + \cdots]$$

Thus,

$$y(x_0 + h) = \frac{y(x_0)}{h}[h + h^2 + \frac{h^3}{3!} + \cdots + \frac{h^n}{n!}]$$

$$= \frac{y(x_0)}{h}[e^h - 1 - \frac{h^2}{2}].$$

To avoid higher-order derivatives a general method is to replace Eq. (7.25) by

$$y_{i+1} = y_i + h_i g(x_i, y_i, h_i) \tag{7.26}$$

Here $h_i = x_{i+1} - x_i$ is the difference between successive tabular points. With these methods the differences can vary at each iteration. These methods are called *Runge-Kutta techniques*. The choice of $g$ is based on the order and accuracy desired. The simplest Runge-Kutta formula for $g$ is obtained by using a linear combination of two functional points of $f$. This is given by

$$g(x_i, y_i, h_i) = \alpha_1 f(x_i, y_i) + (1 - \alpha_1) f(x_i + \frac{h_i}{2\alpha_1}, y_i) + \frac{h_i}{2\alpha_1} f(x_i, y_i) \tag{7.27}$$

where $\alpha_1$ is a constant (often set equal to 1 or a number in the interval (0, 1)). In carrying out calculations, the value of $\alpha_1$ would be inserted and the expression $y_i + h_i f(x_i, y_i)/2\alpha_1$ computed. This is really a prediction of $y_{i+1}$, say, $\tilde{y}_{i+1}$. The value of $\tilde{y}_{i+1}$ is substituted into Eq. (7.27) and then into Eq. (7.26) to obtain a corrected estimate. As equations we would use

$$\tilde{y}_{i+1} = y_i + \frac{h_i f(x_i, y_i)}{2\alpha_1}$$

and

$$y_{i+1} = y_i + h_i k(x_i, y_i, \tilde{y}_{i+1}, h_i) \tag{7.28}$$

where $k(x_i, y_i, \tilde{y}_{i+1}, h_i)$ is $g(x_i, y_i, h_i)$ with the value of $\tilde{y}_{i+1}$ inserted. Runge-Kutta methods are obtained by generating Taylor series for $y_{i+1} - y_i$ and solving the resulting equations by setting coefficients of $h_i^{t'}$, $t' \leq T$, equal. The order of the method is $T$.

The above is an example of a predictor–corrector method. We first predict $y_{i+1}$ and then correct or refine this estimate. The second equation in Eq. (7.28) can be used repeatedly for refinement.

The error in Runge-Kutta methods stems from taking large step sizes ($h_i$ is large). The error itself and, in particular, truncation error is difficult to estimate since we cannot use direct expansion. Bounds on Runge-Kutta methods, however, have been shown to converge. The number of computations involving $f$ at various points is related to the order of the method. With second-order methods, two calculations of functions values are needed. With some higher-order methods, the number of calculations may be less than the order.

Runge-Kutta methods are examples of general predictor-corrector procedures. These methods are often used in satellite tracking in real time where the need for rapid estimates exceeds the desire for very small error.

Computational algorithms and methods for solving differential equations have received emphasis due to the demands for accuracy and speed in real-time and near-real-time tracking. Efficiency is gained by selections of step sizes and parameter values through exercise and simulation.

### 7.2.5 Numerical analysis and operations research

There is a strong connection between numerical analysis and operations research. There is first the direct relation between the solution procedures. This has been exemplified by the simplex procedure and Gaussian elimination. It results from the need of optimization to solve efficiently and accurately mathematical problems of systems of equations, differential equations, and estimation. Some additional examples are mentioned here to reveal the scope of the relationship.

Suppose observations are being taken on the behavior of a function $f(x)$ that is unknown. Examples occur in transportation, medicine, and engineering. The function $f$ could represent the behavior of a system as a function of a specific input or vector of inputs. Of interest is obtaining an estimate of the point at which the maximum of $f$ is attained. From operations research, methods exist for selecting points to observe $f$ based on past observations and an estimate of $f$. From the preceding section on interpolation, an estimate of $f$, $f_n$, can be obtained from observations $x_1, x_2, ..., x_n$. The next point, $x_{n+1}$, can then be selected by the optimization method. A simple example of a procedure would be to select the point $x_{n+1}$ closest to $x_n$ that maximizes $f_n$. Since $f_n$ converges to $f$ as $n$ increases, this procedure will provide a method for estimating a point at which $f$ attains a maximum value. To find the maximum of $f_n$ for $f_n$, a polynomial, we can differentiate $f_n$ and solve for the roots of an $(n - 2)$th degree polynomial. The functional values of the roots can then be compared to select the next estimate.

The example above indicates how numerical methods are used for properties of convergence and precision in operations research. Another example is a tracking system where a numerical analysis approach for solving differential equations is coupled with an integer programming algorithm for scheduling observations from satellites. More specifically, Runge-Kutta-type methods could be employed to estimate tracks of satellites and to predict future locations. These results could be used by an optimization method so that radar stations are not saturated and also do not spend excessive time and power in pivoting the radar antennae.

Numerical analysis can provide information on parameters and coefficients for optimization. The problem of selecting inventory levels and depots is dependent on estimating demand maintenance and other quantities associated with operations. Extrapolation can be employed to predict future values of these quantities.

## 7.3 Programs

The references are divided between numerical analysis textbooks and sources that are more computer oriented. In the latter category, sample programs and printouts are given, and less attention is focused on the theory and more on specific methods.

The text by Hildebrand[3] has been widely used for a number of years. Ralston[6] has one of the more recent textbooks that has oriented the presentation toward the use of computing machinery. The difference due to the use of the computer can be seen in comparing Householder[4] and Ralston.[6] Other texts in numerical analysis are Hamming[1], Henrici[2], and Kopal.[5] Todd[7] contains a collection of interesting papers that cut across many of the areas of numerical analysis.

In the second category of references, Carnahan, Luther, and Wilkes[8] present the basic parts of the methods along with computer solutions of simple problems. This text also contains numerous problems. More emphasis on theory is given in Ralston and Wilf.[11] Forsythe and Moler[9] consider linear systems in detail. McCracken and Dorn[10] give some of the basic numerical methods along with FORTRAN programming.

Some of the available programs from users group are included in the following table:

Table 7-3

| Program | User Group | Language |
|---|---|---|
| Polynomial curve fit | CUBE | ALGOL |
| Nonlinear difference equations | COSMIC | FORTRAN |
| Systems of nonlinear equations | COSMIC | Object |
| Eigenvalues, eigenvectors | COSMIC | FORTRAN |
| Ordinary difference equations | EIN | FORTRAN |
| Polynomial roots | FOCUS | FORTRAN 63 |
| Eigenvalues of real symmetrical matrices | FOCUS | FORTRAN 3600 |
| Gauss–Jordan matrix inversion | FOCUS | FORTRAN 32 |
| Least squares estimation of nonlinear, linear parameters | SHARE | PL/1 |

## REFERENCES

*Textbooks in Numerical Analysis*

1. HAMMING, R. W., *Numerical Methods for Scientists and Engineers.* New York: McGraw-Hill Book Co., 1962.
2. HENRICI, P., *Elements of Numerical Analysis.* New York: John Wiley & Sons, Inc., 1964.
3. HILDEBRAND, F. B., *Introduction to Numerical Analysis.* New York: McGraw-Hill Book Co., 1958.
4. HOUSEHOLDER, A. S., *Principles of Numerical Analysis.* New York: McGraw-Hill Book Co., 1953.
5. KOPAL, F., *Numerical Analysis.* New York: John Wiley & Sons, Inc., 1955.
6. RALSTON, A., *A First Course in Numerical Analysis.* New York: McGraw-Hill Book Co., 1965.
7. TODD, J. (ED.), *Survey of Numerical Analysis.* New York: McGraw-Hill Book Co., 1962.

*Manuals and Texts Related to Computing Methods*

8. CARNAHAN, B., H. A. LUTHER, AND J. Q. WILKES, *Applied Numerical Methods.* New York: John Wiley & Sons, Inc., 1969.
9. FORSYTHE, G. AND C. B. MOLER, *Computer Solution of Linear Algebraic Systems.* Englewood Cliffs, N. J.: Prentice-Hall, Inc., 1967.
10. MCCRACKEN, D. D. AND W. S. DORN, *Numerical Methods and FORTRAN Programming.* New York: John Wiley & Sons, Inc., 1964.
11. RALSTON, A. AND H. S. WILF, *Mathematical Methods for Digital Computers,* New York: John Wiley & Sons, Inc., 1960.

## PROBLEMS

1. A stock market analyst wishes to estimate the price of a stock on a particular day in 1966. The day was the first trading day after the announcement of a particularly unfavorable earnings report. Describe how he should perform this task using monthly closing prices and yearly closing prices. Explain the possible sources of error and relate these to the stock's price during a month and year. Set up some sample data and evaluate your approach.
2. A highway section is being monitored as to the volume of cars over a given time. Data is available for the number of cars passing over a sensor in a 10-minute period. Develop a method for finding the smallest time interval that contains 40% of the total vehicular traffic.
3. An airline wishes to project future traffic load on a particular route from Denver to St. Louis at 6 p.m. Develop a method of projection using some or all of the following available information for the route:

(a) Airline traffic history.
(b) Airline industry traffic history.
(c) Transportation industry history.
(d) Population data.

4. A commercial satellite firm is developing a network of ground stations so as to transmit and receive information from other stations by means of several earth satellites. The accuracy and completeness of information transmittal depends on the ability and accuracy in tracking the satellite and in timing transmissions. Discuss some possible factors and approaches in developing such a tracking system.

5. A production engineer has developed a formula for estimating the cost of producing a single unit of a product type as a function of the labor, size of production run, cost of raw materials, maintenance, and depreciation. Discuss how statistical validation and simulation could be employed to evaluate the formula. Suppose existing data was available along with the function. Describe how interpolation and extrapolation could be used. What would integration and quadrature of this function yield?

6. Use the Fraser diagram to derive the following formula:

    (a) Newton's forward formula:
    $$g(m) = f_0 + (m:1)\,\Delta f_0 + (m:2)\,\Delta^2 f_0 + \cdots + (m:n)\,\Delta^n f_0$$

    (b) Newton's backward formula:
    $$g(m) = f_0 + m\,\Delta f_{-1} + (m+1:2)\,\Delta^2 f_{-2}$$
    $$+ \cdots + (m+n-1:n)\,\Delta^n f_{-n}$$

    (c) Gauss's forward formula:
    $$g(m) = f_0 + m\,\Delta f_0 + (m:2)\,\Delta^2 f_{-1} + (m+1:3)\,\Delta^3 f_{-1}$$
    $$+ \cdots + (m+n-2:n)\,\Delta^n f_{-1}$$

7. Use Lagrangian interpolation to find $f(2.4)$ from the following table

    | $x$ | 0 | 0.5 | 1.0 | 1.5 | 2.0 | 2.5 |
    |---|---|---|---|---|---|---|
    | $f(x)$ | 1.1 | 1.5 | 1.8 | 1.9 | 1.5 | 1.2 |

    Find an error bound if $|f^{(6)}(y)| \leq L$, $|f^{(7)}(y)| \leq M$ for $y \in [0, 2.5]$.

8. Apply Lagrangian interpolation to estimate $f(3.0)$ for the data of Problem 7. Explain the difficulty in obtaining bounds on the error term.

9. Define $g(x, y)$ by
    $$g(x, y) = \int_0^y (1 - x^2 t)\,dt$$

Using this function, the following table of values of g were obtained.

| y \ x | 0 | 1 | 2 | 3 |
|---|---|---|---|---|
| 1 | 1 | 0.5 | −1 | −3.5 |
| 2 | 2 | 0.0 | −6 | −16 |
| 3 | 3 | −1.5 | −15 | −37.5 |
| 4 | 4 | −4 | −28 | −68 |

(a) Interpolate for $g(1.5, 2)$ using a horizontal row of data;
(b) Interpolate for $g(1, 3.5)$ using a vertical column of data;
(c) Develop an approach for interpolating for $g(1.5, 2.5)$ using all the table entries.

10. (a) Express forward differences as a function of backward differences.
    (b) Do the same for central differences in terms of forward differences

11. Find the zero of $f(x)$ between 0.8 and 1.3 using the following data and Gauss's backward formula.

| x | 0.8 | 1.3 | 1.7 | 2.3 | 3.9 |
|---|---|---|---|---|---|
| f(x) | −0.5 | 0.5 | 1.5 | 2.5 | 3.5 |

12. In Problem 9, find the zero of $g(x, 1)$ for $x$ between 1 and 2.

13. An integrated circuit is subjected to continuous stress. Damage is measured at 15-minute intervals. The data is summarized below. Estimate the time at which damage attains the value of 3.6.

| t | 1.2 | 1.5 | 1.6 | 2.1 | 2.5 | 3.1 | 3.4 | 3.6 |
|---|---|---|---|---|---|---|---|---|
| Stress | 0.9 | 1.4 | 1.9 | 2.8 | 2.9 | 3.7 | 3.9 | 4.1 |

14. Write a FORTRAN program to compute forward differences of highest possible order using the following data:

| x | f(x) | x | f(x) |
|---|---|---|---|
| −15 | 3.7 | −8 | −0.6 |
| −14 | 3.2 | −7 | 2.1 |
| −13 | 2.1 | −6 | 2.4 |
| −12 | −0.7 | −5 | 2.9 |
| −11 | −7.4 | | |
| −9 | −2.5 | | |

15. Prove that the Lagrangian polynomial is the unique polynomial passing through the points $\{(x_i, f(x_i)) : 0 \leq i \leq n\}$.

16. It is possible to add tabular points sequentially, for the Lagrangian formula $g(x:x_i, \ldots, x_k)$ denotes the Lagrangian formula for the point $x$ with tabular points $x_1, \ldots, x_k$. Then

$$g(x:x_1, \ldots, x_k) = \frac{1}{x_k - x_{k-1}} \begin{vmatrix} g(x:x_1, \ldots, x-x_{k-1}) \\ \\ g(x:x_1, \ldots, x_{k-2}, x_k) x_{k-1} - x \end{vmatrix}$$

By successively adding points and using this expression, the function $g(x:x_1, \ldots, x_k)$ is obtained. Use this method to solve Problem 7.

17. (a) Write a program to approximate

$$\int_a^b f(x) \, dx$$

by a closed Newton-Cotes formula for four tabular points.

(b) Apply this to approximate

$$\int_0^1 x \cos(\pi x) \, dx$$

18. Use the trapezoid and Simpson's rule to estimate

$$\int_0^1 e^{-x} \sin \pi x \, dx \quad \text{for } n = 3, 4$$

19. Solve the following systems of equations by (i) Gaussian elimination, (ii) Jacobi's method, and (iii) Gauss-Seidel method by writing computer programs for each method.

(a) $4x_1 - 3x_2 + 2x_3 = 9$
$2x_1 + 5x_2 + 3x_3 = 4$
$5x_1 + 6x_2 - 2x_3 = 18$

(b) $x_1 + 2x_2 + 3x_3 = 0$
$2x_1 - x_2 + x_3 = 0$
$5x_1 + 3x_2 - 2x_3 = 0$

(c) $2x_1 + 2x_2 - 2x_3 = 9$
$6x_1 + x_2 + 2x_4 = 8$
$x_2 + x_3 - x_4 = 18$
$2x_1 - x_3 - x_4 = 0$

20. Program and apply the (i) Taylor expansion and (ii) Runge-Kutta second-order methods to the following problems. Use $h = 0.05$ for Taylor's method and $h_i = \frac{1}{10i}$ for $i \geqslant 1$ for the Runge-Kutta method.

(a) $\dfrac{dy}{dx} = \dfrac{-(x - y)}{(x + y)}$

subject to

$$y(0) = 1$$

(b) $\dfrac{dy}{dx} = \dfrac{(2xy + y)}{(x - x^2 + 1)}$

subject to

$$y(0) = 0$$

(c) $\dfrac{d\theta}{dr} = -\dfrac{r + \sin\theta - \cos\theta}{\sin\theta + \cos\theta}$

subject to

$$r(0) = 1$$

(d) $\dfrac{dy}{dx} = \dfrac{2xy}{x^2 - y^2}$

subject to

$$y(0) = 0$$

# A

# LINEAR ALGEBRA AND MATRICES

## A.1 Definitions and Relationships

This section summarizes some of the basic concepts related to linear algebra and matrices. These provide a base for linear programming, regression analysis, and solutions of numerical equations. References in algebra and matrices appear at the end of the chapter.

In the areas above we deal with arrays of numbers or vectors. A vector can be thought of as a directed line segment with both magnitude and direction. Thus, a vector is not a number but can be represented in a coordinate system by a line with an indicated direction. The length of the line indicates magnitude (see Fig. A-1).

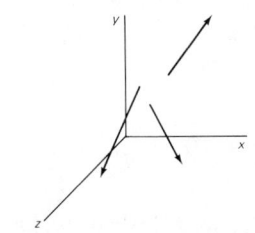

Figure A-1. Examples of vectors.

244 / Linear Algebra and Matrices

Any vector beginning at the origin and terminating at the point $p = (x, y, z)$ can be put in a one-to-one correspondence with the point $(x, y, z)$. Therefore, we shall consider points in coordinate systems rather than physical vectors.

There are certain operations that can be performed with vectors. These include addition between vectors and multiplication of a vector by a real number, and they are defined by

$$\mathbf{x} + \mathbf{y} = (x_1, x_2, ..., x_n) + (y_1, y_2, ..., y_n)$$
$$= (x_1 + y_1, x_2 + y_2, ..., x_n + y_n) \quad (A.1)$$
$$a\mathbf{x} = a(x_1, x_2, ..., x_n) = (ax_1, ax_2, ..., ax_n) \quad (A.2)$$

In Eq. (A.1) and (A.2), $(x_1, ..., x_n)$ and $(y_1, ..., y_n)$ are vectors in $n$-dimensional space denoted by $E^{n\,*}$. The quantity $a$ is any real number. Two vectors, $(x_1, ..., x_n)$ and $(y_1, ..., y_n)$, are equal if and only if their respective coordinates are equal (i.e., $x_i = y_i$ for $1 \leq i \leq n$).

Vectors can be written in either row or column format given by

$$(x_1, ..., x_n) \text{ (row format)} \quad \text{and} \quad \begin{pmatrix} x_1 \\ \vdots \\ x_n \end{pmatrix} \text{(column format)}.$$

Certain vectors are used frequently and are defined here. Let $\mathbf{e}_i$ be a vector in $n$-space with a 1 in the $i$th entry and a 0 in all other entries. Thus,

$$\mathbf{e}_1 = (1, 0, ..., 0)$$
$$\mathbf{e}_2 = (0, 1, 0, ..., 0)$$
$$\vdots$$
$$\mathbf{e}_n = (0, 0, ..., 0, 1) \quad (A.3)$$

---

*This is the set of all points $(x_1, ..., x_n)$ where $\{x_i\}$ are real numbers.

Now for any vector $\mathbf{x} = (x_1, \ldots, x_n)$ we can write x using Eq. (A.1) to (A.3) as a linear combination of the vectors $\{e_i : 1 \leq i \leq n\}$. This follows from the expression

$$\mathbf{x} = (x_1, \ldots, x_n) = x_1 \mathbf{e}_i + \cdots + x_i \mathbf{e}_i + \cdots + x_n \mathbf{e}_n \quad (A.4)$$

Because this is true for all vectors x in $n$-dimensional space, we see that by taking appropriate linear combinations of $\{e_i\}$ using Eq. (A.4) we can obtain any vector in $E^n$. We say that the set of vectors $\{e_i\}$ spans $E^n$ because of this property. $\{e_i\}$ is called a *spanning* or *generating* set of $E^n$. These definitions can be expanded to be applicable to any subset of $E^n$. Formally, let $S$ be a subset of $E^n$. A collection of vectors $V$ in $S$ spans $S$ if for every vector $S$ in $S$ there is a finite set of vectors $\{v_1, \ldots, v_k\}$ in $\mathbf{V}$ and real numbers $a_1, \ldots, a_k$ with

$$s = a_1 \mathbf{v}_1 + \cdots + a_k \mathbf{v}_k$$

In other words, every vector in $S$ can be represented as a linear combination of vectors in $V$.

There may be certain cases where it is impossible for any vector in a set to be written as a linear combination of other vectors in the set. The concept of linear independence is based on this. A set of vectors $V = \{v_i : 1 \leq i \leq m\}$ is *linearly independent* if the only way for equality to hold in the following equation is for all coefficients to be 0.

$$b_1 \mathbf{v}_1 + \cdots + b_m \mathbf{v}_m = 0 \quad (A.5)$$

If the set $V$ is not linearly independent, then it is said to be *linearly dependent*. There are a number of results relating to the concepts that are stated here without proof.

A.1. Any subset of a linearly independent set of vectors is independent.

A.2. Any set of $n + 1$ vectors in $E^n$ is linearly dependent.

A.3. If $(\mathbf{v}_1, \ldots, \mathbf{v}_k) \subset V$ are linearly independent, then vectors in $V$ can be added so that the new, larger set of vectors is linearly independent and spans $V$.

246 / Linear Algebra and Matrices

Combining the concepts of linear independence and spanning sets yields the concept of a basis. A *basis* for a set $V$ is a collection of vectors which span $V$ and which are linearly independent. A basis is then a means for generating all vectors in a set with a linearly independent set of vectors. For example, the collection $\{e_i\}$ is a basis for $E^n$ (show that $\{e_i\}$ are linearly independent). The following results can be derived for a basis.

A.4. Any two bases for a set $V$ have the same number of elements.

A.5. For any $m$ ($< n$) linearly independent vectors in $E^n$ there exist $n - m$ vectors that when combined with the original vectors will constitute a basis for $E^n$.

A vector as we have seen is a one-dimensional array of numbers written vertically or horizontally. This can be generalized to higher dimensions. The general concept is that of a matrix. A *matrix* is defined as a rectangular array of numbers in rows and columns as follows:

$$C = \begin{pmatrix} c_{11} & \cdots & c_{1n} \\ \vdots & & \vdots \\ c_{m1} & \cdots & c_{mn} \end{pmatrix} = (c_{ij}) \qquad (A.6)$$

Here the general element $c_{ij}$ is usually a real number that represents the entry in the $i$th row and $j$th column. If $m = 1$ or $n = 1$, the matrix becomes a vector. A matrix must have an entry in each of the $mn$ locations in the matrix. To indicate the dimension of a matrix $A$, we write $A: m \times n$.

As with vectors we can perform certain operations with matrices. The matrices $A$ and $B$ are equal if $a_{ij} = b_{ij}$ for all $i$ and $j$. Addition and subtraction are defined by

$$A + B = (a_{ij} + b_{ij}) = \begin{pmatrix} a_{11} + b_{11} & \cdots & a_{1n} + b_{1n} \\ \vdots & & \vdots \\ a_{m1} + b_{m1} & \cdots & a_{mn} + b_{mn} \end{pmatrix} \qquad (A.7)$$

and

$$A - B = (a_{ij} - b_{ij}) = \begin{pmatrix} a_{11} - b_{11} & \cdots & a_{1n} - b_{1n} \\ \vdots & \cdots & \vdots \\ a_{m1} - b_{m1} & \cdots & a_{mn} - b_{mn} \end{pmatrix} \quad (A.8)$$

In order to perform the operation, $A$ and $B$ must have the same number of rows and columns. A real number multiplied by a matrix is defined analogously to multiplication by a vector so that

$$aC = \begin{pmatrix} ac_{11} & \cdots & ac_{1n} \\ \vdots & & \\ ac_{mn} & \cdots & ac_{mn} \end{pmatrix} \quad (A.9)$$

Multiplication of two matrices is possible if certain conditions are met. If we wish to multiply two matrices $A$ and $B$ to form $AB$, then the number of columns of $A$ and rows of $B$ must be the same. The reason is based on the definition of matrix multiplication.

If $A(m \times n)$ and $B(n \times p)$ can be multiplied, then the product of $AB$ is given by

$$AB = (c_{ij}) \quad (A.10)$$

where

$$c_{ij} = \sum_{k=1}^{n} a_{ik} b_{kj} \quad (A.11)$$

for $1 \leq i \leq m$, $1 \leq j \leq p$. The product $AB$ has $m$ rows and $p$ columns.

Some examples of matrix operations are given below.

$$\begin{pmatrix} 2 & -1 \\ 3 & 2 \end{pmatrix} + \begin{pmatrix} -1 & 4.5 \\ 6 & -1 \end{pmatrix} = \begin{pmatrix} 1 & 3.5 \\ 9 & 1 \end{pmatrix}$$

$$\begin{pmatrix} 7.2 & \sqrt{3} \\ 0 & 5 \end{pmatrix} - \begin{pmatrix} 2.1 & \sqrt{5} \\ 1 & 2 \end{pmatrix} = \begin{pmatrix} 5.1 & \sqrt{3} - \sqrt{5} \\ -1 & 3 \end{pmatrix}$$

$$\begin{pmatrix} 2 & 1 & 0 \\ 7 & -1 & 0 \end{pmatrix} \begin{pmatrix} -1 & 2 & 1 & 0 \\ 4 & 2 & 3 & 5 \\ 1 & 2 & 1 & 0 \end{pmatrix} = \begin{pmatrix} 2 & 6 & 5 & 5 \\ -11 & 5 & 4 & -5 \end{pmatrix}$$

$$\begin{pmatrix} -1 & 2 & 1 & 0 \\ 4 & 2 & 3 & 5 \\ 1 & 2 & 1 & 0 \end{pmatrix} \begin{pmatrix} 2 & 1 & 0 \\ 7 & -1 & 0 \end{pmatrix} = \text{undefined}$$

Another matrix operation is the transposition of the rows and columns of a matrix. For a matrix $A = (a_{ij}): m \times n$, the *transpose* of $A$, written $A^t$, is defined as

$$A^t = (a_{ji}) = \begin{pmatrix} a_{11} & \cdots & a_{m1} \\ \vdots & & \vdots \\ a_{1n} & \cdots & a_{mn} \end{pmatrix} \quad :n \times m \qquad (A.12)$$

Each column (row) of $A$ becomes a row (column) of $A^t$. A matrix $A$ is *symmetric* if $A = A^t$.

The following laws hold for matrices $A$, $B$, and $C$.

$$A + B = B + A$$
$$A + (B + C) = (A + B) + C$$
$$A(B + C) = AB + AC$$
$$(A^t)^t = A$$
$$(A + B)^t = A^t + B^t$$
$$(AB)^t = B^t A^t$$

It is assumed that the numbers of rows and columns of $A$, $B$, and $C$ permits the operation. It is not true in general that $AB = BA$.

Definitions and Relationships / 249

For a matrix $A$, we could examine parts or submatrices of $A$ by only considering certain rows and columns. For example, if

$$A = \begin{pmatrix} a_{11} & a_{12} & a_{13} \\ a_{21} & a_{22} & a_{23} \\ a_{31} & a_{32} & a_{33} \end{pmatrix}$$

then some submatrices of $A$ are

$$A_1 = \begin{pmatrix} a_{11} & a_{12} \\ a_{21} & a_{22} \end{pmatrix} \quad : \text{ eliminate row 3 and column 3}$$

$$A_2 = \begin{pmatrix} a_{12} & a_{13} \\ a_{22} & a_{23} \\ a_{31} & a_{33} \end{pmatrix} \quad : \text{ eliminate column 1}$$

and

$$A_3 = (a_{32}) \quad : \text{ eliminate columns 1 and 3, rows 1 and 2}$$

It is also possible to decompose a matrix $A$ into submatrices such that the submatrices do not share any common entries and such that every entry of $A$ appears in exactly one submatrix of $A$. A collection of submatrices with this property is called a *partition* of $A$. For $A$, as above, two possible partitions are

$$\begin{pmatrix} a_{11} & a_{12} \\ a_{21} & a_{22} \\ a_{31} & a_{32} \end{pmatrix}, \begin{pmatrix} a_{13} \\ a_{23} \\ a_{33} \end{pmatrix}$$

and

$$(a_{11}), \begin{pmatrix} a_{21} \\ a_{31} \end{pmatrix}, \begin{pmatrix} a_{12} & a_{13} \\ a_{22} & a_{23} \end{pmatrix}, (a_{32} \; a_{33})$$

This leads to $A$ being written, respectively, as

$$A = (A_{11} \mid A_{12})$$

$$A = \left(\begin{array}{c|c} A_{11} & A_{12} \\ \hline A_{21} & A_{22} \end{array}\right)$$

where $A_{11}$, $A_{12}$, $A_{21}$, and $A_{22}$ are the appropriate submatrices.

Partitioning and examining submatrices are particularly valuable for working with large problems. Matrix operations with partitioned matrices can be done if the corresponding row and column sizes permit the operation. For example, if $A$ and $B$ are partitioned as

$$A = \left(\begin{array}{c|c} A_{11} & A_{12} \\ \hline A_{21} & A_{22} \end{array}\right) \text{ and } B = \left(\begin{array}{c|c} B_{11} & B_{12} \\ \hline B_{21} & B_{22} \end{array}\right),$$

then $AB$ is given by

$$AB = \left(\begin{array}{c|c} A_{11}B_{11} + A_{12}B_{21} & A_{11}B_{12} + A_{12}B_{22} \\ \hline A_{21}B_{11} + A_{22}B_{21} & A_{21}B_{12} + A_{22}B_{22} \end{array}\right)$$

if the products $A_{11}B_{11}$, $A_{12}B_{21}$, etc., can be formed. Similar remarks hold for the sum and difference of two partitioned matrices.

Certain matrices are of special interest. For a given positive integer $n$, the *identity matrix* $I_n$ is defined by

$$I_n = \begin{pmatrix} 1 & 0 & 0 & \cdots & 0 & 0 \\ 0 & 1 & 0 & \cdots & 0 & 0 \\ \cdot & \cdot & \cdot & & \cdot & \cdot \\ \cdot & \cdot & \cdot & & \cdot & \cdot \\ \cdot & \cdot & \cdot & & \cdot & \cdot \\ 0 & 0 & 0 & \cdots & 0 & 1 \end{pmatrix} : n \times n \qquad (A.13)$$

The matrix $I_n$ has 1's along the diagonal (northwest–southeast) and 0's elsewhere. The identity matrix derives its name from the property that for any $n \times n$ matrix $A$

$$AI_n = I_n A = A$$

A *diagonal matrix* $D$:$n \times n$ is defined by

$$D = \begin{pmatrix} d_{11} & \cdots & 0 \\ \cdot & \cdot & \cdot \\ \cdot & \cdot & \cdot \\ \cdot & \cdot & \cdot \\ 0 & \cdots & d_{nn} \end{pmatrix} : n \times n \qquad (A.14)$$

The matrix $D$ has real elements along the diagonal and zero elements elsewhere.

Upper and lower triangular matrices $A$ and $B$ are given, respectively, by

$$A = \begin{pmatrix} 0 & a_{12} & \cdots & a_{1n} \\ \cdot & \cdot & & \cdot \\ \cdot & \cdot & & \cdot \\ \cdot & \cdot & & \cdot \\ 0 & 0 & \cdots & a_{mn} \end{pmatrix}$$

and

$$B = \begin{pmatrix} 0 & \cdots & 0 & 0 \\ b_{21} & \cdots & 0 & 0 \\ \cdot & & \cdot & \cdot \\ \cdot & & \cdot & \cdot \\ \cdot & & \cdot & \cdot \\ b_{m1} & \cdots & b_{m,n-1} & 0 \end{pmatrix}$$

Here $A(B)$ has zero-valued elements on and below (on and above) the diagonal.

A system of equations such as given in Eq. (A.15) can be represented in matrix form as Eq. (A.16). The correspondences between Eq. (A.15) and (A.16) is given in Eq. (A.17).

$$a_{11}x_1 + \cdots + a_{1n}x_n = b_1$$
$$\vdots \qquad\qquad \vdots$$
$$a_{m1}x_1 + \cdots + a_{mn}x_n = b_m \tag{A.15}$$

$$\mathbf{Ax} = \mathbf{b} \tag{A.16}$$

$$A = (a_{ij}), \quad \mathbf{x} = \begin{pmatrix} x_1 \\ \vdots \\ x_n \end{pmatrix}, \quad \mathbf{b} = \begin{pmatrix} b_1 \\ \vdots \\ b_m \end{pmatrix} \tag{A.17}$$

A number of areas of applied mathematics and operations analysis depend on functions of matrices. One function of particular interest is based on associating a number with a square matrix such that the actual value of the number depends on the matrix entries. For a square matrix $A$, of $n$ rows this number is called the *determinant* of $A$, written $|A|$. The determinant of $A$ can be defined inductively on the number of rows or columns $n$.

If $n = 2$, then

$$|A| = \begin{vmatrix} a_{11} & a_{12} \\ a_{21} & a_{22} \end{vmatrix} = a_{11}a_{22} - a_{12}a_{21}$$

For $n = 3$

$$|A| = \begin{vmatrix} a_{11} & a_{12} & a_{13} \\ a_{21} & a_{22} & a_{23} \\ a_{31} & a_{32} & a_{33} \end{vmatrix} = a_{11}\begin{vmatrix} a_{22} & a_{23} \\ a_{32} & a_{33} \end{vmatrix} - a_{12}\begin{vmatrix} a_{21} & a_{23} \\ a_{31} & a_{33} \end{vmatrix}$$

$$+ a_{13}\begin{vmatrix} a_{21} & a_{22} \\ a_{31} & a_{32} \end{vmatrix}$$

In general, we can expand the matrix $A$ along a specific row or column. For $n = 3$ the first row was chosen. To do this for the $i$th row, we would have

$$|A| = \sum_{j} (-1)^{i+j} a_{ij} |A_{ij}| \qquad (A.18)$$

where $A_{ij}$ is the submatrix of $A$ obtained by omitting the $i$th row and $j$th column.

Some examples of determinant values are

$$\begin{vmatrix} 1 & 0 \\ 0 & 1 \end{vmatrix} = 1$$

and

$$\begin{vmatrix} 1 & -1 & 2 \\ 0 & -2 & 1 \\ 1 & 2 & 2 \end{vmatrix} = -3$$

The following properties hold for determinants for matrices $A$ and $B$ with $n$ rows and columns:

$$|A| = |A^t|$$

$$|aA| = a^n |A|$$

$$\begin{vmatrix} aa_{11} & \cdots & a_{1n} \\ \cdot & & \cdot \\ \cdot & & \cdot \\ \cdot & & \cdot \\ aa_{n1} & \cdots & a_{nn} \end{vmatrix} = a|A|$$

$$|AB| = |A||B| \qquad (A.19)$$

We say a square matrix $A$ is *singular* if $|A| = 0$ (otherwise, it is said to be *nonsingular*). In solving some problems for a given matrix $(A)$, we need to know if there is a matrix $C$ with the property

## 254 / Linear Algebra and Matrices

$$AC = CA = I_n \qquad (A.20)$$

If such a matrix $C$ exists, satisfying Eq. (A.20), then $C$ is called the *inverse* of $A$ and is denoted by $A^{-1}$. It can be shown that $A^{-1}$ exists if and only if $A$ is nonsingular. Because of the requirement in Eq. (A.20), inverses can exist only for square matrices. Some properties of matrix inversion are given in Eq. (A.21).

$$\begin{aligned}(A^{-1})^t &= (A^T)^{-1} \\ (AB)^{-1} &= B^{-1}A^{-1} \\ (A^{-1})^{-1} &= A \end{aligned} \qquad (A.21)$$

Here $A^{-1}$ and $B^{-1}$ must exist for these to hold.

The *rank* of a rectangular matrix $A$ [denoted $r(A)$] is the number of columns of the largest submatrix of $A$ that is nonsingular. Alternatively, it is the maximum number of linearly independent columns in $A$. The rank of the matrix

$$\begin{pmatrix} 1 & 2 & 0 \\ 0 & 0 & 3 \end{pmatrix}$$

is 2 since at least one 2 × 2 submatrix has a nonzero determinant value; e.g.,

$$\begin{vmatrix} 1 & 0 \\ 0 & 3 \end{vmatrix} \neq 0$$

It cannot exceed 2 since the matrix has only two rows. The matrix

$$\begin{pmatrix} 5 & 2 & 0 \\ 1 & 3 & 0 \\ 4 & 7 & 0 \end{pmatrix}$$

has rank 2 since

$$\begin{vmatrix} 5 & 2 \\ 1 & 3 \end{vmatrix} \neq 0$$

and since the determinant of the entire matrix vanishes because the third column consists entirely of zero elements.

## A.2. Programs

There are numerous references on the linear algebra and matrices. Some of the textbooks at the less advanced levels have been included on p. 255. Usually these texts include convexity and linear equations and so encompass some of the methods of linear programming and numerical analysis.

Some of the available programs in matrix operations and linear algebra from libraries and user groups appear in Table A-1.

Table A-1

| Program Title | User Group | Language |
|---|---|---|
| Matrix operations | CUBE | ALGOL |
| SAMIS—matrix operations for structures | COSMIC | FORTRAN |
| Determinant of matrix | SHARE | FORTRAN |
| Incore matrix package | SHARE | FORTRAN |

## REFERENCES

*Textbooks*

1. AITKEN, A. C., *Determinants and Matrices*. New York: Interscience Publishers, Inc., 1962.
2. BEAUMONT, R. A. AND R. W. BALL, *Introduction to Modern Algebra and Matrix Theory*. New York: Holt, Rinehart and Winston, Inc. 1964.
3. CURTIS, C. W., *Linear Algebra: An Introductory Approach*. Boston: Allyn and Bacon, Inc., 1963.
4. MACLANE, S. AND G. BIRKHOFF, *Algebra*. New York: The MacMillan Co., 1967.
5. MCCOY, N. H., *Introduction to Modern Algebra*. Boston, Mass.: Allyn and Bacon, Inc., 1962.
6. PARKER, W. V. AND J. C. EAVES, *Matrices*. New York: Ronald Press Co., 1960.

## PROBLEMS

1. Determine if the following collections of vectors are linearly independent. Give reasons for your answers. Also describe the space generated by these vectors.

   (a) (1,2)
       (2,1)

   (b) (2, 1, −1)
       (1, 2, 2)
       (3, 7, 1)

   (c) (2, 4, 8)
       (1, 2, 4)
       (4, 8, 16)

   (d) (4, 1, −1, 8)
       (2, 1, 0, 7)
       (5, 3, 1, 6)

2. Determine if the vector (1, 1, 6) can be generated from the following vectors:

   $$(2, 2, 5),\quad (0, 1, 0),\quad (3, 7, 0)$$

3. Find all possible products of any two of the following matrices.

   $$(1\ \ 3\ \ 2),\quad \begin{pmatrix} 1 & 2 & 1 \\ 7 & 4 & -1 \\ 6 & -2 & -3 \end{pmatrix},\quad \begin{pmatrix} -1 & 2 \\ 3 & -9 \end{pmatrix},\quad \begin{pmatrix} 4 & 7 \\ 5 & -7 \\ 1 & 3 \end{pmatrix},\quad \begin{pmatrix} -5 & 4 & 2 \\ 8 & 3 & -1 \end{pmatrix}$$

4. Using the matrices in Problem 3 and their transposes, generate all products.

5. Find the determinants of the following matrices.

   (a) $(\sqrt{3})$

   (b) $\begin{pmatrix} 4 & 0 & 8 & 2 \\ 7 & 1 & 2 & 1 \\ -2 & 4 & 1 & 0 \\ 1 & 6 & 3 & 10 \end{pmatrix}$

   (c) $\begin{pmatrix} 1 & 2 & 3 \\ 2 & -1 & 0 \\ -1 & 4 & 7 \end{pmatrix}$

   (d) $\begin{pmatrix} 1 & 3 \\ -2 & 6 \end{pmatrix}$

6. Write the determinant formula for a general 4 × 4 matrix with expansion along (a) The second row, (b) The third column.

7. Find the rank of the following matrices

   (a) (5)

   (b) $\begin{pmatrix} 6 & 2 & 0 & 1 \\ 1 & 5 & 1 & 6 \end{pmatrix}$

   (c) $\begin{pmatrix} 3 & 1 & 4 \\ -2 & 3 & 1 \\ 1 & 2 & 0 \\ 0 & 1 & 3 \end{pmatrix}$

   (d) $\begin{pmatrix} 1 & 0 & -1 \\ 0 & 0 & 0 \\ -1 & 0 & 1 \end{pmatrix}$

8. Matrices can be used to express nonlinear functions of several variables. Show that the function $f(x_1, x_2)$ defined by

$$f(x_1, x_2) = a_1 x_1^2 + a_2 x_1 x_2 + a_3 x_2^2 + a_4 x_1 + a_5 x_2 + a_6$$

can be represented as

$$f(x_1, x_2) = f + c'x + x'Ax$$

where

$$x = \begin{pmatrix} x_1 \\ x_2 \end{pmatrix} \quad c = \begin{pmatrix} c_1 \\ c_2 \end{pmatrix}$$

$f$ is a constant, and $A$ is a $2 \times 2$ matrix.

9. A function $x'Ax$ is known as a quadratic form. A matrix $A$ is positive definite if

$$x'Ax > 0 \quad \text{for all } x \neq 0$$

The matrix $A$ is nonnegative definite if $x'Ax \geq 0$ for all $x$.

(a) Show that a positive definite matrix is nonnegative definite.

(b) Determine if the following matrices are nonnegative or positive definite:

$$(3) \quad \begin{pmatrix} 2 & 1 \\ 0 & 1 \end{pmatrix} \quad \begin{pmatrix} 2 & 4 \\ 1 & 2 \end{pmatrix}$$

10. Show that the matrix

$$A = \begin{pmatrix} a_{11} & a_{12} \\ a_{21} & a_{22} \end{pmatrix}$$

is positive definite if

$$a_{11} > 0 \quad \text{and} \quad \begin{vmatrix} a_{11} & a_{12} \\ a_{21} & a_{22} \end{vmatrix} > 0$$

11. Using the definition of positive definiteness, relate this property to the convexity of the function $f(x) = x'Ax$ ($A: 2 \times 2$). With this result, give conditions for $x'Ax$ achieving a minimum value at $x_o$.

# B

# NETWORKS AND GRAPH THEORY

## B.1 Network Concepts

In both data management and network analysis, definitions and results of graph theory are frequently encountered. This appendix consists of general definitions for networks along with some basic results. This is followed by a discussion of trees with examples from data management.

A *network* can be viewed as a collection of *nodes* or centers $N$, and a set of *links* connected to some of these nodes $L$. If we denote the set of nodes as $(n_i : 1 \leq i \leq k)$, then a *link* is a connection between two nodes $n_i$ and $n_j$, written $(n_i, n_j)$. Synonyms for node (link) are vertex, point, and activity (edge, branch, or arc). Some examples of networks appear in Fig. B-1.

By listing the set of nodes ($N$) and links ($L$), the network or graph can be expressed as $\mathcal{N} = (N:L)$. This is a description that is equivalent to a diagram such as in Fig. B-1. Some network structures are of particular interest. The network in Fig. B-1(c) is a ring structure and is the network with the minimum number of links such that each node is connected to two other nodes. The star network in Fig. B-1(d)

Examples of Networks:

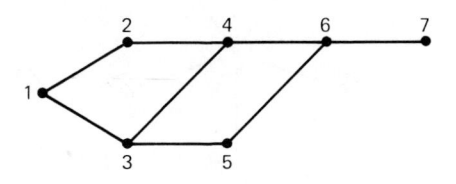

Figure B-1(a). General network.

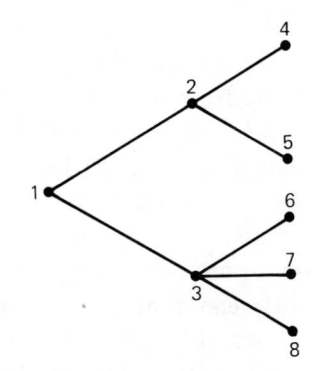

Figure B-1(b). Tree.

is employed in command structures where nodes $n_1$, $n_2$, ..., $n_5$ are peripheral centers that communicate with $n_6$.

Examples of networks include logical relationships between words, highway or transportation systems project planning, petroleum pipelines, and communication systems. Considering a street network, we know street systems are composed of one-way and two-way streets. This indicates that we should differentiate between two-way and one-way links. A two-way link is called an *undirected link* and permits flow of traffic in two directions (from $n_i$ to $n_j$ and from $n_j$ to $n_i$). A one-way link is called a *directed link*.

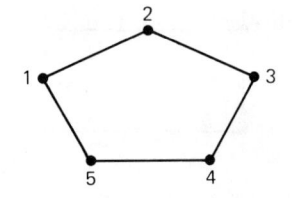

Figure B-1(c). Ring network.

260 / Networks and Graph Theory

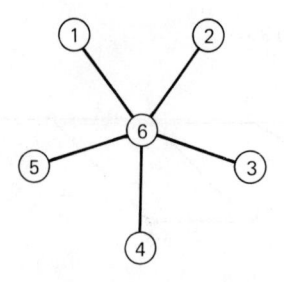

**Figure B-1(d).** Star network.

Occasionally the term *arc* is reserved for directed links. In an arc, traffic can only flow one way from $n_i$ to $n_j$ or $n_j$ to $n_i$. The beginning node is called the *initial node*, while the ending node is the *terminal node*. Figure B-1(b) contains only directed links or arcs. We remark that it is allowable to have a network with both links and arcs. To indicate an arc between $n_i$ and $n_j$, the ordered pair $(n_i, n_j)$ can be used where this represents that an arc exists initiating at $n_i$ and terminating at $n_j$. A general link between $n_i$ and $n_j$ would be $(n_i, n_j)$, which is a shortened form of $(n_i, n_j)$ and $(n_j, n_i)$. By using matrices, we can represent the connections given by a network diagram. This is called an *incidence matrix* for $\mathcal{N}$. It is a matrix whose entries are ±1 and 0. Specifically, let $M(\mathcal{N})$ be the incidence matrix for $\mathcal{N}$ with $m_{ij}(\mathcal{N})$ as the element in the $i$th row and $j$th column. Then

$$m_{ij}(\mathcal{N}) = \begin{cases} +1 & \text{if there is an arc from } n_i \text{ to } n_j \\ -1 & \text{if there is an arc from } n_j \text{ to } n_i \\ 0 & \text{if there is no link between } n_i \text{ and } n_j \end{cases}$$

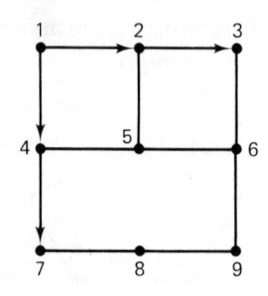

**Figure B-1(e).** Network with both directed and undirected links.

If the network contains no one-way links (undirected network), then we define

$$m_{ij}(\mathcal{N}) = \begin{cases} 1 & \text{if } n_i \text{ and } n_j \text{ are connected by a link} \\ 0 & \text{otherwise} \end{cases}$$

Incidence matrices are used for computer calculations concerning network structures. Some of the properties will be examined later.

In the example in Fig. B-1, the incidence matrices are given, respectively, by

B.1.(a) $M(\mathcal{N}) = \begin{pmatrix} 0 & 1 & 1 & 0 & 0 & 0 & 0 \\ 1 & 0 & 0 & 1 & 0 & 0 & 0 \\ 1 & 0 & 0 & 1 & 1 & 0 & 0 \\ 0 & 1 & 1 & 0 & 0 & 1 & 0 \\ 0 & 0 & 1 & 0 & 0 & 1 & 0 \\ 0 & 0 & 0 & 1 & 0 & 0 & 1 \\ 0 & 0 & 0 & 0 & 0 & 1 & 0 \end{pmatrix}$

(b) $M(\mathcal{N}) = \begin{pmatrix} 0 & 1 & 1 & 0 & 0 & 0 & 0 \\ -1 & 0 & 0 & 1 & 1 & 0 & 0 \\ -1 & 0 & 0 & 0 & 0 & 1 & 1 \\ 0 & -1 & 0 & 0 & 0 & 0 & 0 \\ 0 & -1 & 0 & 0 & 0 & 0 & 0 \\ 0 & 0 & -1 & 0 & 0 & 0 & 0 \\ 0 & 0 & -1 & 0 & 0 & 0 & 0 \end{pmatrix}$

(c) $M(\mathcal{N}) = \begin{pmatrix} 0 & 1 & 0 & 0 & 0 & 1 \\ 1 & 0 & 1 & 0 & 0 & 0 \\ 0 & 1 & 0 & 1 & 0 & 0 \\ 0 & 0 & 1 & 0 & 1 & 0 \\ 0 & 0 & 0 & 1 & 0 & 1 \\ 1 & 0 & 0 & 0 & 1 & 0 \end{pmatrix}$

(d) $M(\mathcal{N}) = \begin{pmatrix} 0 & 0 & 0 & 0 & 0 & 1 \\ 0 & 0 & 0 & 0 & 0 & 1 \\ 0 & 0 & 0 & 0 & 0 & 1 \\ 0 & 0 & 0 & 0 & 0 & 1 \\ 0 & 0 & 0 & 0 & 0 & 1 \\ 1 & 1 & 1 & 1 & 1 & 0 \end{pmatrix}$

**262** / Networks and Graph Theory

(e) $M(\mathcal{N}) = \begin{pmatrix} 0 & 1 & 0 & 1 & 0 & 0 & 0 & 0 & 0 \\ -1 & 0 & 1 & 0 & 1 & 0 & 0 & 0 & 0 \\ 0 & -1 & 0 & 0 & 0 & 1 & 0 & 0 & 0 \\ 1 & 0 & 0 & 0 & 1 & 0 & 1 & 0 & 0 \\ 0 & 1 & 0 & 1 & 0 & 1 & 0 & 0 & 0 \\ 0 & 0 & 1 & 0 & 1 & 0 & 0 & 0 & 1 \\ 0 & 0 & 0 & -1 & 0 & 0 & 0 & 1 & 0 \\ 0 & 0 & 0 & 0 & 0 & 0 & 1 & 0 & 1 \\ 0 & 0 & 0 & 0 & 0 & 1 & 0 & 1 & 0 \end{pmatrix}$

Some network properties can be deduced by examining the incidence matrix. If row $i$ contains no nonzero elements, then node $n_i$ is not connected to any other node in the network. (Show that this holds for column $i$). Suppose a network has two separate parts as in Fig. B-2.

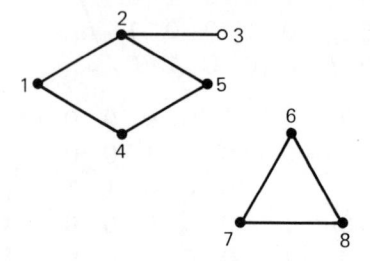

Figure B-2. Network with separate parts.

The incidence matrix is given by

$M(\mathcal{N}) = \begin{pmatrix} 0 & 1 & 0 & 1 & 0 & 0 & 0 & 0 \\ 1 & 0 & 1 & 0 & 0 & 0 & 0 & 0 \\ 0 & 1 & 0 & 0 & 0 & 0 & 0 & 0 \\ 1 & 0 & 0 & 0 & 1 & 0 & 0 & 0 \\ 0 & 1 & 0 & 1 & 0 & 0 & 0 & 0 \\ 0 & 0 & 0 & 0 & 0 & 0 & 1 & 1 \\ 0 & 0 & 0 & 0 & 0 & 1 & 0 & 1 \\ 0 & 0 & 0 & 0 & 0 & 1 & 1 & 0 \end{pmatrix}$

Using Appendix A, we can partition $M(\mathcal{N})$ into

$$M_{11} = \begin{pmatrix} 0 & 1 & 0 & 1 & 0 \\ 1 & 0 & 1 & 0 & 0 \\ 0 & 1 & 0 & 0 & 0 \\ 1 & 0 & 0 & 0 & 1 \\ 0 & 1 & 0 & 1 & 0 \end{pmatrix}, \quad M_{12} = \begin{pmatrix} 0 & 0 & 0 \\ 0 & 0 & 0 \\ 0 & 0 & 0 \\ 0 & 0 & 0 \\ 0 & 0 & 0 \end{pmatrix},$$

$$M_{21} = \begin{pmatrix} 0 & 0 & 0 & 0 & 0 \\ 0 & 0 & 0 & 0 & 0 \\ 0 & 0 & 0 & 0 & 0 \end{pmatrix}, \quad M_{22} = \begin{pmatrix} 0 & 1 & 1 \\ 1 & 0 & 1 \\ 1 & 1 & 0 \end{pmatrix}$$

This separation between the parts is revealed by the property that the submatrices $M_{12}$ and $M_{21}$ have all zero elements. Any link between nodes $n_1, \ldots, n_5$ and $n_6, n_7, n_8$ would appear there.

The example above leads to the definition of subnetwork or subgraph. The network $\mathcal{N}$ above is composed of two parts $\mathcal{N}_1$ and $\mathcal{N}_2$ where $\mathcal{N}_1$ is the network with nodes labeled 1, 2, 3, 4, 5 and $\mathcal{N}_2$ with nodes 6, 7, 8.

Formally, $\mathcal{M} = (M:L_M)$ is a subnetwork of $\mathcal{N} = (N:L_N)$ if $\mathcal{M}$ is a network and $M \subset N$ and $L_M \subset L_N$. That is, every node in $\mathcal{M}$ appears in $\mathcal{N}$ and similarly for every link in $\mathcal{M}$.

Other set theoretic operations hold for networks. Two networks $\mathcal{M}$ and $\mathcal{N}$ are disjoint if they have no nodes in common. The union of two networks, $\mathcal{M}$ and $\mathcal{N}$, denoted $\mathcal{M} \cup \mathcal{N}$ is given by

$$\mathcal{M} \cup \mathcal{N} = \{M \cup N : L_M \cup L_N\}$$

This is the network such that each node (link) lies in $M$ or $N$ ($L_M$ or $L_N$). The intersection of two networks $\mathcal{M}$ and $\mathcal{N}$ is $\mathcal{M} \cap \mathcal{N} = \{M \cap N : L_M \cap L_N\}$.

A collection of subnetworks ($\mathcal{N}_i : 1 \leq i \leq m$) of $\mathcal{N}$ is a decomposition of the network $\mathcal{N}$ if

$$\bigcup_{i=1}^{m} \mathcal{N}_i = \mathcal{N}$$

and

$$\mathcal{N}_i \cap \mathcal{N}_j = \phi$$

The preceding example is an example of a decomposition.

In some applications, such as transportation, decomposition is not possible, while it is frequently encountered in data management. A concept in relating to partitioning a network is that of a *bipartite network*. This is a network (*N:L*) where these are two disjoint subsets of $N$, say, $N_1$ and $N_2$, with the property that for every link $(n_i, n_j)$ in the network $n_i$ is in one subset and $n_j$ is in the other. In the sample network shown in Fig. B-3 we can set $N_1 = (n_1, n_2, n_3)$ and $N_2 = (n_4, n_5, n_6)$ and observe that the network is bipartite.

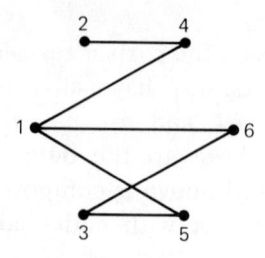

**Figure B-3.**

Another observation is that all diagonal elements of the incidence matrix are zero. This is because no node is connected to itself. A link that connects a node to itself is called a *loop*. An example is shown in Fig. B-4.

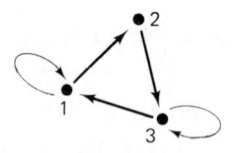

**Figure B-4.**

The incidence matrix for this network is

$$M(\mathcal{N}) = \begin{pmatrix} 1 & 1 & -1 \\ -1 & 0 & 1 \\ 1 & -1 & 1 \end{pmatrix}$$

An undirected network has a symmetric incidence matrix, for if the $(i, j)$ element is 1, then $n_i$ and $n_j$ are linked. Since the network is undirected, there is a 1 in the $(j, i)$th entry in the matrix. Another term for an incidence matrix for an undirected network is a connectivity matrix.

A loop is basically a path from a node to itself without going through any other nodes. More generally, a path connecting two nodes $n_i$ and $n_j$ is a finite collection of intermediate nodes $\{n_{kij}: k = 1, \ldots, p\}$ such that

$$n_{1ij} = n_i, n_{p,i,j} = n_j$$

and $(n_{kij}, n_{k+1,i,j})$ is a link in the network for $k = 1, \ldots, p - 1$. There may be several paths between two nodes. Consider the example in Fig. B-2. To get from $n_1$ to $n_5$, there are several paths including $(n_1, n_2, n_5)$ and $(n_1, n_4, n_5)$. In fact there is at least one path between any two of $n_1, n_2, n_3, n_4, n_5$. There is no path, however between any of these nodes and nodes $n_6, n_7$, and $n_8$. There are no links between these sets of nodes.

A network is *connected* if there is at least one path between any two nodes in the network. The network in Fig. B-2 is then said to be *disconnected*. A *connected subnetwork* of a network is a subnetwork that in itself is connected. Thus, a network may be disconnected but may possess several connected subnetworks. A maximal connected subnetwork is called a *component*. A network is completely connected if there is a link connecting every pair of nodes in the network.

If we consider the possible paths in a network, then some of these will begin and end at the same node. These paths are round trips or *circuits*.

A special type of circuit is one that goes through every node. It is called a *Hamiltonian circuit*. Circuits play a key role in transportation and communication systems since in routing or scheduling it is often a requirement that the commodity being scheduled start from and return to the same location.

It is common to assume that the number of links and nodes in a network is finite. The *moment* of a network is the number of nodes in the network. Each link is really two arcs. Thus, in a network of links, the number of links is the total number of arcs divided by 2. A rough measure of the number of nodes to links is obtained by computing the quotient of the number of links to nodes. In the incidence matrix the number of rows or columns is the moment, while for an undirected network the number of arcs in the network is the number of nonzero elements in the incidence matrix.

## B.2 Tree Structures

A general tree structure is given in Figs. B-1(b) and B-5. The definitions of the previous section can be employed here. A *tree* is a network in which there are no circuits. Thus, in Fig. B-5, it is impossible to return to the starting point. Because of this, all links will be called arcs. Trees are commonly written from left to right and from top to bottom. A *root node* (or root point or parent) is a node with no incoming arcs. The number of root nodes is the *radix*. In Fig. B-5 the radix is 2. Tree theory carries some of the same terms as forestry due to the similarity in structure. On the end of a tree are *leaves*. Thus, a node with no outgoing arcs is a *leaf node*. The *weight* of the tree is the number of leaf nodes. In Fig. B-5 the weight is 8. The *degree* of a node is the number of outgoing arcs from the node. Thus, leaf nodes have degree 0.

In data management a concern is for the levels of data in a hierarchy. Interpreting this for trees, the nodes are aggregated into levels. The dashed lines in Fig. B-5 indicated the levels in the tree. Formally if node $n_i$ is in level $k$ and there is an arc from $n_i$ to $n_j$, then $n_j$ is in level $k + 1$. (If the arc ended at $n_i$, which level would $n_j$ be in?) The number of levels in a tree is the height of the tree.

The notions of subtree and path carry over from the previous section. In Fig. B-5 the following collections of nodes are examples of subtrees: $(n_2, n_5, n_6)$, $(n_3, n_7)$, and $(n_{12}, n_{13}, n_{14}, n_{15})$. Decomposition is also analogous. The structure in the example has two disjoint subtrees $(n_i : 1 \leq i \leq 9)$ and $(n_i : 10 \leq i \leq 15)$.

There is a distinction in the results for tree structures versus general networks. In network problems, we are concerned with some commodity or collection of commodities moving across a network. Thus, we are concerned with maximizing flow, finding shortest paths, and determining bottlenecks. For trees and data management we are involved with labeling schemes and arrangements of nodes in trees. Less flexibility is possible for trees for some data formats than in networks where routes can be chosen quite liberally. In networks, the links have certain physical properties. There may be, for example, a capacity and a distance. For a tree structure a link is a logical connection between one term and another. A geneology tree is a good example of a tree, while collection of streets in a city is an example of a network.

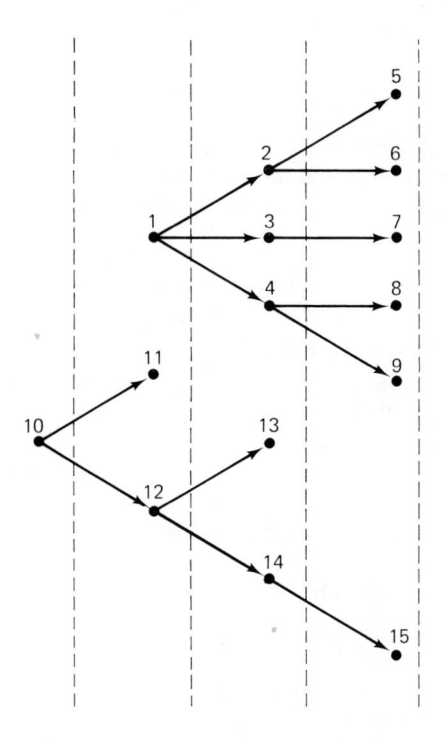

Figure B-5. Diagram of a tree structure.

## REFERENCES

There are several excellent theoretical texts in graph theory and the theory of trees. Several of these are Berge[1] and Ore[2]. Combinatorical methods that relate to these structures are explored in Ryser[3].

In addition, many network analysis and date management texts contain material on graph theory. These are cited in References in Chapters 2 and 4.

Graph theory is one of the active areas of theoretical mathematics; papers in graph theory and combinatorics appear in the journals listed below. A reason for this connection is that many mathematical problems in graph theory involve ordering and properties and arrangement.

## 268 / Networks and Graph Theory

*Journal of Combinatorial Theory*

*Association of Computing Machinery Journals*

*Society of Industrial and Applied Mathematics—
Journal on Applied Mathematics*

*Journal of Franklin Institute*

*Acta Mathematica*

*Canadian Journal of Mathematics*

*Michigan Mathematics Journal*

*Proceedings of American Mathematical Society*

*Textbooks*

1. BERGE, C., *The Theory of Graphs*. London: Methuen & Co., Ltd. 1962.
2. ORE, O., *"Theory of Graphs"* Amer. Math. Society, 38, Colloquium Publications, Providence, R. I., 1962.
3. RYSER, H. J., *Combinatorial Mathematics*, N. Y.: John Wiley & Sons, Inc. (MAA publisher), 1963.

## PROBLEMS

For the following networks, find

(i)   The incidence matrix.

(ii)  Moment.

(iii) All subnetworks.

(iv)  Decompositions (if they exist).

(v)   All circuits from node 1.

(vi)  All components.

(vii) Loops.

Also indicate whether each network is bipartite.

1.

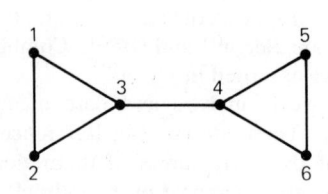

Figure B-4-1

2.

Figure B-4-2

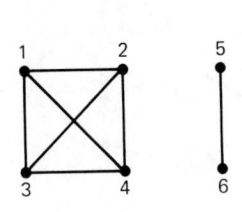

3.

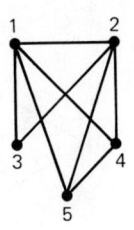

Figure B-4-3

4.

Figure B-4-4

For the following trees, find

    (i)    The incidence matrix.
    (ii)   Moment.
    (iii)  Height.
    (iv)  Radix.
    (v)   Weight.
    (vi)  All leaf points.
    (vii) All levels.

5.

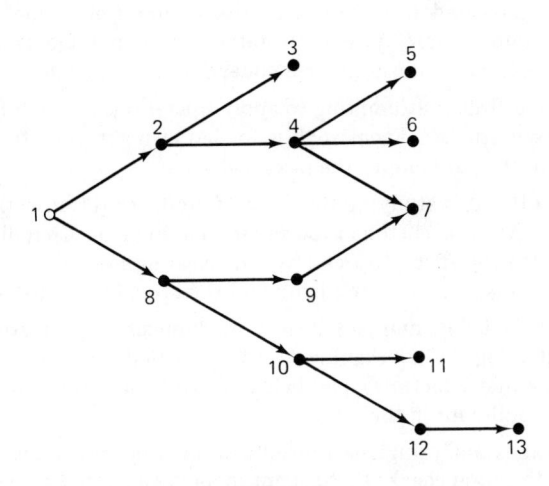

Figure B-4-5

6.

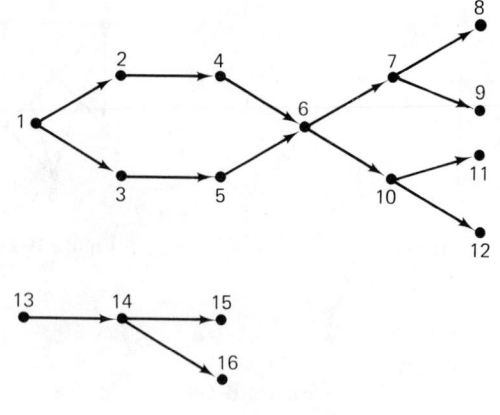

Figure B-4-6

In Problems 7 to 13, establish the situation as a network defining the links and nodes. Determine whether or not the structure is a tree and any special properties of the network.

7. An engineer is in charge of laying out a production program for wing nuts. Each nut goes through five processes including cutting, forming, threading, coating, and packing.

8. A school administrator is attempting to set a computer based file system for the student records. Each student's record will contain his social security number, home address, telephone number, grade point average, courses and individual grades, marital status, class, and units completed. This information is aggregated into personal information (telephone, social security, marital status, address), school status (grade point average, class), units (completed), and courses (course code, date taken, grade).

9. A trucking firm is attempting to apply operations research to the routing of its delivery trucks. Each truck is loaded at night prior to a day's run and returns to the yard empty the next night.

10. A bank official is studying the flow of credit card transactions through the system. After a customer purchases an item on a credit card, a slip is turned into the first of three levels of clearing houses. From the last clearing house it goes to a central bank and then to a branch location.

11. Pollution is being dumped into a medium-sized river from 10 factories arranged along the riverbank. A city is located below the first 3 factories, below the first 7 factories, and below all 10 factories. Each factory dumps a different pollutant in the river.

12. A student is analyzing the procedures involved in a student health center. The health center checks the student in and assigns him to one of seven areas for care. Each area has six distinct procedures for the student. The student then checks out after being treated.

13. Describe two systems or phenomena that can be interpreted in a network context.

In some graph theory applications a tree is constructed where the links have different labels or colors. The result is a *chromatic tree*. Such trees are the subject of Problems 14 and 15.

14. Balls are drawn from an urn. The balls are of three colors: red, white, and blue. As each ball is drawn, it is lined up from left to right. Construct a tree interpretation of this experiment. What is a path? Classify the links and nodes.

15. A radar center receives conflicting reports on the location of an unknown aircraft from each of three radar stations. Interference and conflict occur when two successive observations come in from different centers. Construct a graph-theoretic interpretation of this situation and explain how to determine the number of ways observations can enter the center with interference between all successive pairs of observations.

# C

## TABLE OF STATISTICS AND PSEUDO-RANDOM NUMBERS

Table C-1. BINOMIAL COEFFICIENTS

| $n$ | $\binom{n}{2}$ | $\binom{n}{3}$ | $\binom{n}{4}$ | $\binom{n}{5}$ | $\binom{n}{6}$ | $\binom{n}{7}$ | $\binom{n}{8}$ | $\binom{n}{9}$ | $\binom{n}{10}$ |
|---|---|---|---|---|---|---|---|---|---|
| 2 | 1 | | | | | | | | |
| 3 | 3 | 1 | | | | | | | |
| 4 | 6 | 4 | 1 | | | | | | |
| 5 | 10 | 10 | 5 | 1 | | | | | |
| 6 | 15 | 20 | 15 | 6 | 1 | | | | |
| 7 | 21 | 35 | 35 | 21 | 7 | 1 | | | |
| 8 | 28 | 56 | 70 | 56 | 28 | 8 | 1 | | |
| 9 | 36 | 84 | 126 | 126 | 84 | 36 | 9 | 1 | |
| 10 | 45 | 120 | 210 | 252 | 210 | 120 | 45 | 10 | 1 |
| 11 | 55 | 165 | 330 | 462 | 462 | 330 | 165 | 55 | 11 |
| 12 | 66 | 220 | 495 | 792 | 924 | 792 | 495 | 220 | 66 |
| 13 | 78 | 286 | 715 | 1287 | 1716 | 1716 | 1287 | 715 | 286 |
| 14 | 91 | 364 | 1001 | 2002 | 3003 | 3432 | 3003 | 2002 | 1001 |
| 15 | 105 | 455 | 1365 | 3003 | 5005 | 6435 | 6435 | 5005 | 3003 |
| 16 | 120 | 560 | 1820 | 4368 | 8008 | 11440 | 12870 | 11440 | 8008 |
| 17 | 136 | 680 | 2380 | 6188 | 12376 | 19448 | 24310 | 24310 | 19448 |
| 18 | 153 | 816 | 3060 | 8568 | 18564 | 31824 | 43758 | 48620 | 43758 |
| 19 | 171 | 969 | 3876 | 11628 | 27132 | 50388 | 75582 | 92378 | 92378 |
| 20 | 190 | 1140 | 4845 | 15504 | 38760 | 77520 | 125970 | 167960 | 184756 |

## Table C-2. EXPONENTIAL DISTRIBUTION

$$F(x) = \int_0^x e^{-y}\, dy$$

| $x$ | $F(x)$ | $x$ | $F(x)$ |
|---|---|---|---|
| 0 | 0 | 2.6 | 0.925726 |
| 0.00501 | 0.005 | 2.7 | 0.932794 |
| 0.01005 | 0.01 | 2.8 | 0.939190 |
| 0.05129 | 0.05 | 2.9 | 0.944977 |
| 0.1 | 0.095163 | 2.99573 | 0.95 |
| 0.10536 | 0.10 | 3.0 | 0.950213 |
| 0.2 | 0.181269 | 3.1 | 0.954951 |
| 0.3 | 0.259182 | 3.2 | 0.959238 |
| 0.4 | 0.329680 | 3.3 | 0.963117 |
| 0.5 | 0.393469 | 3.4 | 0.966627 |
| 0.6 | 0.451182 | 3.5 | 0.969803 |
| 0.7 | 0.503415 | 3.6 | 0.972676 |
| 0.8 | 0.550671 | 3.7 | 0.975276 |
| 0.9 | 0.593430 | 3.8 | 0.977629 |
| 1.0 | 0.632121 | 3.9 | 0.979758 |
| 1.1 | 0.667129 | 4.0 | 0.981684 |
| 1.2 | 0.698806 | 4.1 | 0.983427 |
| 1.3 | 0.727468 | 4.2 | 0.985004 |
| 1.4 | 0.753403 | 4.3 | 0.986431 |
| 1.5 | 0.776870 | 4.4 | 0.987723 |
| 1.6 | 0.798103 | 4.5 | 0.988891 |
| 1.7 | 0.817316 | 4.6 | 0.989948 |
| 1.8 | 0.834701 | 4.60517 | 0.99 |
| 1.9 | 0.850431 | 4.7 | 0.990905 |
| 2.0 | 0.864665 | 4.8 | 0.991770 |
| 2.1 | 0.877544 | 4.9 | 0.992553 |
| 2.2 | 0.889197 | 5.0 | 0.993262 |
| 2.3 | 0.899741 | 5.29832 | 0.995 |
| 2.30259 | 0.90 | | |
| 2.4 | 0.909282 | | |
| 2.5 | 0.917915 | | |

Table C-3. NORMAL DISTRIBUTION

$$F(x) = \int_{-\infty}^{x} e^{-y^2/2}(2\pi)^{-1/2}\,dy$$

| $x$ | $F(x)$ | $x$ | $F(x)$ |
|---|---|---|---|
| 0   | 0.50000 | 2.0 | 0.97725 |
| 0.1 | 0.53983 | 2.1 | 0.98214 |
| 0.2 | 0.57926 | 2.2 | 0.98610 |
| 0.3 | 0.61791 | 2.3 | 0.98928 |
| 0.4 | 0.65542 | 2.4 | 0.99180 |
| 0.5 | 0.69146 | 2.5 | 0.99379 |
| 0.6 | 0.72575 | 2.6 | 0.99534 |
| 0.7 | 0.75804 | 2.7 | 0.99653 |
| 0.8 | 0.78815 | 2.8 | 0.99745 |
| 0.9 | 0.81594 | 2.9 | 0.99813 |
| 1.0 | 0.84135 | 3.0 | 0.99865 |
| 1.1 | 0.86433 | 3.1 | 0.99903 |
| 1.2 | 0.88493 | 3.2 | 0.99931 |
| 1.3 | 0.90320 | 3.3 | 0.99952 |
| 1.4 | 0.91924 | 3.4 | 0.99966 |
| 1.5 | 0.93319 | 3.5 | 0.99977 |
| 1.6 | 0.94520 | 3.6 | 0.99984 |
| 1.7 | 0.95544 | 3.7 | 0.99989 |
| 1.8 | 0.96407 | 3.8 | 0.99993 |
| 1.9 | 0.97128 | 3.9 | 0.99995 |
|     |         | 4.0 | 0.99997 |

**Table C-4.** CHI-SQUARE DISTRIBUTION VALUES OF $x$ FOR VARIOUS VALUES OF $F(x)$ AND $n$ DEGREES OF FREEDOM

| $F(x)$ \ $n$ | 0.1 | 0.3 | 0.5 | 0.7 | 0.8 | 0.9 | 0.95 | 0.98 | 0.99 |
|---|---|---|---|---|---|---|---|---|---|
| 1  | 0.016  | 0.148  | 0.455  | 1.074  | 1.642  | 2.706  | 3.841  | 5.412  | 6.635 |
| 2  | 0.211  | 0.713  | 1.386  | 2.408  | 3.219  | 4.605  | 5.991  | 7.824  | 9.210 |
| 3  | 0.584  | 1.424  | 2.366  | 3.665  | 4.642  | 6.251  | 7.815  | 9.837  | 11.345 |
| 4  | 1.064  | 2.195  | 3.357  | 4.878  | 5.989  | 7.779  | 9.488  | 11.668 | 13.277 |
| 5  | 1.610  | 3.000  | 4.351  | 6.064  | 7.289  | 9.236  | 11.070 | 13.388 | 15.086 |
| 6  | 2.204  | 3.828  | 5.348  | 7.231  | 8.558  | 10.645 | 12.592 | 15.033 | 16.812 |
| 7  | 2.833  | 4.671  | 6.346  | 8.383  | 9.803  | 12.017 | 14.067 | 16.622 | 18.472 |
| 8  | 3.490  | 5.527  | 7.344  | 9.524  | 11.030 | 13.362 | 15.507 | 18.168 | 20.090 |
| 9  | 4.168  | 6.393  | 8.343  | 10.656 | 12.242 | 14.684 | 16.919 | 19.679 | 21.666 |
| 10 | 4.865  | 7.267  | 9.342  | 11.781 | 13.442 | 15.987 | 18.307 | 21.161 | 23.209 |
| 11 | 5.578  | 8.148  | 10.341 | 12.899 | 14.631 | 17.275 | 19.675 | 22.618 | 24.725 |
| 12 | 6.304  | 9.034  | 11.340 | 14.011 | 15.812 | 18.549 | 21.026 | 24.054 | 26.217 |
| 13 | 7.042  | 9.926  | 12.340 | 15.119 | 16.985 | 19.812 | 22.362 | 25.472 | 27.688 |
| 14 | 7.790  | 10.821 | 13.339 | 16.222 | 18.151 | 21.064 | 23.685 | 26.873 | 29.141 |
| 15 | 8.547  | 11.721 | 14.339 | 17.322 | 19.311 | 22.307 | 24.996 | 28.259 | 30.578 |
| 16 | 9.312  | 12.625 | 15.339 | 18.418 | 20.465 | 23.542 | 26.296 | 29.633 | 32.000 |
| 17 | 10.085 | 13.531 | 16.339 | 19.511 | 21.615 | 24.769 | 27.587 | 30.995 | 33.409 |
| 18 | 10.865 | 14.440 | 17.339 | 20.601 | 22.760 | 25.989 | 28.869 | 32.346 | 34.805 |
| 19 | 11.651 | 15.352 | 18.339 | 21.689 | 23.900 | 27.204 | 30.144 | 33.687 | 36.191 |
| 20 | 12.443 | 16.266 | 19.337 | 22.775 | 25.038 | 28.412 | 31.410 | 35.020 | 37.566 |
| 21 | 13.240 | 17.182 | 20.337 | 23.858 | 26.171 | 29.615 | 32.671 | 36.343 | 38.932 |
| 22 | 14.041 | 18.101 | 21.337 | 24.939 | 27.301 | 30.813 | 33.924 | 37.659 | 40.289 |
| 23 | 14.848 | 19.021 | 22.337 | 26.018 | 28.429 | 32.007 | 35.172 | 38.968 | 41.639 |
| 24 | 15.649 | 19.943 | 23.337 | 27.096 | 29.553 | 33.196 | 36.415 | 40.270 | 42.980 |
| 25 | 16.473 | 20.867 | 24.337 | 28.172 | 30.675 | 34.382 | 37.652 | 41.566 | 44.314 |

**Table C-5.** $F$ DISTRIBUTION VALUES OF $t_r$ WHERE P $[F \leq t_\gamma] = \gamma$

$\gamma = 0.90$

| | 1 | 2 | 3 | 4 | 5 | 6 | 7 | 8 | 9 | 10 | 12 | 15 | 20 | 24 | 30 | 40 | 68 | 120 |
|---|---|---|---|---|---|---|---|---|---|---|---|---|---|---|---|---|---|---|
| 1 | 39.86 | 49.50 | 53.59 | 55.83 | 57.24 | 58.20 | 58.91 | 59.44 | 59.86 | 60.19 | 60.71 | 61.22 | 61.74 | 62.00 | 62.26 | 62.53 | 62.79 | 63.06 |
| 2 | 8.53 | 9.00 | 9.16 | 9.24 | 9.29 | 9.33 | 9.35 | 9.37 | 9.38 | 9.39 | 9.41 | 9.42 | 9.44 | 9.45 | 9.46 | 9.47 | 9.47 | 9.48 |
| 3 | 5.54 | 5.46 | 5.39 | 5.34 | 5.31 | 5.28 | 5.27 | 5.25 | 5.24 | 5.23 | 5.22 | 5.20 | 5.18 | 5.18 | 5.17 | 5.16 | 5.15 | 5.14 |
| 4 | 4.54 | 4.32 | 4.19 | 4.11 | 4.05 | 4.01 | 3.98 | 3.95 | 3.94 | 3.92 | 3.90 | 3.87 | 3.84 | 3.83 | 3.82 | 3.80 | 3.79 | 3.78 |
| 5 | 4.06 | 3.78 | 3.62 | 3.52 | 3.45 | 3.40 | 3.37 | 3.34 | 3.32 | 3.30 | 3.27 | 3.24 | 3.21 | 3.19 | 3.17 | 3.16 | 3.14 | 3.12 |
| 6 | 3.78 | 3.46 | 3.29 | 3.18 | 3.11 | 3.05 | 3.01 | 2.98 | 2.96 | 2.94 | 2.90 | 2.87 | 2.84 | 2.82 | 2.80 | 2.78 | 2.76 | 2.74 |
| 7 | 3.59 | 3.26 | 3.07 | 2.96 | 2.88 | 2.83 | 2.78 | 2.75 | 2.72 | 2.70 | 2.67 | 2.63 | 2.59 | 2.58 | 2.56 | 2.54 | 2.51 | 2.49 |
| 8 | 3.46 | 3.11 | 2.92 | 2.81 | 2.73 | 2.67 | 2.62 | 2.59 | 2.56 | 2.54 | 2.50 | 2.46 | 2.42 | 2.40 | 2.38 | 2.36 | 2.34 | 2.32 |
| 9 | 3.36 | 3.01 | 2.81 | 2.69 | 2.61 | 2.55 | 2.51 | 2.47 | 2.44 | 2.42 | 2.38 | 2.34 | 2.30 | 2.28 | 2.25 | 2.23 | 2.21 | 2.18 |
| 10 | 3.29 | 2.92 | 2.73 | 2.61 | 2.52 | 2.46 | 2.41 | 2.38 | 2.35 | 2.32 | 2.28 | 2.24 | 2.20 | 2.18 | 2.16 | 2.13 | 2.11 | 2.08 |
| 11 | 3.23 | 2.86 | 2.66 | 2.54 | 2.45 | 2.39 | 2.34 | 2.30 | 2.27 | 2.25 | 2.21 | 2.17 | 2.12 | 2.10 | 2.08 | 2.05 | 2.03 | 2.00 |
| 12 | 3.18 | 2.81 | 2.61 | 2.48 | 2.39 | 2.33 | 2.28 | 2.24 | 2.21 | 2.19 | 2.15 | 2.10 | 2.06 | 2.04 | 2.01 | 1.99 | 1.96 | 1.93 |
| 13 | 3.14 | 2.76 | 2.56 | 2.43 | 2.35 | 2.28 | 2.23 | 2.20 | 2.16 | 2.14 | 2.10 | 2.05 | 2.01 | 1.98 | 1.96 | 1.93 | 1.90 | 1.88 |
| 14 | 3.10 | 2.73 | 2.52 | 2.39 | 2.31 | 2.24 | 2.19 | 2.15 | 2.12 | 2.10 | 2.05 | 2.01 | 1.96 | 1.94 | 1.91 | 1.89 | 1.86 | 1.83 |
| 15 | 3.07 | 2.70 | 2.49 | 2.36 | 2.27 | 2.21 | 2.16 | 2.12 | 2.09 | 2.06 | 2.02 | 1.97 | 1.92 | 1.90 | 1.87 | 1.85 | 1.82 | 1.79 |
| 16 | 3.05 | 2.67 | 2.46 | 2.33 | 2.24 | 2.18 | 2.13 | 2.09 | 2.06 | 2.03 | 1.99 | 1.94 | 1.89 | 1.87 | 1.84 | 1.81 | 1.78 | 1.75 |
| 17 | 3.03 | 2.64 | 2.44 | 2.31 | 2.22 | 2.15 | 2.10 | 2.06 | 2.03 | 2.00 | 1.96 | 1.91 | 1.86 | 1.84 | 1.81 | 1.78 | 1.75 | 1.72 |
| 18 | 3.01 | 2.62 | 2.42 | 2.29 | 2.20 | 2.13 | 2.08 | 2.04 | 2.00 | 1.98 | 1.93 | 1.89 | 1.84 | 1.81 | 1.78 | 1.75 | 1.72 | 1.69 |
| 19 | 2.99 | 2.61 | 2.40 | 2.27 | 2.18 | 2.11 | 2.06 | 2.02 | 1.98 | 1.96 | 1.91 | 1.86 | 1.81 | 1.79 | 1.76 | 1.73 | 1.70 | 1.67 |
| 20 | 2.97 | 2.59 | 2.38 | 2.25 | 2.16 | 2.09 | 2.04 | 2.00 | 1.96 | 1.94 | 1.89 | 1.84 | 1.79 | 1.77 | 1.74 | 1.71 | 1.68 | 1.64 |
| 21 | 2.96 | 2.57 | 2.36 | 2.23 | 2.14 | 2.08 | 2.02 | 1.98 | 1.95 | 1.92 | 1.87 | 1.83 | 1.78 | 1.75 | 1.72 | 1.69 | 1.66 | 1.62 |
| 22 | 2.95 | 2.56 | 2.35 | 2.22 | 2.13 | 2.06 | 2.01 | 1.97 | 1.93 | 1.90 | 1.86 | 1.81 | 1.76 | 1.73 | 1.70 | 1.67 | 1.64 | 1.60 |
| 23 | 2.94 | 2.55 | 2.34 | 2.21 | 2.11 | 2.05 | 1.99 | 1.95 | 1.92 | 1.89 | 1.84 | 1.80 | 1.74 | 1.72 | 1.69 | 1.66 | 1.62 | 1.59 |
| 24 | 2.93 | 2.54 | 2.33 | 2.19 | 2.10 | 2.04 | 1.98 | 1.94 | 1.91 | 1.88 | 1.83 | 1.78 | 1.73 | 1.70 | 1.67 | 1.64 | 1.61 | 1.57 |
| 25 | 2.92 | 2.53 | 2.32 | 2.18 | 2.09 | 2.02 | 1.97 | 1.93 | 1.89 | 1.87 | 1.82 | 1.77 | 1.72 | 1.69 | 1.66 | 1.63 | 1.59 | 1.56 |
| 30 | 2.88 | 2.49 | 2.28 | 2.14 | 2.05 | 1.98 | 1.93 | 1.88 | 1.85 | 1.82 | 1.77 | 1.72 | 1.67 | 1.64 | 1.61 | 1.57 | 1.54 | 1.50 |
| 40 | 2.84 | 2.44 | 2.23 | 2.09 | 2.00 | 1.93 | 1.87 | 1.83 | 1.79 | 1.76 | 1.71 | 1.66 | 1.61 | 1.57 | 1.54 | 1.51 | 1.47 | 1.42 |
| 60 | 2.79 | 2.39 | 2.18 | 2.04 | 1.95 | 1.87 | 1.82 | 1.77 | 1.74 | 1.71 | 1.66 | 1.60 | 1.54 | 1.51 | 1.48 | 1.44 | 1.40 | 1.35 |
| 120 | 2.75 | 2.35 | 2.13 | 1.99 | 1.90 | 1.82 | 1.77 | 1.72 | 1.68 | 1.65 | 1.60 | 1.55 | 1.48 | 1.45 | 1.41 | 1.37 | 1.32 | 1.26 |

$\gamma = 0.95$

| | 161.4 | 199.5 | 215.7 | 224.6 | 230.2 | 234.0 | 236.8 | 238.9 | 240.5 | 241.9 | 243.9 | 245.9 | 248.0 | 249.1 | 250.1 | 251.1 | 252.2 | 253.3 |
|---|---|---|---|---|---|---|---|---|---|---|---|---|---|---|---|---|---|---|
| 1 | 161.4 | 199.5 | 215.7 | 224.6 | 230.2 | 234.0 | 236.8 | 238.9 | 240.5 | 241.9 | 243.9 | 245.9 | 248.0 | 249.1 | 250.1 | 251.1 | 252.2 | 253.3 |
| 2 | 18.51 | 19.00 | 19.16 | 19.25 | 19.30 | 19.33 | 19.35 | 19.37 | 19.38 | 19.40 | 19.41 | 19.43 | 19.45 | 19.45 | 19.46 | 19.47 | 19.48 | 19.49 |
| 3 | 10.13 | 9.55 | 9.28 | 9.12 | 9.01 | 8.94 | 8.89 | 8.85 | 8.81 | 8.79 | 8.74 | 8.70 | 8.66 | 8.64 | 8.62 | 8.59 | 8.57 | 8.55 |
| 4 | 7.71 | 6.94 | 6.59 | 6.39 | 6.26 | 6.16 | 6.09 | 6.04 | 6.00 | 5.96 | 5.91 | 5.86 | 5.80 | 5.77 | 5.75 | 5.72 | 5.69 | 5.66 |
| 5 | 6.61 | 5.79 | 5.41 | 5.19 | 5.05 | 4.95 | 4.88 | 4.82 | 4.77 | 4.74 | 4.68 | 4.62 | 4.56 | 4.53 | 4.50 | 4.46 | 4.43 | 4.40 |
| 6 | 5.99 | 5.14 | 4.76 | 4.53 | 4.39 | 4.28 | 4.21 | 4.15 | 4.10 | 4.06 | 4.00 | 3.94 | 3.87 | 3.84 | 3.81 | 3.77 | 3.74 | 3.70 |
| 7 | 5.59 | 4.74 | 4.35 | 4.12 | 3.97 | 3.87 | 3.79 | 3.73 | 3.68 | 3.64 | 3.57 | 3.51 | 3.44 | 3.41 | 3.38 | 3.34 | 3.30 | 3.27 |
| 8 | 5.32 | 4.46 | 4.07 | 3.84 | 3.69 | 3.58 | 3.50 | 3.44 | 3.39 | 3.35 | 3.28 | 3.22 | 3.15 | 3.12 | 3.08 | 3.04 | 3.01 | 2.97 |
| 9 | 5.12 | 4.26 | 3.86 | 3.63 | 3.48 | 3.37 | 3.29 | 3.23 | 3.18 | 3.14 | 3.07 | 3.01 | 2.94 | 2.90 | 2.86 | 2.83 | 2.79 | 2.75 |
| 10 | 4.96 | 4.10 | 3.71 | 3.48 | 3.33 | 3.22 | 3.14 | 3.07 | 3.02 | 2.98 | 2.91 | 2.85 | 2.77 | 2.74 | 2.70 | 2.66 | 2.62 | 2.58 |
| 11 | 4.84 | 3.98 | 3.59 | 3.36 | 3.20 | 3.09 | 3.01 | 2.95 | 2.90 | 2.85 | 2.79 | 2.72 | 2.65 | 2.61 | 2.57 | 2.53 | 2.49 | 2.45 |
| 12 | 4.75 | 3.89 | 3.49 | 3.26 | 3.11 | 3.00 | 2.91 | 2.85 | 2.80 | 2.75 | 2.69 | 2.62 | 2.54 | 2.51 | 2.47 | 2.43 | 2.38 | 2.34 |
| 13 | 4.67 | 3.81 | 3.41 | 3.18 | 3.03 | 2.92 | 2.83 | 2.77 | 2.71 | 2.67 | 2.60 | 2.53 | 2.46 | 2.42 | 2.38 | 2.34 | 2.30 | 2.25 |
| 14 | 4.60 | 3.74 | 3.34 | 3.11 | 2.96 | 2.85 | 2.76 | 2.70 | 2.65 | 2.60 | 2.53 | 2.46 | 2.39 | 2.35 | 2.31 | 2.27 | 2.22 | 2.18 |
| 15 | 4.54 | 3.68 | 3.29 | 3.06 | 2.90 | 2.79 | 2.71 | 2.64 | 2.59 | 2.54 | 2.48 | 2.40 | 2.33 | 2.29 | 2.25 | 2.20 | 2.16 | 2.11 |
| 16 | 4.49 | 3.63 | 3.24 | 3.01 | 2.85 | 2.74 | 2.66 | 2.59 | 2.54 | 2.49 | 2.42 | 2.35 | 2.28 | 2.24 | 2.19 | 2.15 | 2.11 | 2.06 |
| 17 | 4.45 | 3.59 | 3.20 | 2.96 | 2.81 | 2.70 | 2.61 | 2.55 | 2.49 | 2.45 | 2.38 | 2.31 | 2.23 | 2.19 | 2.15 | 2.10 | 2.06 | 2.01 |
| 18 | 4.41 | 3.55 | 3.16 | 2.93 | 2.77 | 2.66 | 2.58 | 2.51 | 2.46 | 2.41 | 2.34 | 2.27 | 2.19 | 2.15 | 2.11 | 2.06 | 2.02 | 1.97 |
| 19 | 4.38 | 3.52 | 3.13 | 2.90 | 2.74 | 2.63 | 2.54 | 2.48 | 2.42 | 2.38 | 2.31 | 2.23 | 2.16 | 2.11 | 2.07 | 2.03 | 1.98 | 1.93 |
| 20 | 4.35 | 3.49 | 3.10 | 2.87 | 2.71 | 2.60 | 2.51 | 2.45 | 2.39 | 2.35 | 2.28 | 2.20 | 2.12 | 2.08 | 2.04 | 1.99 | 1.95 | 1.90 |
| 21 | 4.32 | 3.47 | 3.07 | 2.84 | 2.68 | 2.57 | 2.49 | 2.42 | 2.37 | 2.32 | 2.25 | 2.18 | 2.10 | 2.05 | 2.01 | 1.96 | 1.92 | 1.87 |
| 22 | 4.30 | 3.44 | 3.05 | 2.82 | 2.66 | 2.55 | 2.46 | 2.40 | 2.34 | 2.30 | 2.23 | 2.15 | 2.07 | 2.03 | 1.98 | 1.94 | 1.89 | 1.84 |
| 23 | 4.28 | 3.42 | 3.03 | 2.80 | 2.64 | 2.53 | 2.44 | 2.37 | 2.32 | 2.27 | 2.20 | 2.13 | 2.05 | 2.01 | 1.96 | 1.91 | 1.86 | 1.81 |
| 24 | 4.26 | 3.40 | 3.01 | 2.78 | 2.62 | 2.51 | 2.42 | 2.36 | 2.30 | 2.25 | 2.18 | 2.11 | 2.03 | 1.98 | 1.94 | 1.89 | 1.84 | 1.79 |
| 25 | 4.24 | 3.39 | 2.99 | 2.76 | 2.60 | 2.49 | 2.40 | 2.34 | 2.28 | 2.24 | 2.16 | 2.09 | 2.01 | 1.96 | 1.92 | 1.87 | 1.82 | 1.77 |
| 30 | 4.17 | 3.32 | 2.92 | 2.69 | 2.53 | 2.42 | 2.33 | 2.27 | 2.21 | 2.16 | 2.09 | 2.01 | 1.93 | 1.89 | 1.84 | 1.79 | 1.74 | 1.68 |
| 40 | 4.08 | 3.23 | 2.84 | 2.61 | 2.45 | 2.34 | 2.25 | 2.18 | 2.12 | 2.08 | 2.00 | 1.92 | 1.84 | 1.79 | 1.74 | 1.69 | 1.64 | 1.58 |
| 60 | 4.00 | 3.15 | 2.76 | 2.53 | 2.37 | 2.25 | 2.17 | 2.10 | 2.04 | 1.99 | 1.92 | 1.84 | 1.75 | 1.70 | 1.65 | 1.59 | 1.53 | 1.47 |
| 120 | 3.92 | 3.07 | 2.68 | 2.45 | 2.29 | 2.17 | 2.09 | 2.02 | 1.96 | 1.91 | 1.83 | 1.75 | 1.66 | 1.61 | 1.55 | 1.50 | 1.43 | 1.35 |

$\gamma = 0.99$

|  | 1 | 2 | 3 | 4 | 5 | 6 | 7 | 8 | 9 | 10 | 12 | 15 | 20 | 24 | 30 | 40 | 68 | 120 |
|---|---|---|---|---|---|---|---|---|---|---|---|---|---|---|---|---|---|---|
| 1 | 4052 | 4999.5 | 5403 | 5625 | 5764 | 5859 | 5928 | 5982 | 6022 | 6056 | 6106 | 6157 | 6209 | 6235 | 6261 | 6287 | 6313 | 6339 |
| 2 | 98.50 | 99.00 | 99.17 | 99.25 | 99.30 | 99.33 | 99.36 | 99.37 | 99.39 | 99.40 | 99.42 | 99.43 | 99.45 | 99.46 | 99.47 | 99.47 | 99.48 | 99.49 |
| 3 | 34.12 | 30.82 | 29.46 | 28.71 | 28.24 | 27.91 | 27.67 | 27.49 | 27.35 | 27.23 | 27.05 | 26.87 | 26.69 | 26.60 | 26.50 | 26.41 | 26.32 | 26.22 |
| 4 | 21.20 | 18.00 | 16.69 | 15.98 | 15.52 | 15.21 | 14.98 | 14.80 | 14.66 | 14.55 | 14.37 | 14.20 | 14.02 | 13.93 | 13.84 | 13.75 | 13.65 | 13.56 |
| 5 | 16.26 | 13.27 | 12.06 | 11.39 | 10.97 | 10.67 | 10.46 | 10.29 | 10.16 | 10.05 | 9.89 | 9.72 | 9.55 | 9.47 | 9.38 | 9.29 | 9.20 | 9.11 |
| 6 | 13.75 | 10.92 | 9.78 | 9.15 | 8.75 | 8.47 | 8.26 | 8.10 | 7.98 | 7.87 | 7.72 | 7.56 | 7.40 | 7.31 | 7.23 | 7.14 | 7.06 | 6.97 |
| 7 | 12.25 | 9.55 | 8.45 | 7.85 | 7.46 | 7.19 | 6.99 | 6.84 | 6.72 | 6.62 | 6.47 | 6.31 | 6.16 | 6.07 | 5.99 | 5.91 | 5.82 | 5.74 |
| 8 | 11.26 | 8.65 | 7.59 | 7.01 | 6.53 | 6.37 | 6.18 | 6.03 | 5.91 | 5.81 | 5.67 | 5.52 | 5.36 | 5.28 | 5.20 | 5.12 | 5.03 | 4.95 |
| 9 | 10.56 | 8.02 | 6.99 | 6.42 | 6.06 | 5.80 | 5.61 | 5.47 | 5.35 | 5.26 | 5.11 | 4.96 | 4.81 | 4.73 | 4.65 | 4.57 | 4.48 | 4.40 |
| 10 | 10.04 | 7.56 | 6.55 | 5.99 | 5.64 | 5.39 | 5.20 | 5.06 | 4.94 | 4.85 | 4.71 | 4.56 | 4.41 | 4.33 | 4.25 | 4.17 | 4.08 | 4.00 |
| 11 | 9.65 | 7.21 | 6.22 | 5.67 | 5.32 | 5.07 | 4.89 | 4.74 | 4.63 | 4.54 | 4.40 | 4.25 | 4.10 | 4.02 | 3.94 | 3.86 | 3.78 | 3.69 |
| 12 | 9.33 | 6.93 | 5.95 | 5.41 | 5.06 | 4.82 | 4.64 | 4.50 | 4.39 | 4.30 | 4.16 | 4.01 | 3.86 | 3.78 | 3.70 | 3.62 | 3.54 | 3.45 |
| 13 | 9.07 | 6.70 | 5.74 | 5.21 | 4.86 | 4.62 | 4.44 | 4.30 | 4.19 | 4.10 | 3.96 | 3.82 | 3.66 | 3.59 | 3.51 | 3.43 | 3.34 | 3.25 |
| 14 | 8.86 | 6.51 | 5.56 | 5.04 | 4.69 | 4.46 | 4.28 | 4.14 | 4.03 | 3.94 | 3.80 | 3.66 | 3.51 | 3.43 | 3.35 | 3.27 | 3.18 | 3.09 |
| 15 | 8.68 | 6.36 | 5.42 | 4.89 | 4.56 | 4.32 | 4.14 | 4.00 | 3.89 | 3.80 | 3.67 | 3.52 | 3.37 | 3.29 | 3.21 | 3.13 | 3.05 | 2.96 |
| 16 | 8.53 | 6.23 | 5.29 | 4.77 | 4.44 | 4.20 | 4.03 | 3.89 | 3.78 | 3.69 | 3.55 | 3.41 | 3.26 | 3.18 | 3.10 | 3.02 | 2.93 | 2.84 |
| 17 | 8.40 | 6.11 | 5.18 | 4.67 | 4.34 | 4.10 | 3.93 | 3.79 | 3.68 | 3.59 | 3.46 | 3.31 | 3.16 | 3.08 | 3.00 | 2.92 | 2.83 | 2.75 |
| 18 | 8.29 | 6.01 | 5.09 | 4.58 | 4.25 | 4.01 | 3.84 | 3.71 | 3.60 | 3.51 | 3.37 | 3.23 | 3.08 | 3.00 | 2.92 | 2.84 | 2.75 | 2.66 |
| 19 | 8.18 | 5.93 | 5.01 | 4.50 | 4.17 | 3.94 | 3.77 | 3.63 | 3.52 | 3.43 | 3.30 | 3.15 | 3.00 | 2.92 | 2.84 | 2.76 | 2.67 | 2.58 |
| 20 | 8.10 | 5.85 | 4.94 | 4.43 | 4.10 | 3.87 | 3.70 | 3.56 | 3.46 | 3.37 | 3.23 | 3.09 | 2.94 | 2.86 | 2.78 | 2.69 | 2.61 | 2.52 |
| 21 | 8.02 | 5.78 | 4.87 | 4.37 | 4.04 | 3.81 | 3.64 | 3.51 | 3.40 | 3.31 | 3.17 | 3.03 | 2.88 | 2.80 | 2.72 | 2.64 | 2.55 | 2.46 |
| 22 | 7.95 | 5.72 | 4.82 | 4.31 | 3.99 | 3.76 | 3.59 | 3.45 | 3.35 | 3.26 | 3.12 | 2.98 | 2.83 | 2.75 | 2.67 | 2.58 | 2.50 | 2.40 |
| 23 | 7.88 | 5.66 | 4.76 | 4.26 | 3.94 | 3.71 | 3.54 | 3.41 | 3.30 | 3.21 | 3.07 | 2.93 | 2.78 | 2.70 | 2.62 | 2.54 | 2.45 | 2.35 |
| 24 | 7.82 | 5.61 | 4.72 | 4.22 | 3.90 | 3.67 | 3.50 | 3.36 | 3.26 | 3.17 | 3.03 | 2.89 | 2.74 | 2.66 | 2.58 | 2.49 | 2.40 | 2.31 |
| 25 | 7.77 | 5.57 | 4.68 | 4.18 | 3.85 | 3.63 | 3.46 | 3.32 | 3.22 | 3.13 | 2.99 | 2.85 | 2.70 | 2.62 | 2.54 | 2.45 | 2.36 | 2.27 |
| 30 | 7.56 | 5.39 | 4.51 | 4.02 | 3.70 | 3.47 | 3.30 | 3.17 | 3.07 | 2.98 | 2.84 | 2.70 | 2.55 | 2.47 | 2.39 | 2.30 | 2.21 | 2.11 |
| 40 | 7.31 | 5.18 | 4.31 | 3.83 | 3.51 | 3.29 | 3.12 | 2.99 | 2.89 | 2.80 | 2.66 | 2.52 | 2.37 | 2.29 | 2.20 | 2.11 | 2.02 | 1.92 |
| 60 | 7.08 | 4.98 | 4.13 | 3.65 | 3.34 | 3.12 | 2.95 | 2.82 | 2.72 | 2.63 | 2.50 | 2.35 | 2.20 | 2.12 | 2.03 | 1.94 | 1.84 | 1.73 |
| 120 | 6.85 | 4.79 | 3.95 | 3.48 | 3.17 | 2.96 | 2.79 | 2.66 | 2.56 | 2.47 | 2.34 | 2.19 | 2.03 | 1.95 | 1.86 | 1.76 | 1.66 | 1.53 |

**Table C-6.** PSEUDO-RANDOM NUMBERS*

| | | | | | | | | | | | | | | |
|---|---|---|---|---|---|---|---|---|---|---|---|---|---|---|
| 15 | 17 | 01 | 64 | 69 | 69 | 58 | 40 | 81 | 16 | 60 | 20 | 00 | 84 | 22 | 28 | 26 | 46 | 66 | 36 | 86 | 66 | 17 | 34 | 49 |
| 85 | 40 | 51 | 40 | 10 | 15 | 33 | 94 | 11 | 65 | 57 | 62 | 94 | 04 | 99 | 05 | 57 | 22 | 71 | 77 | 99 | 68 | 12 | 11 | 14 |
| 47 | 69 | 35 | 90 | 95 | 16 | 17 | 45 | 86 | 29 | 16 | 70 | 48 | 02 | 00 | 59 | 33 | 93 | 28 | 58 | 34 | 32 | 24 | 34 | 07 |
| 13 | 26 | 87 | 40 | 20 | 40 | 81 | 46 | 08 | 09 | 74 | 99 | 16 | 92 | 99 | 85 | 19 | 01 | 23 | 11 | 74 | 00 | 79 | 41 | 69 |
| 10 | 55 | 33 | 20 | 47 | 54 | 16 | 86 | 11 | 16 | 59 | 34 | 71 | 55 | 84 | 03 | 48 | 17 | 60 | 13 | 38 | 71 | 23 | 91 | 83 |
| 05 | 06 | 67 | 26 | 77 | 14 | 85 | 40 | 52 | 68 | 60 | 41 | 94 | 98 | 18 | 62 | 20 | 94 | 03 | 71 | 60 | 26 | 45 | 17 | 92 |
| 65 | 50 | 89 | 18 | 74 | 42 | 07 | 50 | 15 | 69 | 86 | 97 | 40 | 25 | 88 | 14 | 17 | 73 | 92 | 07 | 93 | 11 | 93 | 45 | 15 |
| 59 | 68 | 53 | 31 | 55 | 73 | 47 | 16 | 49 | 79 | 69 | 80 | 76 | 16 | 60 | 58 | 53 | 07 | 04 | 53 | 66 | 94 | 94 | 18 | 13 |
| 31 | 31 | 05 | 36 | 48 | 75 | 16 | 00 | 21 | 11 | 42 | 44 | 84 | 46 | 84 | 83 | 20 | 49 | 17 | 12 | 21 | 93 | 34 | 61 | 16 |
| 91 | 59 | 46 | 44 | 45 | 49 | 25 | 36 | 12 | 07 | 25 | 90 | 89 | 55 | 25 | 83 | 47 | 17 | 23 | 93 | 99 | 56 | 14 | 39 | 16 |
| 63 | 59 | 73 | 21 | 67 | 80 | 00 | 25 | 58 | 25 | 72 | 06 | 12 | 96 | 74 | 54 | 79 | 70 | 85 | 88 | 71 | 58 | 21 | 98 | 48 |
| 89 | 72 | 47 | 46 | 94 | 78 | 56 | 10 | 65 | 97 | 84 | 79 | 42 | 31 | 49 | 94 | 15 | 31 | 13 | 09 | 45 | 43 | 03 | 82 | 81 |
| 70 | 51 | 21 | 03 | 18 | 50 | 21 | 99 | 49 | 73 | 06 | 99 | 19 | 24 | 96 | 39 | 43 | 10 | 14 | 12 | 94 | 08 | 55 | 54 | 70 |
| 14 | 15 | 99 | 60 | 44 | 62 | 72 | 38 | 18 | 36 | 63 | 92 | 61 | 55 | 93 | 77 | 66 | 82 | 10 | 91 | 81 | 51 | 67 | 01 | 47 |
| 92 | 46 | 90 | 39 | 99 | 64 | 08 | 00 | 97 | 27 | 54 | 96 | 63 | 40 | 54 | 34 | 70 | 27 | 48 | 18 | 68 | 59 | 91 | 83 | 32 |
| 81 | 23 | 17 | 13 | 01 | 37 | 57 | 92 | 16 | 34 | 15 | 80 | 90 | 25 | 64 | 67 | 77 | 29 | 95 | 84 | 80 | 84 | 86 | 87 | 22 |
| 87 | 54 | 42 | 46 | 56 | 28 | 89 | 02 | 07 | 97 | 59 | 90 | 75 | 14 | 38 | 98 | 66 | 23 | 20 | 23 | 90 | 55 | 31 | 83 | 48 |
| 74 | 73 | 84 | 98 | 13 | 11 | 48 | 25 | 33 | 39 | 27 | 36 | 08 | 99 | 57 | 60 | 42 | 88 | 68 | 25 | 22 | 89 | 67 | 83 | 16 |
| 94 | 55 | 14 | 00 | 97 | 32 | 51 | 92 | 47 | 03 | 92 | 33 | 73 | 20 | 21 | 29 | 77 | 37 | 06 | 98 | 64 | 63 | 34 | 31 | 43 |
| 69 | 21 | 94 | 26 | 20 | 73 | 90 | 70 | 92 | 76 | 49 | 14 | 60 | 34 | 43 | 90 | 51 | 72 | 11 | 07 | 75 | 94 | 19 | 49 | 40 |
| 82 | 36 | 36 | 89 | 29 | 87 | 70 | 08 | 71 | 98 | 49 | 00 | 89 | 89 | 99 | 29 | 08 | 02 | 72 | 32 | 68 | 16 | 29 | 82 | 19 |
| 25 | 06 | 22 | 30 | 87 | 87 | 44 | 48 | 90 | 91 | 38 | 53 | 10 | 60 | 29 | 40 | 07 | 58 | 97 | 84 | 09 | 04 | 33 | 56 | 72 |
| 82 | 37 | 97 | 60 | 92 | 76 | 39 | 17 | 84 | 34 | 67 | 65 | 52 | 89 | 90 | 62 | 97 | 04 | 33 | 81 | 91 | 27 | 56 | 46 | 35 |
| 83 | 71 | 07 | 22 | 15 | 17 | 55 | 56 | 82 | 62 | 88 | 83 | 86 | 38 | 14 | 63 | 89 | 39 | 81 | 90 | 25 | 62 | 58 | 68 | 87 |
| 73 | 13 | 79 | 15 | 12 | 18 | 34 | 22 | 24 | 75 | 56 | 47 | 45 | 22 | 81 | 30 | 82 | 38 | 34 | 52 | 57 | 48 | 30 | 34 | 17 |

Appendix C / 279

## 280 / Table of Statistics and Pseudo-Random Numbers

| | | | | | | | | | | | | | | |
|--|--|--|--|--|--|--|--|--|--|--|--|--|--|--|
| 91 | 73 | 34 | 04 | 53 | 99 | 77 | 72 | 90 | 07 | 01 | 88 | 50 | 78 | 70 | 15 |
| 33 | 89 | 69 | 69 | 32 | 37 | 46 | 71 | 09 | 19 | 20 | 42 | 93 | 78 | 74 | 64 |
| 56 | 96 | 28 | 50 | 90 | 12 | 16 | 31 | 89 | 99 | 98 | 63 | 34 | 04 | 40 | 77 |
| 88 | 91 | 45 | 71 | 89 | 30 | 65 | 45 | 03 | 72 | 98 | 52 | 27 | 04 | 00 | 74 |
| 87 | 47 | 37 | 84 | 37 | 85 | 76 | 07 | 36 | 92 | 41 | 53 | 98 | 91 | 49 | 89 |

| | | | | | | | | | | | | | | |
|--|--|--|--|--|--|--|--|--|--|--|--|--|--|--|
| 32 | 69 | 09 | 25 | 76 | 89 | 37 | 38 | 29 | 37 | 37 | 84 | 48 | 33 | 03 | 22 |
| 44 | 48 | 83 | 00 | 48 | 58 | 45 | 69 | 33 | 31 | 87 | 30 | 20 | 96 | 59 | 99 |
| 94 | 16 | 22 | 88 | 58 | 42 | 89 | 61 | 78 | 07 | 24 | 82 | 24 | 83 | 88 | 11 |
| 13 | 80 | 21 | 04 | 76 | 88 | 29 | 61 | 42 | 18 | 85 | 59 | 11 | 41 | 62 | 90 |
| 78 | 63 | 13 | 25 | 99 | 53 | 96 | 06 | 99 | 99 | 31 | 21 | 70 | 71 | 05 | 57 |

| | | | | | | | | | | | | | | |
|--|--|--|--|--|--|--|--|--|--|--|--|--|--|--|
| 44 | 13 | 82 | 45 | 40 | 22 | 38 | 86 | 13 | 80 | 44 | 17 | 50 | 15 | 74 | 19 |
| 79 | 33 | 34 | 16 | 71 | 16 | 99 | 42 | 85 | 14 | 59 | 49 | 19 | 56 | 84 | 20 |
| 87 | 15 | 06 | 89 | 00 | 68 | 44 | 59 | 63 | 62 | 94 | 98 | 72 | 68 | 20 | 84 |
| 85 | 80 | 55 | 74 | 85 | 54 | 26 | 25 | 88 | 90 | 40 | 98 | 83 | 83 | 08 | 90 |
| 43 | 12 | 07 | 91 | 16 | 35 | 35 | 35 | 65 | 94 | 98 | 32 | 43 | 25 | 38 | 23 |

| | | | | | | | | | | | | | | |
|--|--|--|--|--|--|--|--|--|--|--|--|--|--|--|
| 37 | 43 | 98 | 51 | 69 | 22 | 78 | 60 | 50 | 68 | 51 | 64 | 12 | 14 | 71 | 99 |
| 43 | 21 | 14 | 34 | 29 | 16 | 90 | 25 | 65 | 00 | 00 | 75 | 48 | 95 | 65 | 33 |
| 21 | 50 | 87 | 97 | 70 | 68 | 79 | 11 | 06 | 17 | 29 | 27 | 75 | 64 | 06 | 85 |
| 50 | 09 | 93 | 69 | 39 | 54 | 29 | 43 | 75 | 27 | 08 | 30 | 37 | 25 | 10 | 42 |
| 09 | 91 | 28 | 52 | 24 | 35 | 31 | 86 | 06 | 21 | 47 | 87 | 66 | 12 | 11 | 84 |

| | | | | | | | | | | | | | | |
|--|--|--|--|--|--|--|--|--|--|--|--|--|--|--|
| 91 | 73 | 80 | 69 | 24 | 63 | 43 | 23 | 02 | 92 | 37 | 17 | 88 | 50 | 68 | 92 |
| 33 | 28 | 76 | 38 | 33 | 84 | 78 | 33 | 74 | 45 | 86 | 41 | 30 | 43 | 08 | 93 |
| 56 | 03 | 47 | 03 | 19 | 17 | 79 | 30 | 73 | 20 | 60 | 33 | 96 | 39 | 26 | 46 |
| 88 | 47 | 88 | 35 | 72 | 82 | 29 | 81 | 15 | 19 | 94 | 08 | 24 | 99 | 98 | 27 |
| 87 | 03 | 33 | 20 | 14 | 50 | 31 | 63 | 55 | 89 | 07 | 69 | 12 | 56 | 67 | 00 |

| | | | | | | | | | | | | | | |
|--|--|--|--|--|--|--|--|--|--|--|--|--|--|--|
| 21 | 95 | 38 | 12 | 92 | 30 | 57 | 00 | 21 | 28 | 32 | 44 | 38 | 12 | 42 | 04 |
| 05 | 31 | 77 | 21 | 08 | 57 | 62 | 55 | 47 | 61 | 88 | 66 | 40 | 24 | 52 | 82 |
| 67 | 27 | 26 | 70 | 64 | 38 | 32 | 25 | 44 | 08 | 77 | 30 | 85 | 85 | 48 | 38 |
| 21 | 50 | 34 | 69 | 82 | 29 | 02 | 52 | 08 | 40 | 84 | 13 | 48 | 19 | 91 | 91 |
| 02 | 59 | 69 | 07 | 51 | 62 | 23 | 88 | 63 | 84 | 05 | 27 | 19 | 05 | 78 | 42 |

| | | | | | | | | | | | | | | |
|--|--|--|--|--|--|--|--|--|--|--|--|--|--|--|
| 35 | 57 | 57 | 34 | 82 | 08 | 15 | 21 | 30 | 39 | 34 | 02 | 30 | 43 | 96 | 87 |
| 04 | 64 | 47 | 59 | 01 | 13 | 23 | 88 | 43 | 52 | 38 | 96 | 02 | 77 | 30 | 43 |
| 60 | 15 | 41 | 61 | 41 | 79 | 67 | 08 | 77 | 85 | 16 | 30 | 96 | 84 | 43 | 77 |
| 12 | 60 | 38 | 46 | 65 | 00 | 09 | 40 | 84 | 48 | 24 | 88 | 30 | 77 | 84 | 71 |
| 05 | 80 | 67 | 75 | 85 | 99 | 05 | 84 | 19 | 22 | 22 | 68 | 06 | 05 | 58 | 80 |

| | | | | | | | | | | | | | | |
|--|--|--|--|--|--|--|--|--|--|--|--|--|--|--|
| 15 | 45 | 68 | 46 | 99 | 40 | 46 | 36 | 62 | 89 | 31 | 36 | 81 | 54 | 48 | 23 |
| 34 | 72 | 80 | 83 | 13 | 20 | 36 | 57 | 57 | 44 | 91 | 57 | 43 | 65 | 97 | 97 |
| 30 | 46 | 46 | 32 | 69 | 59 | 57 | 43 | 80 | 92 | 98 | 98 |  |  |  |  |
| 06 | 60 | 48 | 46 | 55 | 71 | 87 | 14 | 39 | 89 | 45 | 79 | 03 | 98 | 04 | 40 |
| 16 | 21 | 63 | 04 | 58 | 89 | 81 | 15 | 92 | 02 | 50 | 69 | 56 | 04 |  | 66 |

| | | | | | | | | | | | | | | |
|--|--|--|--|--|--|--|--|--|--|--|--|--|--|--|
| 89 | 32 | 53 | 82 | 20 | 36 | 95 | 48 | 09 |  |  |  |  |  |  |  |
| 26 | 57 | 95 | 07 | 74 | 10 | 96 | 43 | 97 |  |  |  |  |  |  |  |

Appendix C / 281

```
15 62 38 72 92  03 76 09 30 75  77 80 24 54 60  10 26 21 60 03  48 14
77 81 15 14 67  55 24 22 20 55  26 93 69 37 22  43 32 56 15 75  25 12
18 87 05 09 96  45 14 72 41 46  12 67 72 02 59  06 17 73 28 23  52 48
08 58 53 63 66  13 07 04 48 71  39 07 96 40 20  86 79 88 11 15  23 17
16 07 79 57 61  42 19 68 15 12  60 21 12 07 04  99 88 39 16 69  13 84

54 13 05 17 39  05 51 24 53 57  46 51 14 17 21  39 89 35 47 87  36 62
95 27 23 17 80  80 24 44 48 93  75 94 77 23 09  75 91 03 55 51  74 47
22 39 44 74 11  25 95 28 63 90  41 19 48 44 46  12 97 83 35 83  17 29
69 95 21 30 97  98 81 38 00 53  41 40 04 72 16  29 83 18 30 44  37 64
75 63 63 97 12  11 57 05 86 52  82 72 47 78 14  72 69 75 72 52  51 81

08 74 79 30 80  70 11 66 79 25  88 01 94 31 38  98 57 38 12 84  01 54
04 88 45 98 60  90 92 74 77 87  40 18 65 37 08  62 68 08 84 18  68 18
97 35 74 05 75  42 13 49 48 38  74 19 06 60 20  90 79 20 18 51  27 27
53 09 93 28 29  80 19 68 30 45  94 49 42 21 93  71 93 30 52 65  40 13
26 36 68 48 09  37 69 26 22 80  23 34 10 70 83  07 51 99 62 96  42 64

49 16 57 15 79  56 63 22 94 28  11 39 69 38 53  06 97 06 09 14  43 48
03 51 79 78 74  75 23 73 75 98  47 85 07 02 61  28 01 28 14 12  67 22
21 88 87 28 48  23 44 03 03 80  53 89 07 93 30  17 84 17 16 53  39 01
56 41 73 33 41  59 16 59 50 98  24 24 87 75 99  52 09 52 86 25  50 94
72 39 19 70 17  01 04 01 22 33  04 84 63 65 84  39 45 39 95 88  90 37

97 28 25 81 49  71 69 22 04 51  56 46 56 10 69  59 99 59 33 50  93 09
18 87 02 72 08  74 52 16 03 82  20 19 66 62 37  51 04 37 32 19  85 57
53 40 11 75 45  13 56 85 31 37  09 17 71 79 39  50 79 39 71 14  53 03
60 49 03 41 56  78 33 77 28 92  21 90 10 01 97  06 45 97 95 12  18 52
09 16 12 75 04  39 69 95 00 48  26 85 28 73 08  92 10 66 62 61  82 57
```

## 282 / Table of Statistics and Pseudo-Random Numbers

| | | | | | | | | | | | | | | | | | | | |
|---|---|---|---|---|---|---|---|---|---|---|---|---|---|---|---|---|---|---|---|
| 64 | 20 | 19 | 87 | 54 | 88 | 15 | 12 | 54 | 24 | 06 | 99 | 57 | 07 | 28 | 51 | 35 | 54 | 98 | 50 | 70 | 88 | 02 | 86 | 48 |
| 31 | 28 | 07 | 58 | 77 | 03 | 98 | 26 | 76 | 09 | 10 | 44 | 57 | 61 | 28 | 60 | 29 | 85 | 70 | 79 | 80 | 29 | 19 | 98 | 92 |
| 80 | 04 | 28 | 47 | 76 | 35 | 73 | 67 | 78 | 28 | 09 | 39 | 88 | 63 | 74 | 41 | 26 | 92 | 42 | 33 | 06 | 80 | 06 | 33 | 84 |
| 24 | 60 | 22 | 51 | 19 | 34 | 54 | 08 | 24 | 73 | 86 | 72 | 11 | 44 | 69 | 76 | 90 | 81 | 17 | 85 | 57 | 47 | 35 | 16 | 84 |
| 59 | 16 | 11 | 26 | 29 | 18 | 97 | 78 | 44 | 43 | 58 | 92 | 78 | 70 | 80 | 09 | 65 | 32 | 68 | 26 | 65 | 73 | 90 | 50 | 46 |
| 58 | 54 | 29 | 98 | 27 | 40 | 51 | 92 | 07 | 13 | 58 | 41 | 59 | 56 | 94 | 16 | 32 | 51 | 42 | 54 | 77 | 37 | 13 | 85 | 19 |
| 20 | 18 | 34 | 22 | 73 | 57 | 40 | 67 | 17 | 28 | 63 | 57 | 74 | 36 | 18 | 65 | 55 | 25 | 50 | 68 | 35 | 90 | 00 | 03 | 38 |
| 53 | 90 | 46 | 56 | 19 | 50 | 58 | 33 | 84 | 53 | 14 | 74 | 17 | 40 | 73 | 86 | 11 | 04 | 02 | 04 | 02 | 28 | 49 | 62 | 36 |
| 97 | 16 | 93 | 94 | 65 | 70 | 95 | 95 | 83 | 20 | 91 | 42 | 57 | 95 | 63 | 00 | 98 | 29 | 02 | 53 | 02 | 27 | 86 | 70 | 95 |
| 72 | 55 | 71 | 70 | 92 | 04 | 22 | 53 | 19 | 29 | 67 | 29 | 13 | 56 | 70 | 45 | 73 | 45 | 05 | 04 | 32 | 43 | 30 | 93 | 41 |
| 99 | 19 | 72 | 58 | 35 | 49 | 09 | 26 | 00 | 74 | 26 | 42 | 94 | 52 | 02 | 83 | 31 | 85 | 65 | 66 | 31 | 97 | 67 | 52 | 15 |
| 48 | 21 | 49 | 72 | 97 | 79 | 19 | 64 | 81 | 82 | 78 | 92 | 51 | 96 | 51 | 28 | 79 | 13 | 20 | 82 | 34 | 81 | 39 | 46 | 86 |
| 52 | 37 | 68 | 15 | 53 | 22 | 98 | 30 | 16 | 31 | 83 | 24 | 87 | 69 | 29 | 24 | 85 | 44 | 25 | 50 | 75 | 62 | 83 | 95 | 41 |
| 97 | 50 | 52 | 53 | 52 | 26 | 78 | 21 | 68 | 69 | 57 | 79 | 42 | 40 | 89 | 55 | 81 | 75 | 24 | 52 | 51 | 32 | 79 | 97 | 05 |
| 36 | 05 | 09 | 18 | 11 | 71 | 01 | 63 | 17 | 60 | 11 | 65 | 19 | 43 | 07 | 44 | 86 | 19 | 58 | 92 | 23 | 71 | 32 | 96 | 19 |
| 20 | 79 | 70 | 09 | 30 | 81 | 14 | 53 | 80 | 93 | 71 | 94 | 10 | 18 | 14 | 83 | 69 | 76 | 53 | 25 | 27 | 36 | 65 | 65 | 05 |
| 13 | 07 | 89 | 72 | 08 | 00 | 37 | 75 | 14 | 94 | 83 | 85 | 06 | 72 | 66 | 07 | 47 | 30 | 17 | 11 | 16 | 02 | 63 | 97 | 30 |
| 94 | 26 | 82 | 37 | 43 | 34 | 23 | 00 | 14 | 00 | 96 | 85 | 41 | 17 | 71 | 69 | 20 | 15 | 98 | 82 | 79 | 69 | 68 | 50 | 31 |
| 13 | 55 | 88 | 38 | 43 | 75 | 37 | 46 | 83 | 85 | 53 | 74 | 54 | 62 | 99 | 68 | 93 | 74 | 43 | 95 | 06 | 26 | 79 | 78 | 87 |
| 02 | 44 | 24 | 97 | 71 | 97 | 93 | 12 | 70 | 80 | 42 | 52 | 33 | 24 | 91 | 05 | 87 | 53 | 15 | 77 | 49 | 92 | 83 | 97 | 80 |
| 34 | 90 | 96 | 63 | 54 | 22 | 84 | 36 | 38 | 39 | 85 | 36 | 25 | 03 | 27 | 49 | 24 | 72 | 10 | 50 | 95 | 14 | 18 | 26 | 64 |
| 13 | 67 | 06 | 34 | 98 | 04 | 20 | 80 | 12 | 04 | 01 | 18 | 54 | 20 | 76 | 92 | 10 | 47 | 04 | 65 | 54 | 45 | 82 | 42 | 90 |
| 18 | 75 | 55 | 82 | 66 | 34 | 77 | 28 | 71 | 09 | 67 | 65 | 85 | 92 | 68 | 16 | 43 | 83 | 18 | 74 | 12 | 48 | 68 | 87 | 22 |
| 91 | 25 | 52 | 57 | 15 | 21 | 54 | 40 | 05 | 60 | 67 | 51 | 66 | 45 | 69 | 84 | 72 | 74 | 32 | 30 | 17 | 70 | 40 | 90 | 24 |
| 76 | 24 | 00 | 14 | 92 | 14 | 29 | 12 | 17 | 13 | 77 | 46 | 44 | 24 | 30 | 48 | 50 | 36 | 30 | 24 | 93 | 08 | 01 | 39 | 37 |

*This table was generated from a discrete uniformly distributed variable on the integers 0, 1, ..., 99 using a form of

# INDEX

**A**

Abadie, J., 96
Access arm, 5
Access key, 34
Access time, 36
ACM, Journal of, 268
Acta Mathematica, 268
Activity, 258
ACUTE, 16
AFIPS Conference Proceedings, 124
Aircraft scheduling, 52-53, 68-69
Airline crew scheduling, 20, 39-43, 49
Aitken, A., 255
ALCHE, 17
ALGOL, 7
Alternative hypothesis, 140
American Mathematical Society,
  Proceedings of, 268
Analysis of variance, 149ff
APL, 7
Arc, 258
Array, 22
Articulation level, 104
Ashton, T., 158

Association of Computing Machinery, 12, 13
Australian Computer Journal, 95
Automatic flowcharting, 8
Average query time, 38

**B**

Backward differences, 220
Balinski, M., 96
Ball, R., 255
BASIC, 7
Basic feasible solution, 62
Basis, 246
Batch processing, 6
Beale, E., 78, 96
Beaumont, R., 255
Bell, E., 92
Bell Systems Technical Journal, 124
Bellman, R., 125
Benders, J., 78
Benes, V., 125
Bent, D., 162
Berge, C., 267, 268
Bernoulli distribution, 134

Beta distribution, 134
Binary search, 27, 28
Binary tree search, 28, 29
Binomial distribution, 134
BIO, 17
Bipartite graph, 264
Birkhoff, G., 255
Bit, 2
Blending of raw materials, 54, 55
BMD programs, 160, 161
Branch, 258
Brennan, R., 211
Brownlee, K., 161
Brunk, H., 161
Buckley, D., 158

## C

Canadian Journal of Mathematics, 268
CAP user group, 15
Capacity, 105
Carnahan, B., 237
Central finite differences, 220
Central limit Theorem, 138
CEPA, 17
Chain structure, 35
Chakravarti, I., 161
Chapin, N., 20, 35
Charnes, A., 92
Checkout compiler, 8
Chien, R., 126
$\chi^2$ goodness of fit test, 145
Chromatic graph, 271
Circuit, 265
Clancy, J., 211
Closed set, 57
COBOL, 7, 19
Cochran, W., 161
CODASYL, 19
Combinational Theory, Journal of, 268
Command systems, 105
COMMON user group, 15
Communications of ACM, 44, 45, 124
Compiler, 7
Component, 265
Composite formula, 227
Composite hypotheses, 142
Computer, 1
Computer Bulletin, 3
Computer Decisions, 45
Computer Journal, 13, 44
Computer Physics Communications, 13
Computer Programs Directory, 12

Computers and Biomedical Research, 13
Computers and Operations Research, 95
Computer system, 1
Computer World, 45
Computing Report, 13
Computing Reviews, 13, 44
Computing Surveys, 44
Confidence interval, 139
Connected network, 265
Construction, program, 9
Contamination, (see Numerical contamination)
Contingency table, 147
Control Data Corporation, 92, 93
Conveyer module, 172, 174
Convex hull, 59
Convex set, 58
Cooper, W., 92
Core, 2
Correlation coefficient, 145
Cosmic, 12
Covariance, 145
Cox, G., 161
Cox, J., 206, 212
cpu, 7
Crew scheduling (see airline crew scheduling)
Critical path method (CPM), 118
CRT, 169
Cuadra, C., 45
CUBE user group, 12
Curtis, C., 255
Cut, 105
Cut set, 104
Cutting plane, 76
Cycle, 7
Cylinder, 5

## D

Daellenbach, H., 92
Dahl, O., 206, 212
Dantzig, G., 92
Data base, 18
Data management, 10, 11, 18ff
Datamation, 45
Data structure, 19
Day, D., 15
Debugging, 7, 9
Decomposition, 69-71, 263
DECUS user group, 15

Index / 285

Degenerate, 64
Degree, 266
Dennis, J., 125
Density function, 133
Determinant of a matrix, 252
DEUA, 15
Diagonal matrix, 251
Differential equation, 215, 233ff
Directed link, 259
Direct methods, 228
Disconnected network, 265
Disk, 4, 5
Distribution, free, 153
Distribution function, 133
Dodd, J., 34
Dorn, W., 237
Double chain, 35
Double linked structure, 34, 35
Drum, 5
Dual version of linear programming, 65
Dutton, S., 206, 213
Dynamic programming, 113
DYNAMO, 204

E

Eaves, J., 255
ECHO, 17
Econometrika, 92
Edge, 258
EDUCOM, 17
Efficiency of data management system, 21
Efficiency of files structures, 36-39
Eigenvalues, 215
Eigenvectors, 215
EIN, 12
Electronic data processing, 1
Electrooptical systems design, 79
Elmaghraby, S., 226
Empirical distribution function, 153
Employee records, 19, 21
Encrypting, 19
Enshoff, J., 206, 212
Entering variable, 62
Environment, 10
Euler's method, 233
Event, 132
Event to event simulation, 179
Execution time, 7
Exiting variable, 63
Expectation of variable, 133
Experiment, 131

Exponential distribution, 134
Extrapolation, 143, 215

F

Faden, B., 15
Feasible solution, 57
Field, 2
FIFO, 194
File, 20
File selection, 34ff
Fineberg, M., 201
Finite differences, 219ff
Finney, O., 161
Flores, I., 14, 15, 45
FMPS - MIP, 95
Focus, 12, 15
Ford, Jr. L., 125
Forsythe, G., 237
FORTRAN, 7, 203ff
Forward finite differences, 219
Fourcans, A., 200, 213
Frank, H., 113
Franklin Institute, Journal of, 268
Fraser diagram, 220
Fraser, J., 92, 100
Free, V., 42
Freund, J., 161
Frisch, I., 113
Fulkersun, D., 125

G

Gambling, 55, 56
Gamma distribution, 134
GANTT chart, 120
GASP, 204, 205
Gass, S., 72
Gaussian elimination, 67, 228
Gaussian-type quadrature, 224
Gauss-Seidel method, 232
Generating set, 245
Geoffrion, A., 78, 96
Geometric distribution, 134
GET, 15
Gomory, R., 76, 78
Goodness-of-fit, 145, 169, 183
Gorden, G., 206, 212
Gorry, G., 78
GPSS, 204
Graph theory enumeration, 75
Graves, G., 96
Greenburg, S., 212

Gretzkow, H., 206, 213
Gruenberger, F., 45
GUIDE, 16

## H

Hadley, G., 6, 92, 125
Hamiltonian circuit, 265
Hammer, P., 96
Hamming, R., 237, 238
Hardware sorting, 33
Hash cook, 30
Hashing, 30
Height, 20
H – 800 user group, 12
Henrici, P., 237, 238
Herroelen, W., 122, 126
H – 400, 1400 user group, 12, 16
Hierarchy, 20
Hildebrand, F., 237, 238
Hillier, F., 92, 105, 125, 190, 212
Hindelang, T., 200, 213
Hord, W., 79
Horizontal hierarchy, 34
Householder, A., 237, 238
Housner, B., 212
Howard, R., 125
Hu, T., 95, 108, 113, 125
HUG user group, 16
Hull, C., 162
Hull, T., 15
Hurst, N., 213
Hypothesis, 139, 140

## I

IBM, 92
IBM Systems Journal, 45
ICP Quarterly, 12, 43
Identity matrix, 250
IEEE Transactions on circuit theory, 124
IEEE Transactions on Communication Technology, 124
IEEE Transactions on Computers, 45
IFIPS Proceedings, 45
ILLIAC computer, 70
Implementation model, 10
IMPRESS, 161
IMS, 43, 44
Incidence matrix, 260
Independence, test of, 148
Independent events, 137

Independent random variables, 137
Index dictionary, 34
Indexed sequential files, 34
Infeasibility, 71
Information and Control, 45
Information retrieval (*see* Retrieval)
Initial node, 260
Input, (*see* I/O)
Integer programming, 67ff
Integration, 215
Integrity, 19
Interpolation, 214, 215, 217ff
Inverse of matrix, 254
Inverted file structure, 31
Inverted list structure, 34, 35
I/O, 2

## J

Job control languages (JCL), 8
Joint Computer Conferences, 44
JUG, 17

## K

Karlin, S., 212
Karr, H., 212
Kennedy, O., 198, 213
Kim, W., 126
Kiriat, H., 205, 212
Kleinrock, L., 126
Knuth, B., 14, 15, 45
Kopal, F., 237
Krasnow, H., 203, 211
$k$-removed, 114
Kronmal, R., 153

## L

Lagrangian interpolation, 218
Larson, R., 199, 213
Lasdon, L., 96
Leaf node, 266
Leaf point, 20, 72
Least squares, 145
Lee, A., 212
Legendre polynomial, 224
Lehmer congruential method, 181
Library, 19
Lieberman, G., 92, 105, 125, 190, 212
Lientz, B., 158
LIFO, 194
Likelihood ratio, 141

Linear approximation, 216
Linear dependence, 245
Linear independence, 245
Linear programming problem, 51
Linear search, 26
Linebarger, R., 211
Link, 258
Lipschitz condition, 233
LISP, 24
List file structure, 22, 34
Loeve, M., 153
Loop, 264
Lubin, J., 203, 211
Luther, H., 237
Lyon, J., 45

## M

MacLane, S., 255
Magnetic tape, 2, 3
Management information system, 20, 39-43
Management Science, 13, 95, 124
Mann-Whitney test, 154-155
Mark IV, 43, 44
Markowitz, H., 212
Marsten, R., 78, 96
Mass function, 133
Master event list, 175
Mathematical Biophysics, Bulletin of, 124
Mathematical Programming, 95
mathematical programming, 49ff
Matrix, 246
Matrix operations, 246ff
Maurer, W., 45
Max flow – min cut theorem, 111
Maximal flow, 105ff
Maximum entry search, 30-31
McCoy, N., 255
McCracken, D., 237
Meadow, C., 38, 45
Menke, W., 201, 213
Merging, 22, 25, 33-34
Merikallio, R., 203, 211
Messick, S., 206, 213
Michigan Mathematical Journal, 268
MIDAS, 2, 95
Minicomputer, 14
Minimal spanning tree, 117
Minimax, 218
Minimum variance unbiased estimate, 138

Mize, J., 206, 212
Model, 10
Modularity, 11
Modulo, 181
Molar, C., 237
Moment, 135, 265
Monte Carlo sampling, 180
MPS, 93-94
MPS-X, 93-94
Multicommodity flow, 112
Muth, J., 96, 100
Multilist, 34, 35

## N

Natural input/output, 7
Naval Research Logistics Quarterly, 95, 124
Naylor, T., 205, 212
Neman, T., 42
Nemhauser, G., 126
Networks, 124
networks, 102ff, 258ff
Newton-Cotes quadrature formula, 225
Nie, N., 162
Node, 72, 102, 258
Nonsingular matrix, 253
Normal distribution, 134
Null hypothesis, 140
Numerical contamination, 8
Nygaard, K., 206, 212

## O

O'Neil, B., 91, 101
One way analysis of variance, 150
On-line processing, 6
Operating system, 7, 8
Operationally optimal, 50
Operations Research, 13, 95, 125
Operations systems, 1, 9
OPHELIE II, 94, 95
Optimization problems, 51ff
Optimization Theory and Applications, Journal of, 95
Ore, O., 267, 268
Output, (see I/O)

## P

Pack, disk, 4
Paper tape, 4
Parameter, 133
Parker, W., 255

Partition, matrix, 249
Parzen, E., 153, 161
Path search, 9
PDQ-LP, 94
PERT, 118
Phillips, C., 126
PL/1, 7, 203ff
Point, 258
Pointer, 22
Poisson distribution, 134
Poisson process, 186, 187
Power of test, 140
Predictor-corrector methods, 235
Pritsker, A., 205, 212
Probability, 132
Problem generator, 41
Program construction, 9
Program duration, 121
Program planning, 118ff
Pruning of branches, 75
Pugh, A., 212
Push down list, 23, 24

## Q

Quadrature, 123ff, 215
Queuing theory, 185ff

## R

Radix, 20, 266
Ralston, A., 237
Random access file, 34
Random number generator, 180ff
Random variable, 133
RAND table of random digits, 180
Rank of matrix, 228, 254
Rapid access device, 5
Rational approximation, 216
RCA-CUA user group, 12
Record, 20
Register, 2
Regression analysis, 143
Relaxation of problem, 71
Reliability, 84ff
Report generation, 42
Residual sum of squares, 151
Response time, 21
Retrieval, 21
Rice, J., 14, 15
Ring structure, 34, 35
RIP-30C, 95
Rolle's theorem, 218

Root of tree, 266
Round-off error, 216
Routing logic in simulation, 178
Rudeanu, S., 96
Runge-Kutta methods, 234, 235
Runs test, 157
Russell, E., 101
Ryser, H., 267, 268

## S

Sample mean, 138
Sample space, 132
Samuelson, K., 39
Scheffe, H., 161
Schmidt, J., 206, 213
Searching, 25
Searching and sorting, 24ff
Security, 19
Sequential file, 34
SERCUS user group, 16
Set of events, 132
Shapiro, J., 78, 101
SHARE user group, 12, 16, 91
Shortest path, 113
Sign test, 155
Simplex method, 60ff
Simplex tableau, 65
Simpsons's rule, 226
SIMSCRIPT, 204, 205
SIMULA, 204, 206
Singular matrix, 253
Sink, 104
Sisson, R., 206, 212
Size of problem, 11
Size of test, 140
Skip search, 27
Slack variable, 61
SNUG user group, 16
Society of Industrial and Applied
 Mathematics, Journal, 268
Software World, 12
Sorted list, 23
Sorting, 22ff
Sorting, hardware, 33
Sorting by maximal element, 32
Sorting by reordering, 32, 33
Source node, 104
Spanning set, 245
Spanning tree, 117
Sparse matrix, 228
Spielberg, K., 96
SPSS, 160, 161

Starbuck, W., 206, 213
Stationary increments, 186
STATPAK, 161
Steady state, 190
Stone-Weierstrass theorem, 216
Sublist, 23
Submatrix, 250
Sullivan, E., 82-84, 101
Sum of squared error, 217
Sum of squares, 143
Surplus variable, 63
Symmetrix matrix, 248
System, 9
SYSTEM 2000, 43, 44

T

Tableau, 65
Tabular points, 215
Tape, (see Magnetic tape or Paper tape)
Tartar, M., 153
Taylor, R., 206, 213
Teichroew, D., 203, 211
Terminal node, 260
Test statistic, 142
Thompson, E., 96, 102
Time headway, 158
Time sharing, 7
Time slicing, 180
Tocher, K., 203, 206, 212
Todd, J., 237
Tomkins, S., 206, 213
TOTAL, 43, 44
Track, 5
Transportation Research, 125
Transportation Science, 125
Transpose of a matrix, 248
Trapezoid rule, 226
Tree, 20, 73, 266
Truncation error, 216
Turnaround time, 7
Type I error, 140
Type II error, 140

U

Unbiased estimate, 138
Undirected link, 259
Uniform distribution, 134
USE user group, 16
Utility programs, 43, 44
UUA user group, 12, 16

V

Validation, 10
Validation of simulation model, 168, 169
Variance of random variable, 135
Vector, 243
Vector operations, 244ff
Vertex, 258
Vertical hierarchy, 34
VIM user group, 16
Virtual memory, 6
VSP, 123
VSP-X, 123

W

Wagner, H., 91, 108
Walsh, J., 161
Wegner, P., 15, 45
Weight, 266
Weissman, C., 24
Wilf, H., 237
Wilkes, J., 237
Wolfe, P., 96, 99
Woolsey, G., 96
Word, 2

X-Y-Z

XDS user group, 12, 16
Zero of a function, 222